Ernest Hemingway

ERNEST HEMINGWAY

FLAWED GENIUS

Aubrey Malone

FONTHILL

First published in Great Britain in 2025 by
Fonthill
An imprint of
Pen & Sword Books Ltd
Yorkshire – Philadelphia

ISBN 978-1-78155-935-2

A CIP catalogue record for this book is available from the British Library.

The Publisher's authorised representative in the EU for product safety is
Authorised Rep Compliance Ltd., Ground Floor, 71 Lower Baggot Street, Dublin D02 P593, Ireland.
www.arccompliance.com

For a complete list of Pen & Sword titles please contact

PEN & SWORD BOOKS LIMITED
47 Church Street, Barnsley, South Yorkshire, S70 2AS, England
E-mail: enquiries@pen-and-sword.co.uk
Website: www.pen-and-sword.co.uk
or
PEN AND SWORD BOOKS
1950 Lawrence Road, Havertown, PA 19083, USA
E-mail: uspen-and-sword@casematepublishers.com
Website: www.penandswordbooks.com

Acknowledgements

I am indebted to Ken Clay for his help in the preparation of this book. Special thanks also to Melissa Gooley. Thank you to John Whelan, Michelle Walker, Ty Sheehy, Joseph Hendaye, James Mitchell Lear, Aoife Hart, and all the librarians at Donaghmede. Thank you also to Sarah Fordham for her sourcing of background material, and to Alan Goodrich and Maryrose Grossman of the John F. Kennedy Library in Massachusetts for their assistance with the illustrations.

Contents

Introduction

Hemingway scoured the world in search of trophies. Some of these took the form of big fish and jungle animals. His women were trophies to him as well. So were his books. Everything was embraced under one gigantic umbrella. He reinvented himself with each safari, each marriage, each novel.

Africa was like Michigan to him just as the Gulf Stream was an extension of the Big Two-Hearted River. The pop gun his father gave him in his childhood may have been replaced by a Winchester when he went hunting, but it was in the early years on Lake Walloon that the lust for the hunt was formed. It was here, listening to the woodchucks in the trees and feeling the breaking twigs underfoot, that he mapped out his future in whatever corner of the globe an animal waited to be tracked or a fish to be hooked.

'A life of action,' he said when he was sixty, 'is much easier to me than writing. In action I don't worry, but writing is something that you can never do as well as it can be done. It's a perpetual challenge.' It cannibalised him until everything else became secondary. He once told Maxwell Perkins he only went to the Second World War to get a book out of it.

George Seldes said, 'Forgive him everything—he writes like an angel.'[1] According to Tobias Wolff, 'He changed the furniture in the room.' More important to him than anything else was the ability to tell the truth 'without screaming'. Screaming, he allowed, may have been necessary to attract attention to suffering, but it could never be a literary tool.

He once told his friend Arnold Samuelson, 'I can do many things better than I can write but when I don't write I feel like shit.' There were many times that it became a duty rather than a pleasure to him. He goaded it along like a recalcitrant animal, teasing it out tortuously. At such times he felt himself as much a victim of the process as an instigator of it. When he was lucky, he found the right sentences. When he was luckier again, they found him.

The only reason he made any money at writing, he told Samuelson, was because he was a literary pirate. Out of every ten stories he wrote, he claimed, only one was any good. He threw the other nine away but charged highly for the good one. 'The editors want my stuff,' he bragged, 'I've got them in a position where they bid for it. I play off one against the other until they pay for the one as if they had bought all ten.'[2]

He told Samuelson he believed all the best stories were invented. In real life only a small minority of people ever had anything happening to them that would make good fiction. If you wrote about yourself, he said, you lived and died once and then you were through, but if you wrote about others, you could die a thousand deaths.[3]

He believed his writing represented the purest part of himself. It was his way of atoning for his sins, his purification ritual. That was why he worked so hard at it.

This is how he put it to Samuelson: 'A writer has to be made up of two different persons. As a man you can be any kind of a son of a bitch you like. You can hate and condemn a person and shoot his head off the next time you see him. But as a writer you have to see him absolutely as he is. You've got to understand his viewpoint completely and learn how to present him accurately without getting your own reactions mixed up in it.' In this sense, the artist was more than a see-r. He was a seer.

'Any good man,' he wrote, 'would rather take chances with his life than with his livelihood.' That was what differentiated the professional from the amateur. The true professional had to live on the edge, pushing the boat out like Santiago from *The Old Man and the Sea* until one day he went too far and had to sacrifice himself for his art.

Writing was like music for Hemingway. Though he was never adept at playing an instrument, he inherited from his mother an appreciation for rhythm that he applied to his prose. This is prose we read as much for its sound as its sense.

An old theory of writing says, 'No tears in the writer, none in the reader.' Hemingway's tears were usually hidden. He liked his characters to grin and bear it. *Il faut d'abord durer*.[4]

He saw writing as a competition. He claimed he started out quietly until he outclassed Turgenev. 'Then I trained hard and I beat Mr de Maupassant. I've fought two draws with Mr Stendhal and I think I had an edge in the last one. But nobody's going to get me in the ring with Tolstoy unless I'm crazy or I keep getting better.'[5]

He looked on literature roughly the same way he viewed hunting and fishing. The great white hunter had to write the great white novel. Catching the big marlin had to be followed by penning the big blockbuster.

The style he minted was sharp, the sentences short. Repetition created a musical quality that drew you in almost without you realising it. Many people tried to copy this. Ivan Kashkeen said: 'He liked to try on an eccentric garb only to discard it, while the imitators continued for a long time to parade the clothes he'd cast off.'

H. E. Bates put it more strongly: 'Little Hemingways, attracted by the street-corner toughness of the style, sprang up everywhere, slick copyists of the surface line, not one in a thousand of them understanding that the colder and harder a man writes, the more deeply and more movingly emotional the result is likely to be.'

Such imitators, in Bates' view, took his language 'straight off the earth, the saloon floor, the café table, the factory bench, the street and the drugstore counter, not bothering to wipe off the colloquial dirt or the spittle, the common dust or the colour, the wit or the fantastically apt metaphor, the slickness or the slang.' Most of them achieved only the primitiveness and the flip quip. What they missed was the richness of texture.

Hemingway brought the eye of the reporter to a poetic sensibility. He stylised the vernacular. He was inside that shark-infested domain but also outside it. Few entered the belly of the beast with as much relish as he did. He gave readers a form of writing bathed in the blood of its protagonists. His was a modern sensibility hankering for the tug of the primeval. It was like Babe Ruth written by Tolstoy.

His flouting of the rules of grammar led critics to dub him a mock-primitive writer. He created an anti-intellectual veneer—but there were almost 5,000 books in his library in the Finca Vigia. Most of them were well-thumbed.

Preparing to write a book was like training for a fight to him. He employed the same discipline, even cutting down on his drinking as he got ready to start. This was a major sacrifice for such a tippler as he was.

He put as much effort into rewriting his books as writing them. Such rewrites were often arduous. 'When a writer first starts out,' he propounded in 1947, 'he gets a big kick from the stuff he does and the reader doesn't get any. After a while, the writer gets a little kick and the reader gets a little kick. Finally, if the writer is any good, he doesn't get any kick at all and the reader gets everything.'[6]

Hemingway spent his life searching for 'the one true sentence'. Into that sentence he promised to put 'a thousand intelligibles'. A line in *Islands in the Stream* goes, 'Even when you break from the straight line of a great painting it's always there to help you.' He went back to basics when he found himself in trouble, regressing to patterns he was able to regurgitate from memory.

'All my life,' he told people, 'I look at words as though I were seeing them for the first time.'

Morley Callaghan described his style of writing as similar to a pool player who lines up the balls with his cue and sinks them cleanly. It had that sense of control, like chess with words.

His philosophy was simple: delete, delete, delete. It was one he learned from journalism. A common phenomenon among writers, he claimed, was 'Guys who think they're geniuses because they've never learned to say no to a typewriter.' (Or as he sometimes called it, 'a writetyper.') It was no accident, he pointed out, that the Gettysberg address was so short.

He told Lillian Ross that the test of a good book was how much you could throw away: 'People think I'm an ignorant bastard who doesn't know the ten dollar words.' He knew them all right, he assured her, but there were 'older and better words which, if you arrange in the proper combination, you make stick.' He finished by telling her, 'Anyone who pulls his education on you hasn't any.'[7] Art concealed art. If it looked like work, it was no good. What you had to aspire to was writing that 'didn't go off like stale fish'.

Every time you see a Hemingway line you feel he wants to say something more than what we see. His characters are often quiet. When they talk, it may often be about things that are trivial. The manner in which they focus on inconsequential details conceals a multitude. He never seems to be commenting on them. The comments are couched in their actions.

This is more obvious in the stories than the novels. These have the stamp of his tight lip. They often begin *in medias res* and end in mid-air. The impression is of life going on rather than plots being enacted. The endings are usually casual or mock-casual, often after momentous events. We could be forgiven for imagining a page of text had gone missing somewhere.

Hemingway would have agreed with the man who said that all good writing should have a beginning, a middle, and an end, but not necessarily in that order. 'With other writers,' Maxwell Geismar believed, 'The word is a catharsis. With Hemingway it seems rather a weapon of coercion.' From this springs his technique of concealment.

After his creative powers diminished, sadly, this turned into an affectation. The formality became mannered, especially in the dialogue. His effects were starting to become too obvious for comfort.

When George Plimpton asked him who his influences were in 1958, he replied, 'Mark Twain, Flaubert, Stendhal, Bach, Turgenev, Tolstoy, Dostoevsky, Chekhov, Andrew Marvell, John Donne, Maupassant, the good Kipling, Thoreau, Captain Marryat, Shakespeare, Mozart, Quevedo, Dante, Virgil, Tintoretto, Hieronymous Bosch, Breughel, Patinier, Goya, Giotto, Cezanne, Van Gogh, Gauguin, San Juan de la Cruz, Gongora. It would take a day to remember everyone.'[8]

By now he was turning away from the minimalism that made his name. His style swaggered just as he did himself. Behind the posturing there was a kind of panic. Old age was creeping on. The Reaper lurked.

Hadley Richardson, his first wife, thought he was one of the most sensitive people she ever met. Embarrassed by his shyness, she thought, he put on a pose of truculence to conceal it. She believed he had a lifelong inferiority complex, that he overacted the part of a he-man in order to suppress his compassion.

Norman Mailer saw him as 'a mid-western boy seized by success and ripped out of every root. He spent his life trying to relocate some of his old sense of *terra firma* by following each movement of the wind through his talent and his dread.' Mailer owed much of his style to him, as did writers like Raymond Chandler, Raymond Carver, Dashiell Hammett, Charles Bukowski, and countless others.

Today we have Hemingway lookalike contests in Key West. We have wannabe novelists aping the hardboiled style but forgetting why it was created in the first place. We have boudoir worthies enquiring of their girlfriends if the earth moved. We have purgatorial exegeses on hidden meanings in his books by critics he would have taken great pleasure in decking if he met them. We even have competitions where people try to see who can ape his style best, with stories carrying titles like 'The Snooze of Kilimanjaro', 'Into the River and up to your Knees', and 'A Farewell to Lunch'.[9] So far we have been spared the T-shirts or key chains but his work will live as long as people read. And he left us at least three classics.

The central mystery of his life remains the most obvious one. How could somebody who believed in doing everything to excess manage to remain so reticent in his books?

1

Beginnings

Ernest Miller Hemingway was born in the front bedroom of 439 North Oak Park, Chicago, at 8 a.m. on 2 July 1899, where his parents lived with his mother's widowed father. It was just six months before the new century. The date, James Nagel wrote, was 'too late for the frontier and too soon for outer space'. That left only the 'country within himself to explore'.[1] He weighed 9.5 pounds and was 23 inches in length.

The 'Ernest' was from his maternal grandfather, Ernest Hall, the 'Miller' from his great grandfather. Both names, significantly came from his mother's side of the family. In this as in most other decisions made while he was growing up, she was the prime arbiter.

Ernest's father, Clarence, more frequently known as 'Ed', was a doctor and, later, an obstetrician. He was 6 feet tall with powerful shoulders and a barrel chest. Though physically strong, his personality was timid. There was a rumour that in his childhood he had been chased into his own home by a school bully and beaten by his mother afterwards for cowardice. He manicured his nails daily and trimmed his neat beard, which he grew to cover a weak chin. He hunted and fished in his spare time and also kept snakes, which he preserved in alcohol in sealed glass jars. He was also interested in Indian culture and collected artifacts from the local mound of the Potawatomi tribe.

Ernest's mother, Grace, was a formidable woman both in her build and her personality. She had a fine contralto voice and, before her marriage, had taken professional lessons in singing in New York. A contract from the Metropolitan Opera resulted in a concert she gave at Madison Square Gardens in 1895. Unfortunately, the strong lights of the venue stung her eyes so much she cried. They had been weakened by her having scarlet fever as a child, which had blinded her for several months after she contracted it. It was this more than anything else that cut her singing career short. The following year she finally said yes to Clarence's marriage proposal. They had known one another since the days they both attended Oak Park High School. It was her voice, Clarence always told people, that he first fell in love with.

After Grace's father died in 1905, she used his inheritance money to buy another house. This was a grey stucco, wood-trimmed residence at 400 Kenilworth Avenue with two storeys and fifteen rooms. She wanted it designed to her specifications and spared no expense in achieving this, employing an architect to enhance it, with particular emphasis on her thirty square foot music room, where she intended to give lessons.

Oak Park was a conservative suburb of the more liberal Chicago, characterised by the sturdy oak trees that lined its streets. It was situated ten miles west of it and inhabited mainly by upper-class Lutherans, Baptists, Methodists, and Presbyterians. Each sect built its own church. An 1899 proposal that it merge with Chicago was strenuously ruled out by the local council.

The new house's bedrooms would be filled in subsequent years as more children arrived. Ernest already had an older sister, Marcelline, born in 1898, and a younger one, Madelaine (also known as Sunny), born in 1904. Carol was born in 1911. Finally there was another boy, Leicester. He arrived in 1915. This was far too late to be someone Ernest could have bonded with. Ursula was his favourite. He nicknamed her Uru.

Ernest's problems began on the day of his christening. He always hated his name, associating it with Oscar Wilde's play *The Importance of Being Earnest*. Couple this with the fact that his mother would have preferred him to be a girl so she could realise her fantasy of having twins. Could these two events, trivial and all as they may appear now, have caused him to overreact by creating a persona that highlighted his male qualities?

He also bridled against the values of Oak Park, an area as durable in its values as the oaks themselves.

It was surrounded by a broad expanse of nature with rolling fields. Clarence did his house calls on horseback, continuing to use this method of travelling even after he bought a car, one of the few in the area. Horses were thankfully free of engines that broke down in emergencies. Neither were cars able to find their way home if he had to leave them in a hurry.[2]

Oak Park, Ernest would later claim, was full of 'wide lawns and narrow minds'. It was a place where cinemas closed on Sundays and the sale of alcohol was forbidden.

Its streets were unpaved. There was no electricity. The residents were forbidden to buy cigarettes or even play billiards. A curfew was imposed at night.[3]

No prostitutes resided in the area nicknamed 'Saint's Rest'.[4] There were no punch-drunk fighters there nor contract killers nor alcoholics nor matadors nor thieves. It was, in other words, anathema to the characters who would people the fiction of its most famous son in years to come.

Oak Park, for Hemingway, was as dull and predictable as its architecture. It was full of houses, as his future friend James Joyce might have put it, 'conscious of the decent lives being lived inside them'.

Rude language was frowned on. If anyone used it, their mouths were washed out with soap.[5] Smoking was forbidden in most houses.[6] The word 'virgin' was even deemed too contentious to appear in school textbooks.

Clarence was more Victorian in his ways than Grace. He even had a problem with people dancing—particularly in ballet—or playing cards. Grace had more common sense in this regard. She saw dancing as a healthy exercise and card-playing as a pleasant pastime, though she agreed with her husband that it was wrong if played for money.[7] Clarence drove Ernest and Marcelline to Saturday dancing glasses with great reluctance, muttering epithets like 'Leads to hell and damnation' and 'It's all your mother's idea' through gritted teeth.

The fact that Hemingway came from such a Bible-thumping background made him an unlikely candidate for becoming a standard-bearer for a generation of disaffected souls. He inherited his love of the outdoors from his father but little else. He hardly got his drinking habits from him as Clarence was a teetotaller. Neither did he inherit his left-wing views from him, or his sexual infidelities, or his fondness for expletives, or his ribald sense of humour.

From his mother he got his poor eyesight and some character traits like stubbornness and pugnacity. He had more in common with her than he cared to admit.

His association with guns began early. When he was a baby, she fired a toy pistol at him with her left arm while she held him with her right one. As early as his fourth birthday, his grandfather was talking about 'Ernest, the great hunter.' A few years later, target practice became a ritual at the Hemingway household. His paternal grandfather presented him with a rifle on his tenth birthday. The fact that he fought in the Civil War meant the young Ernest was steeped in stories of combat. Both of his grandfathers had fought in the war, serving with distinction in the Union army.

Ernest was given a fishing rod when he was three. A few years later, he was sleeping rough in the woods and stuffing dead animals. His father taught him how to do this, and to shoot well. Ernest looked up to him for his strength and gentleness—two qualities he would come to possess himself in varying degrees in time.

Clarence was a kindly soul who gave his services free to local charities. He designed a laminectomy forceps once to replace the cruder instruments that were being used at the time but refused to patent it, believing it would be wrong to make money from anything altruistic.[8]

Grace 'twinned' Ernest with Marcelline. An early photograph of him carries the caption, 'Summer Girl.'[9] It has him dressed in girl's clothes and with hair as long as hers. He always feared it would surface somewhere during his lifetime, or that the world would see photographs of him in his female curls. He was six before he got his first haircut.

The twinning might strike us as odd today, but in the early years of the last century, it was a fairly common practice to dress family members of different sexes similarly. Where Grace differed from most mothers of her time was in continuing to put Ernest in girl's clothes as he grew up.

She kept Marcelline in kindergarten an extra year so she could be in the same high school class as him. The twinning process was reversed when Marcelline was five. Grace now dressed and coiffed her daughter as a boy.[10]

When Grace went shopping, she bought two of everything.[11] Ernest and Marcelline slept in the same room in twin white cribs. They had dolls that were similar, and played with china tea sets that had exactly the same pattern.

During their high school years, Grace did everything in her power to encourage them to be social partners, even to the extent of forbidding Marcelline to go to parties with other boys so Ernest would have to accompany her. Her actions drove the two of them farther and farther apart as the years went on, familiarity breeding contempt.

As early as three years old, Ernest was already aware of the fact that something was wrong about the way he looked. One day he told Grace he was worried Santa Claus might not recognise him at Christmas. He was afraid of being given a doll instead of the pop gun he asked for.

If we look at photographs of him from Grace's scrap album, we can see a staggering difference between the way he appeared in 1902, where he could have been mistaken for a little girl in his long pink dress, and one of a year later where he stands on top of a boat with a rifle in his hand.

Grace upset him hugely by having him taken out of school one year so he could concentrate exclusively on the cello.[12] He stopped playing it as soon as he could. The same applied to the clarinet, another instrument she foisted on him. 'A music nut' was a term he applied to her when he became old enough to know what was going on. She also directed the local church choir.

Ernest flaked off her. He wanted to be Huckleberry Finn, someone who crawled out from under his Aunt Sally's apron-strings to make a name for himself.

'Grace under pressure' was a term that would always be associated with his attitude to life. In his early years, 'Pressure under Grace' was more applicable.

Whatever damage she did to him was more than compensated for by the hunting and fishing expeditions Clarence organised for him.

When Ernest was four, Grace tried to lull him to sleep by singing 'Onward Christian Soldiers' to him. She had little success. 'I don't want to be an Onward Christian Soldier when I get to be a big boy,' he vowed, 'I want to go with Dad and shoot lions and wolves.' At five he was asked if there was anything he feared. He replied, 'Fraid a nothing.'[13] Over the next half century, in greater or lesser degrees, he would continue to prove that, or at least appear to.

Clarence may have been Ernest's most obvious role model in the sense that he gave him his love of hunting and fishing, but a more influential one was his grandfather, Anson. Clarence liked to shoot, but he never shot at anything that could attack him, unlike his father—and his son. Hemingway always preferred people who shot at something that ran 'both ways', like jungle animals. One could also be attacked by human beings in war, as his grandfathers would have experienced.

His habit of telling tall tales began early. At the age of five, he boasted to Anson of having stopped a runaway horse single-handedly. Anson said, 'With an imagination like that, you'll either end up famous or in jail.'[14]

Ernest had an amazing memory. When he reached six, he was alleged to have known the names of an incredible number of birds in Latin. In years to come, such a memory would stand him in good stead. He told Leicester, 'I've always made things stick that I wanted to stick. I've never kept notes or a journal. I just push the recall button and there it is. If it isn't there it isn't worth keeping.'

The things he found not worth keeping mostly came from Grace. He argued with her growing up, feeling a resentment not only over his twinning with Marcelline but the way she tried to quell his spirit at every turn. Happiness for him meant not seeing her. The best time he ever had in Oak Park, he told people, was when she was laid up with typhoid fever.

In many ways Grace was a woman before her time. She raised a few eyebrows when she cycled down the streets of Oak Park on her penny farthing bicycle. Ambitious to a fault, she made little secret of the fact that, while marriage to an obstetrician might have been a step up the social ladder for some women, for her it was more like a setback.

She found it difficult having to substitute the glory days of Madison Square Gardens for a life of being 'merely' a teacher of music and a composer of songs.

Housekeeping she saw as beneath her. Clarence was prevailed upon to bring her breakfast in bed and do domestic chores in between his medical rounds. Like the young Ernest, he sought refuge from her in the woods surrounding Oak Park when things got too much. There was nobody to bully them there. Both Ernest and Clarence released their tensions by shooting wild birds and eating food without having to worry about washing up afterwards.

Grace also had a financial hold over Clarence. He only had a little money when they married. Their house was paid for with an inheritance she received from her father's estate. She made it clear from early on in the marriage that the Hemingway household was her 'show'. The money she commanded from her music classes also vastly outstripped Clarence's meagre earnings from medicine. He earned only $50 a month, as opposed to her $1,000, gleaned from tutoring over fifty pupils at $8 an hour.

Clarence lacked the backbone to take her down from her high horse. As well as the woods, work was his escape from her. He went out on calls at all hours of the day and night to escape her shrieking directives. In his darker moments, he fell prey to depression, his natural good humour reverting to sullenness when she barked instructions at him.

He lost his temper with her sometimes, the frustration of his repression under her boiling over inside him. Occasionally he reared up at Ernest too. Many cowards become bullies, Hemingway believed. Clarence had elements of both qualities in him.

Grace conducted concerts in the house on occasion. Clarence sat listening to her like an extra child as she did so. The impression she created at these was that she was the important member of the household, not he.

He changed diapers when she was too tired to. Despite the responsibilities of his career, her concerns were always paramount. If she felt unwell she ran to her room, pulling down the shades and turning off the lights so she could rest in the dark.

One year Clarence told her he was thinking of practising medicine abroad. She poured cold water on the idea. She had sacrificed her singing career for him, she huffed. The least he could offer her in return was domestic stability.

The young Ernest took all this in, setting his mother's narcissism off against his father's silent suffering. He assured himself that his own life would be different. He could never have married a woman like Grace. If he did, the marriage would end before she became too fond of her control.

He watched his father taking bullets out of people's legs and then becoming cowed with the harridan he married. How, he wondered, could somebody be so powerful and powerless at the same time?

Ernest's admiration for Clarence was tempered by his disappointment that he allowed Grace to ride roughshod over him. This made his shows of temper less bearable. He told his friend Bill Smith that he sometimes sat in a shed aiming a loaded shotgun at Clarence's head on days when he had been punished by him.

Grace was like the male element in the Hemingway household and Clarence like the female one. The fact that Ernest was getting confused signals from his parents could have given rise to the strong theme of sex reversal in his work. It could also explain why he set such store by a life of action. Asked once what was the main reason for his success, he replied, 'I owe it all to the idle hours I spent in the music room playing "Pop Goes the Weasel" on my cello.'[15]

One of the myths of his youth, probably propagated by himself, was that he ran away from home to become a prize-fighter.[16] Nothing could have been farther from the truth. Neither did he jump trains, as was also alleged. Anytime he left home he kept in almost constant touch with his parents. He even brought stamped postcards from Clarence on some of his trips. The warmth of his comments on these communications hints at a warmth towards Clarence—and even Grace—that he discounted in later years.

The letters are awash with a kind of Lardneresque prose. This stands in marked contrast to the tight-lipped nature of his fiction. He made bad puns (like 'Alum Markus' for Alma Mater) and used quasi-Shakespearean dialect like 'Hie thee to a spaghettery.'

Hemingway was a notoriously bad speller. Sometimes he misspelled words deliberately, as, for instance, when he wrote 'situation' as 'sitshooation'.

The running away myth might have had its root in an incident that took place one day in 1916 when he accused Grace of serving him 'slop' for lunch. She ordered him to leave the table and not return until he apologised. Hemingway never liked being told what to do and that day was no exception. Instead he went to a friend's house, staying there for several days.

Another myth of his youth was that at one time he had been engaged to the screen siren Mae Marsh. Hemingway nurtured these stories like any good fiction writer. After a time, not even he himself seemed to be sure where fact ran towards fantasy.

Writing gave him an early opportunity to exhibit his personality. He contributed to the school magazine. The editor was short of a feature one time so Hemingway invented a Boy's Rifle Club to fill the space. Each week afterwards, the paper carried a column about the non-existent club.

He was unexceptional in class and neither did he excel athletically, being a clumsy footballer. His good looks should have given him confidence with girls but for some reason they failed to. Like many writers, he was shy at base.

He was also slow to develop sexually. Marcelline thought this was because he had so many sisters hovering around him in his early years. She said it made him slow to seek out girlfriends. The fact that Marcelline was both taller and stronger than Ernest for many years—and also brighter academically—shattered his confidence.

He liked telling people he slept around early in his life. A more likely possibility is that his first sexual experiences were a one-night stand with a waitress from Horton Bay and an equally brief dalliance with Prudence Bolton, an Indian girl who worked as a cook for his family.

Bolton appears as 'Trudy' in his story 'Fathers and Sons'. She's the girl who 'did first what no one has ever done better'.[17] Hemingway always claimed she was the first girl he 'pleasured'.[18] There has been some speculation about this. In his story 'Summer People', he claims to have slept with a character modelled on her.

In 1914, he had his first official date. It was with a girl called Dorothy Davies. Afterwards he took a shine to another girl, Frances Coates. Neither of these developed into relationships. He was more comfortable in the presence of his male friends.

Dancing was the main place where boys met girls in Oak Park. What dances usually meant to Ernest was acting as a chaperone for Marcelline. Neither was dancing his favourite activity. His big feet made him as clumsy on the floor as he was on the football pitch.

But few people in Oak Park had better personalities than Ernest. He had charisma and wit and was able to talk knowledgeably on many subjects—literature, boxing, baseball, and anything else that struck his fancy.

Most of the people who knew him felt he was going to make his mark on life in some shape or form. His squibs in the school magazine suggested writing might be the key, but he also threw himself into many outdoor pursuits—not only football but water polo. He also appeared in school plays and did some amateur boxing.

On 6 April 1917, America declared war on Germany. Two months later, Hemingway graduated from school. He got high marks in most subjects. His parents wanted him to go to university, but he had little interest in this.

His main ambition was to go to the war. It was like the ultimate football game to him. He was determined to get a place on the military 'team' by hook or by crook. 'I can't let a show like this go on without getting into it,' he told Marcelline.

He was too young to be drafted into military service. A defective left eye was another impediment. When he heard that one of his friends, Ted Brumback, became an ambulance driver at the front, he saw a way of experiencing combat without being an official soldier.

Brumback had a glass eye. It was caused by a golf ball hitting him after rebounding from a tree. The injury ruled him out of official military service just as Hemingway's defective vision did. But when Brumback became an ambulance driver in France, Hemingway decided to follow suit.

He applied to Italy—or 'Wopland' as he called it—rather than France. He said the reason for this was that there was less chance of getting killed there.

He drove an ambulance for the Red Cross in Schio, a town situated in the foothills of the Southern Alps, but he wanted to get closer to where the action was. The frontline was at a town called Fossalta on the Piave river. He asked to be moved to that location.

On 8 July, just a couple of weeks before his nineteenth birthday, he underwent the first major trauma of his life. As he was cycling towards the troops with some cigarettes and candy, an enemy mortar knocked him off his bicycle, rendering him unconscious and killing one of the soldiers standing beside him.

He was unconscious for a few moments. When he came to, he saw a man near him writhing in agony and he went to his aid. When he lifted him up, he was hit by machine gun fire into his left leg. He continued carrying the soldier to the trench. Then he collapsed. Afterwards, he was taken to hospital.

Over 200 pieces of shell lay lodged in his leg. Most of them were too small to cause any serious damage, but two of them cut into his knee and one into his right foot.

For carrying the injured man back to his dug-out, he was awarded the *Croce di Guerra* and also the more prestigious *Medaglia d'argento al valor militaire*. He said later that he threw them into the bowl beside his hospital bed 'with all the other scrap metal', i.e. the pieces of shrapnel that were taken from his leg. The 'aw-shucks' nature of his comment failed to mask his delight.

He spent his nineteenth birthday recuperating in a hospital in Milan. Grace wrote to him saying it was 'great to be the mother of a hero' and reassuring to know her boy was 'every inch a man'.[19]

One finds it difficult to know how he was able to carry a man to the safety of a dug-out after his knee had been shot to pieces. This has caused much sniping among biographers about the deservability of his medals. Some people said he exaggerated the details of the incident. But if he did, why was he awarded so much for courage? Some of his detractors felt he was decorated lavishly because the Italians needed an American hero to ensure U.S. support for them in the war. This is a point worth pondering. In *A Farewell to Arms*, a character asks his alter ego Frederic Henry, 'Didn't you carry anybody on your back?' He replies, 'I didn't carry anybody. I couldn't move.' The doctors at the hospital, however, knew how seriously he was injured. Amputation of his leg was even considered for a time.

As he convalesced, he removed the Red Cross identification labels from his uniform and replaced them with U.S. military ones. He then—contrarily—draped an Italian cloak over it, leading people to imagine he was in the Italian army.[20]

He held court like a king on his throne recalling the incident. As he did so, he took out some of the smaller pieces of shrapnel from his leg with a penknife. Nips from a bottle of cognac dulled the pain. One visitor claimed he prised out over 200 pieces altogether, placing them in a pillbox for people to admire

He wrote the following words to his parents: 'Maybe you didn't appreciate me when I used to reside in the bosom.' The war had made a nobody into a somebody. He added that the experience was 'the next best thing to getting killed and reading your obituary'.

In another letter, he wrote:

> The 227 wounds I got from the trench mortar didn't hurt a bit at the time, only my feet felt like I had rubber boots full of water and my knee was acting queer. The machine gun bullet just felt like a sharp smack on the leg with an icy snowball. They thought I was shot thru my chest because of my bloody coat. When they took off my coat they saw the old torso was intact. Then they said I'd probably live. That cheered me up any amount.

News of his actions spread round Oak Park like wildfire. Marcelline was at a film with a friend one night when she saw him on the Pathe News waving a crutch at the camera. She was so mesmerised she stayed at the cinema when the main feature was over and asked the projectionist to run it again. The next night she went back again with her parents.

Hemingway was in a lot of pain at this time. Copious doses of alcohol helped to dull it. He was attended to by no less than eighteen nurses. One took his fancy, a pretty girl called Agnes von Kurowsky, who was a number of years older than him. She was the daughter of a Polish aristocrat who emigrated to America after his family went bankrupt. He was treated by her mainly at night but night-time was when his demons struck. She saw him at his most vulnerable, becoming like a second mother to him—or maybe a first.

He fell head over heels in love with her. They even talked of marriage. He felt sure they could continue their romance in America. She gave him no reason to think not. Her letters to him have survived. The ones he wrote to her are lost. She also wrote about him in her diaries.

He gushed about her in a letter he wrote to his friend Bill Smith: 'Listen to what kind of girl I have. She heard about me hitting the alcohol and she said, "Kid, we're going to be partners. If you're going to drink, I am too." Bill, this is some girl. I'm glad I got crucked [*sic*] so I met her.'[21]

In one of her letters, she signed off with the words, 'Yours Till the War Ends.' It was a significant phrase. Was Hemingway merely filling in time for her until something better came along? It hardly sounded like that when she wrote, 'No letter from you since Sun. afternoon so I'll probably expire gaspingly tomorrow if none is forthcoming by noon.'[22] This was the same woman who wrote a few months later, 'Dear Ernie, you are to me a wonderful boy & when you add on a few years and some dignity and calm, you'll be very much worthwhile. I only fear all the Chicago femmes will be willing you away from your night nurse.'[23] Here she seems to be preparing him for a future rejection.

'I'm looking to you to do big things,' she continued, 'Don't worry & fret over me & get silly ideas in your imaginative brain. Carry on and you'll get farther than you would if you sat down & thought of me all the time.'

The tone in the diaries is harder than the one she employs in the letters. She may have been flattered by his attentions and indulged him temporarily, not having the courage to tell him directly how she felt about him.

She gave him a ring that he wore as proudly as his military attire. One imagines her being amused at this. Agnes basically saw Hemingway as a mixed-up child. A term of endearment she used for him, 'bambino', shows she was all too well aware of the age gap between them. Her feelings were fortified by the nurse/patient context in which their relationship blossomed. Lying immobilised on his back at the age of nineteen was hardly the way to try and seduce a worldly-wise woman like Agnes.

She wrote him no less than fifty-two letters between September 1918 and March 1919. 'You certainly are the champion love letter writer, old furnace man,' she said in one of them. She usually signed off as 'Mrs Kid' or 'Mrs Hemingstein'.[24]

In one of them she referred to him as 'The Light of my Existence.'[25] He was, she praised, 'about the nicest man I know or ever will know.'

She was eventually transferred to a hospital in Florence. Hemingway stayed in Italy as he recuperated, watching military developments from the sidelines. Eventually he went home, feeling secure in the knowledge that Agnes would follow him back to America.

He was given a hero's welcome when he came home. Clarence referred to his wound as a 'miraculous deliverance'. He went back to his *alma mater* to tell his fellow pupils about his experiences and they lapped them up. They gasped audibly when he passed his blood-spattered uniform around for them to examine. 'We hail you the victor,' they sang in a welcoming song, 'Hemingway ever winning the game!'

He spoke at social clubs, church societies, meetings of women's groups associated with his mother.[26] He even charged a fee for some of these. Melodrama reigned supreme. He came out with memories like, 'When the thing exploded it seemed as if I was moving off somewhere in a red din. I said to myself, "Gee, Stein, you're dead." Then I began to feel myself pulling back to earth.' ('Stein' was his nickname for himself.)

A year earlier he would have been far too shy to do things like that. He grew into a man in Italy. The war gave him standing. Before it, he was a drifter and a layabout. The wounding was little more than an 'industrial accident', but it became his *entrée* into a world he dreamed about, a slice of publicity he could hardly have orchestrated better. Each piece of shrapnel was like a brownie point he notched up on the way to becoming one of America's best-known war heroes.

He exaggerated the circumstances as the weeks went on. The pieces of shrapnel lodged inside him grew in the telling. So did the number of operations necessary to get them out. In the way he beefed up incidents, people were witnessing the beginning of the Hemingway myth.

He kept his uniform on through all the weeks of recuperation. That was in case anyone might forget his heroics. He gave a speech to a civic group in Petoskey dressed in it, posing for photographs afterwards in full military regalia.

There were twenty pieces of mortar shell inside him, but the idea that he was one of the most wounded Americans in the war was spectacularly untrue. He disavowed it some years down the road when he had other wounds to boast about.

His fascination with his hero status may be gleaned from details like the fact that he went fishing in Michigan after he recuperated. To do so, he dressed in his Italian service beret and combat boots. Here again he embellished the story of his wounding to locals. He told them he needed the boots because his leg was still troubling him.[27]

He told a reporter from the *Oak Parker* newspaper that he got over thirty .45-calibre bullet wounds and that twenty-eight of these were removed without an anaesthetic. This was untrue.[28] He blithely told lies to people while keeping a straight face. To his friend Guy Hickok he talked about the circumstances of his wound in almost Cartesian fashion: 'I felt my soul or something coming right out of my body like you'd pull a silk handkerchief out of a pocket by one corner. It flew around and then came back and went in again and I wasn't dead anymore.'

Though he acted nonchalant after his wounding, he experienced traumas from the incident right through his life. He had to sleep with a light on for a long time after it happened. Ursula—or rather 'Uru'—sat by his bed. Sometimes she climbed in beside him when his demons struck. He developed a phobia that if he fell asleep in the dark, he might never wake up. He was suffering from what was then called shellshock and is now termed post-traumatic stress disorder. He wrote about it in detail in the semi-autobiographical story, 'A Way You'll Never Be'.

His hero's return to Oak Park was followed by a period of inertia. The practical reality was that he had no job. His school friends were embarking on careers. His own literary one was yet to take off.

When the allure of his status wore off, he became, like the character of Krebs from his story 'Soldier's Home', like a beached whale. The 'somebody' invented lies to avoid sliding back into being a 'nobody' again. Nothing was more boring than war heroes who lived in the past. 'I'm willing to die for this great and glorious nation,' he wrote to his friend Jim Gamble, 'but I hate like the deuce to live in it.'[29]

Grace asked him what his plans for the future were. He told her he had none.

On 7 March 1919, he received a 'Dear John' letter from Agnes. In it she wrote that what happened between them was just a 'boy-girl' thing: 'I am still very fond of you but it is more as a mother than as a sweetheart.' It was the first major blow to his ego, laying the foundation for a philosophy of love that would form the cornerstone of his work. The philosophy was this: if you gave too much of your heart to any woman you would die emotionally. 'I tried hard to make you understand what I was thinking,' Agnes wrote, 'but you acted like a spoiled child & I couldn't keep on hurting you.'[30]

When people speak of Hemingway's war wound, maybe they should be talking of Agnes as much as Fossalta. He was hers too. He hounded her after her promise to marry him.

He threw up after he received the letter, feeling like 'a hermit crab in its borrowed shell'.

He wrote to his friend Bill Horne:

> She doesn't love me, Bill. She takes it all back. Oh Bill I can't kid about it. I'm just smashed. The devil of it is it wouldn't have happened if I hadn't left Italy. Never leave your girl until you marry her. I loved Ag. She was my ideal. I forgot about religion and everything else because I had her to worship. Now the bottom has dropped out of the whole [*sic*]. I'm writing this with a dry mouth and a lump in the old throat. Aw Bill I can't write about it 'cause I love her so damned much.

He got over his grief the following month, adopting a more philosophical attitude in a letter he wrote to Jim Gamble: 'Through good fortune I escaped matrimony so why should I grumble? I'm now free to do whatever I want. I can fall in love with anyone I wish, which is a great and priceless privilege.'

Agnes afterwards became engaged to an Italian artillery officer. He was the heir to a Neapolitan dukedom. Their liaison came to an end when his mother decided her son was 'too good' for Agnes. Hemingway tried to sound sorry for her. 'Poor damned kid,' he wrote to Howell Jenkins, 'I'm sorry as hell for her but there's nothing I can do. I loved her once and then she gypped me. That's all behind me now, long ago and far away.'[31]

More surprising than her rejection, maybe, was the fact that she believed she could attach herself to nobility this easily. Hemingway had given her immense confidence in herself.

He suspected her engagement was responsible for her dumping of him. Up to now she was keeping her options open. It was as if the gauche war hero would 'do' if nothing better turned up.

When he read the letter, his nervous system went to pieces. He developed a fever as a result. Afterwards the pain changed to rage. He wrote in a letter to his friend Elsie MacDonald that when Agnes returned to New York, he wanted her to trip on the boat and knock out all her front teeth.[32] He claimed to have cauterised her memory out of himself with a course of booze and other women.[33] That was how he dealt with most of his problems in life.

Writing was another form of therapy. Could he make a living from it? Journalism was where the immediate money was but his main interest was in fiction. That paid less. The last thing he wanted was to end up like his father, doing work without reward. When he cut grass or did his paper round with *Oak Leaves*, the local gazette, people paid him. Why should writing be different?

Edgar Rice Burroughs lived near him. He was famous for his *Tarzan* novels. One of them had been made into a film. Hemingway had more interest in people like Ring Lardner. He read the writers most people of his era read—Shakespeare, Thackeray, Robert Louis Stevenson, Emerson, Hawthorne. Of the last two, he said, 'They had minds, yes. Nice, dry, clean minds.'[34]

His parents still wanted him to go to college. He had even less inclination for that now than before the war. His mother grew frustrated as she watched him frittering away whatever small amounts of money he earned. She importuned him to remember his duties to 'God and your saviour Jesus Christ.'

He fished at Horton Bay during the summer. When it ended, he stayed at Walloon Lake. This was his first time there in the autumn. It was attractive to him being on his own. He was free to go hunting, to witness the autumn storms, to shoot grouse. When he felt like company, he hung out with a waitress called Marjorie Bump and her younger sister, Georgina. Georgina was better known as Pudge. There was a rumour he was engaged to Marjorie for a time, but they were really just friends.

Another good friend was Grace Quinlan. She had a crush on him.[35] They dated for a while. He shared his thoughts with her about what he wanted to do with his life. He wrote to her, sounding like a cross between Jack London and Eugene O'Neill:

> I'm for the open road and the long sea swells, and an old tramp steamer hull down on the oily seas. And waking up in the morning in strange ports with new delightful smells and a tongue you don't understand. And the rattle of shifting cargo in the hold. And tall glasses and siphons and rare new stories and old pals in far places. And hot nights on deck with only pyjamas on. And cold nights when the wind roars outside and

> the waves smash against the thick glass of the portholes and you walk on deck in the flying scuds and have to shout to make yourself heard. And laying chin down on the grass on a cliff and looking out over the sea.[36]

He borrowed a typewriter from Bill Smith and started writing more stories. They were mainly amateurish pieces about activities like boxing and bootlegging. He wrote some detective stories as well.

Hemingway's early style was far removed from the one we now associate with him. It took him years to find his voice. In his juvenilia he borrowed from writers like Lardner, Mark Twain, and Horatio Alger. His early stories were rejected by editors at all the outlets he could think of: *The Dial*, *Black Cat*, *The Saturday Evening Post.*

Life at home was bad for him at this time. He spent a lot of his time arguing with Marcelline. She sided with his mother against him. Ursula was more supportive. She rebelled against her mother in the same ways he did. They formed a bond together against the stuffiness of Oak Park.

He hung around with Marge and Pudge Bump to get away from the house, entertaining them with his war stories. He collected Marjorie from school some days and took her to dances at the weekends. His wound was still bothering him. He put a bandage around his knee for support when it pained him. Bits of shrapnel sometimes squeezed their way to its surface. He had to go to the hospital in Boyne City to have them removed.

His final lecture about the war took place at Petoskey Library to the Ladies Aid Society. A woman called Harriet Connable attended it. She was in town to visit her mother, her home being in Canada. Her husband, Ralph, was originally from Chicago. He was now the manager of the successful Woolworth stores in Toronto. They had a son who was also called Ralph. He was disabled as the result of a high forceps birth. It left him with a lame leg and an impaired right arm.

His parents were looking for a tutor for him. They were planning to go on holiday for a month to Palm Beach. Hemingway looked like being a good candidate for the job. They wanted him to bring Ralph to concerts and to teach him how to box. It was thought he would be a good friend to him, maybe even an inspiration.

Hemingway jumped at the offer. He went to live in their Toronto mansion in January 1920. It had a billiard table in one of the rooms. Another one had a pipe organ three times the size of his mother's. Outside the house there was a tennis court that had been flooded. It was now used for ice skating.

Hemingway became friendly with the Connables before they set off for Palm Beach, spending some of his time playing billiards with Ralph Senior. He also got to know Dorothy Connable, Ralph's twenty-six-year-old sister. She worked with the YMCA in France and Germany after the war. That fact gave him an immediate empathy with her. He joked that they were both 'young old soldiers'.

No sooner was he settled in than he got a letter from his father. 'Write to me often, dear boy,' he wrote, adding weirdly, 'and if Ralph needs a walloping, now is the time while his folks are away.'

It was the easiest job Hemingway ever had in his life. There were no official chores to be performed in the mornings. He used this time to write. The nights took care of themselves with events and outings that had been pre-planned for Ralph by his parents.

Hemingway's personality clashed with his. America's especial alpha male was never going to hit it off with a lame person—unless he was wounded in a war. He preferred playing billiards with his father than trying to teach Ralph Junior how to box.

When the Connables returned to Canada the following month, Ralph introduced Hemingway to the staff of the *Toronto Star Weekly.* He thought he might be able to get him a job there. The features editor was a man called Gregory Clark. Clark was originally dubious about Hemingway's eccentric style of writing but he ran some of his pieces. He denied him money and even a byline at the beginning. Then he grew on him. The pair of them became friends in time, even going on skiing and fishing expeditions together.

Hemingway's style of writing captivated readers. That was more important to him than what he was earning. He was doing what he wanted. His articles had no clear-cut themes. He wrote about everything from crime to where to get a good haircut.

He went back to Walloon Lake in the summer. In October, he moved to Chicago for a time, sending journalistic dispatches to Chicago's *Daily Star* during that month. As was the case with the *Toronto Star Weekly*, he wrote about anything that struck his fancy—crime, boxing matches, how best to fish.

It became a pattern for him having one home in the winter and another in the summer. He was always in love with change. 'It's like shooting a lion,' he said, 'After a while you think of your next one.' The shooting of lions was far from him yet, but he was thinking that way.

The stuffiness of Oak Park became increasingly oppressive to him. Clarence's nerves got worse. This resulted in Grace distancing herself more and more from him.

She developed a notion of having a cottage built near their home. It was a way of having a life separate from Clarence. He thought it was impractical. How would she carry groceries and water up the hill? 'I want the view,' she demanded, 'It's worth going without water and food to have peace and quiet—and a place to be alone.'[37] He thought it was a needless expense.

Grace brought one of her music students, a woman called Ruth Arnold, into Oak Park to live with her now. This upset Clarence. Like the construction of the cottage, it seemed to be part of her growing away from him. Arnold became like a sister to Grace in time. There were even rumours of a lesbian relationship between them.

Hemingway did some painting and wallpapering of the cottage when he felt like it but neglected the more important chores like chopping wood and digging holes for the garbage. 'You're doing the jobs your sisters can do,' Grace chastised, 'instead of the laborious ones.' He also went off fishing at any opportunity.

His mind was on bigger things than housework now. A notion formed in his mind of going to China. He discussed the idea with Bill Smith and Ted Brumback. They agreed to go with him along with a third friend, Jack Pentecost. He asked his mother for the money for a passport and his fare to San Francisco. That was where the ship was sailing from.[38]

She refused. Hemingway had now been a year and a half without working except for his brief time in Canada. 'Your wounds are healed,' she scolded, 'You need to get a regular job.'

Her frustration with his lackadaisical lifestyle boiled over in the summer of 1920. He had just celebrated his twenty-first birthday on Lake Walloon.

One night Ursula and Sunny told him they were planning to have a midnight party in the cottage with some friends. It was in Windemere. He offered to row them across the lake and join them for the party. A fun time was had by all. They came back at 4 a.m. Two women spotted them rowing home. They informed Grace, who blamed Hemingway for it all.[39]

He told her the party had been their idea, but she refused to believe him. That infuriated him. He used all the four-lettered words he could think of to abuse her. She accused him of corrupting Ursula and Sunny. 'You trade on your good looks,' she accused, 'to fool gullible young girls.'[40] She ordered him off the premises.

He went off in a huff, staying at a friend's house. Shortly afterwards she wrote him a letter outlining her problems with him. She compared love to a bank account on which he overdrew. He regarded this as melodrama. All that happened on the night in question, he explained, was some innocent horseplay, the kind of thing that might be expected of any adolescent children. Grace's reaction made it appear as if he breached some sacred law. 'I didn't even want to go to the bludy [*sic*] thing,' he insisted.

He felt she had an ulterior motive in turning on him. 'Mother was glad of an excuse to oust me,' he told Grace Quinlan, 'ever since I opposed her throwing two or three thousand seed away to build a new cottage for herself.' ('Seed' was his term for dollars.) He said he wanted the money to be used to send Ursula to college. Grace treated this idea with derision.

She said he would only be allowed back to Windemere when he learned not to curse and swear at her 'whether that be in this world or the next'. That scary phrase came at the end of the letter. She read it in its entirety to Clarence. He thought it was a masterpiece.

Hemingway never forgave Grace for banning him from the cottage. It was where he wrote many of his early stories. That gave it a special place in his heart. Now that it was gone from him, he thought, what was the point of being in Michigan at all?

He only went back to Oak Park five more times during the rest of his life. His future lay elsewhere. The days 'up in Michigan' were drawing to a close.

By driving him away from Windemere, Grace probably made him a better writer than he would otherwise have been. Everything he achieved after that became intensified by the knowledge that he was creeping out from under her shadow. He let her know that if She failed to appreciate him, the greater world outdoors would.

Nelson Algren thought Hemingway would have been an expatriate even if he never left Oak Park. 'His exile,' he suggested, 'wasn't from a land but from a way of living. His need wasn't for a country but for the company of men.'

'There was no place on earth he wasn't at home,' wrote E. L. Doctorow, 'except perhaps his birthplace. His parents' mid-West provincialism made independence an easy passage for him.' 'When you stop having fun,' he said, 'you might as well be dead.' The rainbow's end was waiting somewhere for the young man who was determined to have 'the good things now'.[41]

He sat over campfires with Ted Brumback. They ate the fish they caught as they discussed their futures.

After Hemingway left Michigan he lived for a time on the outskirts of Chicago, eating in cheap Italian restaurants and working out in gyms. When his money ran out, he shared a room with Bill Horne. He wrote some articles for the *Chicago Tribune* to make ends meet at this time.

Horne also did some journalism. Afterwards the two of them moved into a house on East Chicago Street owned by an advertising copywriter called Y. Kenley Smith. Hemingway met many writers there, including Sherwood Anderson.

He never saw Agnes again. She wrote to him once after he started to make a name for himself. 'We were good friends once, weren't we?' she said in her letter, 'How proud I will be some day in the not-very-distant future to say, "Oh, yes, Ernest Hemingway. I knew him quite well during the war."'

In later years she lived less than a mile from him but stopped short of seeking him out. She knew there would have been no point. 'Ernest never forgave me for deserting him,' she sighed.

2

Two Parts of the One Person

Hemingway now met Hadley Richardson, a woman who would figure hugely in his life. She was a St Louis girl, something that in time seemed to be a prerequisite for being a Hemingway wife. She met him at a party thrown by Katy Smith, Y.K.'s sister. Hadley had been at school with her.

Hadley had lived a tough life. She fell out of a window as a young girl. When she was twelve her father shot himself from depression over business losses. This was an incident which would have huge resonance for Hemingway. A sister of hers, Dorothea, had also died young. She was pregnant at the time. A brush fire had broken out and spread to her home. She was wearing a loose-fitting kimono on the day in question. As she tried to put out the blaze it caught fire. A few days later she died from her burns. Her baby was stillborn.[1]

When Hemingway met Hadley, she was after spending six months caring for her terminally ill mother. She had Bright's disease. After such a traumatic experience, she needed some joy in her life.

Hemingway fell in love with her at first sight. He was fascinated by her beauty and her auburn hair. Hair was always important to him. This is evident in many of his novels and stories. It seemed to be the first thing he saw in a woman.

Hadley was attracted to him at first sight too. She liked the way he rocked on his feet as he talked to her. He rolled his head from side to side like a boxer. When he laughed, his mouth stretched from ear to ear.[2]

When he talked to her, he made her feel like the only person in the room. He hit her at her 'soul's centre'.

Her attraction to him was easy to understand. He was handsome, he had vitality, he was full of mirth and yarns. Intelligent as well as charismatic, there was a huge mystique about him. 'He was the kind of man,' she said, 'to whom men, women, children and dogs were attracted.'

He was more confident with Hadley than when he was lying on his back in a hospital in Italy being ministered to by Agnes. He saw culture and refinement in her. She was like a breath of fresh air to him, a timely antidote to the small-mindedness of his mother and the cruelty of Agnes.

She was everything his mother was not—sweet, gentle, and a good listener. The only thing she had in common with Grace was a love for the piano. He described her as 'a terribly fine article'.

He was wearing his Italian officer's cape on the night he met her. She suspected he was a shy soul behind it. They bonded immediately. In no time at all, they seemed sure they wanted to be in a serious relationship with one another.

Hadley's main worry about anything developing between them was that Hemingway was seven years younger than her. She tried to play this down by telling him she felt he knew more about life than she did, that she would enjoy learning from him.

If he was older than his years, she was younger than hers. Her life had hardly begun yet. There was a lot of repressed energy inside her waiting to explode. 'I have never taken an attitude of olderness to your youngerness,' she told him in one of the quirky expressions that seemed to come naturally to her.

When they got to know one another better they discovered they had more than a little in common. Hadley's mother, like Hemingway's, had had six children. She also had a promising musical career cut short by marriage.

Hadley told Hemingway about the bad things in her past. Falling out of the window had left her wheelchair-bound for a year. Her mother treated her like a cripple during that time. She also had a failed romance with a piano teacher who rejected her. Hemingway identified with this because of his experience with Agnes. They were both coming to the relationship from a position of being emotionally scarred.

He only saw her seven times in the nine months of their courtship. They communicated mainly by letter. In those nine months, they wrote one another over 1,000 pages. As was the case with Agnes, Hemingway came to depend on receiving a letter from her almost every day. Sometimes he got more than one.

Hadley threw herself passionately into the writing of them. This was in the days before long-distance phone calls were common. 'Oh Mr Hemingway I love you,' she wrote in one of her more breathy missives,

'How exciting you are. What a lot of things happen around you. I love the way you love me.' She didn't take that love for granted, adding, 'Maybe your work calls for a harder wreckage. You're not going to get that from me.'

He gave her a life that was light years away from anything she experienced in St Louis. Up until now, all she did was read and play the piano.

In an unpublished story, Hemingway wrote, 'Those days to me were wonderful. I was awakening from a sleep which I thought was everlasting.' Hadley mellowed him at a time of his life when he had many resentments about his past. She was 'the chink in his armour of telling the world to go to hell'.

Like Cathy and Heathcliff in *Wuthering Heights*, they spoke of being like two parts of the one person. Such identification patterns would find their way into much of Hemingway's fiction in the future. We can see these all the way from *A Farewell to Arms* to *For Whom the Bell Tolls*. Those two novels have heroines partly modelled on Hadley.

Almost single-handedly, Hadley renewed Hemingway's faith in women. She was, as he put it, 'the best and truest and loveliest person that I have ever known'.

Hadley had *joie de vivre*. Hemingway evinced the same thirst for living in his gung-ho pursuits. Both of them wanted to attack life. They were prevented from doing so until they met up. Now they could do it together.

When he brought her on a visit to meet his parents they were delighted. The potential ne'er-do-well had come good, finding himself a 'nice girl' from St Louis. Grace fawned over her. Hadley was polite to her but Hemingway's problems with her were obviously going to get in the way of them ever having a strong bond. 'He trained me to dislike her,' she revealed.[3]

One day during the visit he showed Marcelline a poem of his that had been published in a magazine. 'You wanta see something, Marce?' he offered, holding the magazine out to her almost shyly. 'Of course,' she enthused. 'Look at the table of contents, kid,' he said, 'Your old [*sic*] brother is a poet. Neat, huh?'[4] His excitement over such a modest publication showed how much it meant to him.

Hemingway and Hadley were married on 3 September 1921. Not wanting the fuss of a St Louis wedding, they opted for a more humble ceremony at Horton Bay instead. Hadley was late for it. She went swimming that morning and got delayed. When she arrived at the church, her hair was dripping wet.

Over 100 people attended the wedding. Bill Smith was the best man. Katy Smith and Ursula were the bridesmaids. Hadley's surviving sister, Fonnie, was maid of honour.

Hemingway was nervous. 'His heavy white trousers,' Leicester recalled, 'seemed to have a serious case of the shivers.'

He had a problem kneeling down in the pew due to a trick knee. As they left the church, he stepped on one of Hadley's slippers. She thought this was a bad omen for the marriage.[5]

A friend loaned them a car to go to Lake Walloon for their honeymoon. Grace's expulsion of him from the cottage was lifted for the occasion. As they drove to the lake, tin cans rattled off the rear bumper until the string broke. When they got to it, they decided to take the boat to the cottage. Clarence had hidden the oars behind a tree in case they were stolen. They had some difficulty finding them but eventually they did. Hadley was excited going across the lake. When they got to the cottage, they French-kissed. Hemingway wrote about this in one of his stories: 'She kissed him back the way he taught her, with her mouth a little open so their tongues could play with each other.'

The honeymoon was a disaster. Both of them felt unwell and the weather was overcast. Anyone they met seemed to focus on Hadley's age. It made her feel like 'an old hag of thirty'.[6] Before they were married, she asked Hemingway to make up a 'magnificent lie' about it in case anyone was curious enough to enquire.[7]

He introduced her to his former girlfriends Grace Quinlan and Marjorie Bump.[8] He expected her to be impressed by seeing women he threw over for her, but it had the opposite effect. Both women felt awkward. Quinlan, Hadley recalled, 'just stood by her kitchen table the whole time we visited her. She looked embarrassed and ill at ease.'[9]

Afterwards they moved to an apartment in Dearborn Street in Chicago. Hemingway wrote to Agnes from there to tell her how happy he was. There was a sting in the letter. It was almost like revenge for what she did to him. He now had the upper hand. Such things were always important to him. Life was a battle you won both on the battlefield and in the civilian world. Love bore many resemblances to war for him.

The first year of their marriage was one of the happiest. Hemingway worked hard at his writing and Hadley played the role of the dutiful wife. She bought him a typewriter for his next birthday. It held pride of place in the apartment. A piano she liked to play on was shoved into a corner. It was an early gesture of what was going to be the centre point of their lives.

Grace visited them one day. She took Hadley aside, lecturing her about how to best please Hemingway. Hadley baulked at her interference.

They were invited to Oak Park for Grace and Clarence's twenty-fifth wedding anniversary in October. Hadley bought a dress for it but Hemingway prevailed on her not to wear it. She dressed down. It was a gesture of disrespect to Grace.[10] At a more casual party the following week, she wore the dress she bought for the anniversary, again at Hemingway's behest. This made things even more pointed to Grace.

Hemingway and Hadley now made plans to move to Paris. Their main problem, Hemingway thought, would be financial. He wanted to chuck in journalism and try to live off his creative writing. That was hardly feasible considering he had little or no published work to his credit at this stage.

He started saving whatever money he earned from his journalism and converting it into foreign currency. Hadley had a trust fund worth $3,000 a year. That helped enormously. An uncle of hers died at this time as well, leaving her a further $8,000.

Hemingway's reliance on Hadley to be the early breadwinner was like a replay of his parent's marriage where Grace's earnings from singing exceeded those of her physician husband. The difference was that Clarence allowed Grace to play on this to give her dominance over him. His son took care not to make the same mistake.

Hadley occupied the traditional role of mother and wife in a way none of Hemingway's subsequent spouses would. She provided an ideal working environment for him and significantly advanced his 'artoostic kareer', as she dubbed it. She also made it possible for him to entertain his dream of living in Europe. Here he expected to find the ideal milieu for his burgeoning talent.

Hemingway was impatient to make what he called 'the bold dash' to Paris. That was where, as Gertrude Stein put it, 'the twentieth century was'. Hemingway may not have known it then, but he was about to define that century just as much as it would him.

3

Published Author

Hemingway came from left field in his writing style even if its subject matter was often more like an emanation from *Field and Stream* magazine. When he got to France, he met up with those at the cutting edge of the *avant-garde*.

In Paris, Henry James wrote, the very air was suffused with style.[1] Hemingway arrived there armed with letters of introduction from Sherwood Anderson addressed to three people: Gertrude Stein, Sylvia Beach, and Ezra Pound. He told Anderson he was going to launch the letters like a flock of ships in enemy territory. 'I was born to enjoy life,' he wrote to his parents in 1918, 'but the Lord neglected to have me born with money. I've got to make it on my own.' The incumbent scribe was going to earn his daily bread on what he called his 'write machine'.

He was struggling to get his stories printed at this point. That was why he was glad to have his letters of introduction. He was aware of the fact that knowing the right people was as important a factor in the world of books as it was in any other business. But he was cautious about approaching the people Anderson had referred him to, particularly Stein and Pound. Both of them had reputations for being eccentric.

Pound, he felt, would be a particularly useful contact. He had already established himself as a friend to struggling writers as well as being an intelligent editor of their writings. T. S. Eliot called him *Il Miglior Fabbro* after his herculean work on *The Waste Land*. Hemingway had little respect for that poem, but he knew that Pound was probably his best shot at getting in with the right people.

The Paris of 1922 was awash with dilettantes. Between 1920 and 1927, it was estimated that as many as 35,000 Americans emigrated there. They were seduced by its sense of freedom. It was relatively cheap to have a good time there. The dollar was worth fifteen francs in 1920. There were also the cafes and the fruit markets and the wine—not to mention the entertaining chatter of *boulevardiers*.[2]

The city had been a port of call to Hemingway's grandfathers in the last quarter of the nineteenth century. He himself had passed through it on his way to the war in 1918. 'If you are lucky enough to have lived in Paris as a young man,' he wrote, 'then wherever you go for the rest of your life, it stays with you, for Paris is a moveable feast.'[3] He referred to it as his mistress. Not only was it the epicentre of bohemianism, it was a melting-pot where the literary talents of the time could come to compare notes. They could also philosophise about their books, backbite one another, and, perhaps most importantly, drink.

Hemingway's first residence in the city was on the fourth floor of an old building in a working-class street called Rue de Cardinal Lemoine. Its most noticeable feature was an enormous mahogany bed. 'The French,' Hadley reflected, 'believe in sleeping—and all the other things you can do in bed.'

They also liked to eat. Hemingway remarked that there were '3,000 shiny pots and pans' in the kitchen.

Their concierge, who lived across the corridor, was having an affair with the local policeman. When Hemingway passed their apartment and the door was open, he saw his horse-hair plumed helmet on a chair.

Though hardly flush with money, they were able to employ a *femme de menage* to cook and clean for them. Hemingway referred to her as 'a feminine menagerie'. He credited her with cooking 'the best meals you ever put into your mouth from all the things we've never heard of'.

He saw Paris as a state of mind as much as a place. A conduit for the countercultural expatriates of the time, it provided him both with an endorsement of what he had already done and the promise of better things to come under the tutelage of his literary heroes. 'Paris was always Paris,' he wrote, 'and you changed as it changed.'

He picked up snatches of French, speaking it whenever he could to try and master it. It found its way into his conversations and his writing, often with comic effect if he mixed it with English.

The city was an ideal environment for writing. He woke early and breakfasted on toast and coffee. Hadley had to stay quiet as he contemplated his work. 'We had a great deal of silence,' she remembered, 'Good silence.'

In the afternoons they played tennis. Hadley, or 'Hash' as he called her, was better at this than he was. She could also beat him at billiards. Her catches when they went fishing for trout were even better than his.

At night he read her what he wrote that day. If his muse deserted him, there might be only a few lines, but writing was on his mind all the time. Some nights when they were snuggled up in in bed together and she thought he was trying to sleep, she looked behind her and saw him reading a folded-up newspaper behind her back.[4]

They drank often. 'We got so tight,' she recalled, 'We'd throw up together.' Prohibition was still in force in America. In Paris different laws applied. They frequently lowered a bottle of wine at lunch, following it up with aperitifs before dinner. More wine would be consumed then.

Hadley had as good a tolerance for alcohol as Hemingway. One day when they were on a hike, they stopped at a village inn where a beer-drinking competition was taking place. Hadley out-drank all the other entrants, including her husband. She was so sozzled she passed out. When she woke up, she was informed she'd won a cow.

Hemingway carved out his stories wherever he could—in his apartment, in parks, in a café on the Closerie des Lilas where he went many mornings with his notebooks and his well-sharpened pencils. 'The marble-topped tables,' he wrote, 'the smell of early morning sweeping out and mopping and luck were all you needed.'[5] Observations were jotted down in notebooks with the blunt ends of pencils and put into stories later on. He sent them off to obscure journals, anywhere to make his mark. Often such stories were returned. They came through the slot in the door of the bare room where he sat at an old wooden table.

'A rejection slip is very hard to take,' he said, 'There were times when I'd sit at that table and read one of those cold slips that had been attached to a story I loved and worked on very hard and believed in and I couldn't help crying.'[6] Hadley kept his spirits up. So did his belief that one day the world would take notice of his style.

For pin money, he wrote journalism on and off for *The Toronto Star* as its foreign correspondent. He had a roving commission there, covering everything from trout fishing in Europe to the effects of inflation on the German mark. He brought a whimsical approach to the subjects he wrote about.

Meeting people was part of his brief. He interviewed Benito Mussolini at a time when that demagogue was being exalted by many. 'Mussolini is running a disgraceful business,' he wrote in one of his dispatches, 'Lead pipe government, and everybody that squeals gets bumped off.'

Hemingway always insisted the most essential gift for a writer was 'a built-in, shock-proof crap detector'.[7] Here he showed it was already functioning. After he met Mussolini, he wrote: 'There is something wrong, even histrionically, with a man who wears white spats with a black shirt.'[8] Time would verify such an assessment.

He now approached Gertrude Stein, meeting her in her house at 27 Rue de Fleurus on March 1922 armed with Anderson's letter. Anderson himself had received a letter of introduction to her from Sylvia Beach some years earlier. She was impressed by his charm. Most people were.

They formed an unlikely friendship. He was fascinated by her appearance—her strong features and peasant-like head. She also had enormous breasts which fascinated him, telling Hadley that he imagined they must have weighed 10 pounds each.

Stein lectured him on writing while Hadley chatted to her live-in love, Alice B. Toklas. Toklas was slightly built. She had a hook nose and a Joan of Arc haircut. Hemingway insisted on calling her 'Miss Tocraz'.

When he showed Stein his work, she told him he needed more discipline. This was choice considering the fact that he was arguably the most fastidious writer of his time and she a veritable model of chaos. He sat at her feet listening to her declaiming about Dadaism and other art forms.

He visited her regularly after he got to know her. She seemed androgynous to him. 'All women who are truly famous and who are of conspicuous mental ability,' he wrote, 'reveal some bodily resemblance to a man. The woman who attracts and is attracted by other women is herself half male.' Already he was showing an interest in sexual inversion.

From Stein he learned the art of 'conscious omission'. This was something he would put to good use in his stories. The idea was that the material he left out of them would strengthen them, making readers feel more than they understood. He replicated her penchant for repetition as well, and her quirky phraseology. Journalism had honed his literary skills into a compressed format. She persuaded him to unlearn the stern dictates of newspaper reportage.

The fact that she became his adoptive mother was coincidental. Long before meeting her, he referred to his actual mother as 'Mrs Stein'. They had similar personalities. Both liked to dominate conversations, to enwreathe auditors in their respective webs.

Pablo Picasso was another visitor to Stein. When he painted a portrait of her, she said, 'It doesn't look like me.' He replied, 'It will.' One night he brought her some poems he wrote. After reading them, she looked at him and said witheringly, 'Go home and paint.'[9]

Hemingway also met James Joyce at this time. The pair of them saw little enough of one another in the years to come, but he was a great admirer of his work. 'As for immortality,' he mused, 'that's something we have to die to find out about. But Joyce for *Dubliners* and the end of *Ulysses* is the surest bet for anyone now living.'[10]

Joyce threatened the establishment when he wrote about sex. 'The influence of his work was what changed everything,' Hemingway told an interviewer, 'in the days when words were barred to us and we had to fight for them. He made it possible for us to break away from the restrictions.'

Meeting Ezra Pound was another watershed for him. Like Joyce, he was a perfectionist, someone more concerned with 'getting it right' on the page than selling out his vision for the reader's shilling. Hemingway was two months in Paris before he met him. When he did, he found he was more interested in talking about politics than anything else. He sounded off about the ills of society in an acerbic manner.

Though he had a crusty shell, he was soft inside. He had a genuine affection for Hemingway that was reciprocated. He liked his bluntness and his colourful language. Hemingway learned much from his imagistic style of writing. He also learned from Stein and Joyce. They were all pioneers in their way.

Pound and Hemingway boxed together. Hemingway put as much effort into this as he did into his writing. It was all grist to the mill. The perfect fight was like the perfect story. There were winners and losers outside the ring as well as inside it. What mattered was outlasting the opposition. If war and boxing were both blood sports, so was the activity of putting words on paper for a living.

Hemingway also struck up a friendship with Ford Madox Ford at this time. He was an expatriate British author who edited *The Transatlantic Review*. It would become an outlet for much of Hemingway's fiction in the future.

'I only had to read six words of his,' Ford stated, 'before I decided to publish anything he sent me.' These were heartening words for a writer who had experienced so much rejection up to this. 'One of his pages,' Ford noted, 'has the effect of a brook bottom into which you look down through the flowing water. The words form a tessellation, each in order beside the other.'[11]

A generation of critics would say much the same thing in a variety of different ways in the years to come. For now, Hemingway was just one of many young hopefuls having a limited degree of success in magazines which were largely ignored by the reading public.

No more than Joyce with Dublin, he seemed to be able to see Michigan more clearly when he was out of it. 'Never write about a place until you're away from it,' he told his Cuban fishing friend Arnold Samuelson, 'because that gives you perspective. Immediately after you've seen something, you can give a photographic description of it and make it accurate. That's good practice but it isn't creative writing.' There was a point where the novelist took over from the journalist. He went into that grey area, that twilight zone where reportage became alchemised into the stuff of art.

Hadley continued to tell him his stories were marvellous but the truth of the matter was that they were far from the kind of thing she usually liked reading. They cut just that little bit too close to the bone for comfort. Her natural preference was for writers like Henry James. Hemingway agreed with William Faulkner that James was 'the grand old lady of American letters'.

Life was good for him now. He was in a beautiful city with the woman he loved and soaking up the heady vibrations that came from his fellow writers. He was also more economically comfortable than one might have thought, despite his claim that he was 'very poor'.[12] The stories that went around about his poverty were largely fictitious. It was said that Bumby slept in a dresser drawer, that Hadley walked around Paris with holes in her shoes, that Hemingway engaged in boxing sessions with seasoned boxers for ten francs a round. It was even rumoured that he smuggled a pigeon out of a public park under a baby's blanket one day so he could bring it home to cook.

Stories about writers starving in garrets were attractive to people. Similar ones were trotted out about James Joyce. Hemingway chortled at the idea of Joyce moaning about poverty and then dining out with 'the whole Celtic crew' in fashionable restaurants.[13] He told Gertrude Stein of an Irish woman whose son struck gold in the Klondyke. 'Oh my poor son Joey,' she groaned, 'He's got so much money.' Hemingway enjoyed that one. 'The damned Irish,' he denigrated, 'They have to moan about something or other but you never heard of an Irishman starving.' (Was he not aware of the Great Famine?)

Like Joyce, Hemingway seemed to be able to find money when he wanted to, even if both he and Hadley dressed scruffily by Parisian standards—and lived on the wrong side of the Seine.

Being 'very poor', in effect, meant having his own cook, dining out with famous writers, nipping over to Spain for bullfights when the desire arose, and going to bicycle races locally. He also went skiing regularly in the Vorarlberg region of Austria.

One of his skiing companions was a military man called 'Chink' Dorman-Smith. Edward was his real name. 'Chink' was an affectionate soubriquet. He later changed his surname to O'Gowna.

He was an officer in the British Army in the Second World War but was pensioned off early. Recklessness was the reason given. Hemingway felt it was because he was too intelligent. 'Having brains always made you suspect in any army,' he said, 'I've never known a fighting man with a good brain to ever come to a good end.'

Chink's ancestors were from County Cavan in Ireland. (O'Gowna is Gaelic for Smith.) He became especially close to Hemingway when he talked of freeing Ireland from Britain. 'My intention,' he said boldly to him one day, 'is to get the British out of our last six counties and, having taken Belfast, to march on Dublin and purge it of the neo-Georgian takers.' Ireland was only granted twenty-six of their thirty-two counties from Britain after the uprising of 1916. Hemingway always went out to bat for the rights of small nations.

With regard to his own circumstances, Hadley and himself were both rich *and* poor in these years. As he explained in a letter to Bill Horne regarding delayed revenue, 'Sometimes we'd have to wait a month from the time I'd send in my expense account to *The Star* and we'd live on ten francs a day. Then [we'd] be rich as hell when the five or six hundred seed came.'

Hadley hated this kind of inconsistency. She put up with it for Hemingway's sake. If her man was happy, she was too.

Things became more worrying when he gave up journalism to concentrate on his fiction. Chucking in 'the day job' resulted in him having to cut his cloth. The regularity of Hadley's trust fund meant he was jumping with a safety net. Part of him felt this 'easy money' cut in on the purity of his writing. Maybe it even threatened it.

In December 1922, an incident took place that almost put him 'out of business' (to use one of his favourite expressions) for good. He was at a conference in Lausanne at the time, and temporarily away from Hadley. While travelling from Paris to meet him for a skiing holiday, she took his writings with her so he could work on them in between spells on the slopes.

She stuffed everything into a valise before heading for the train station at Gare de Lyon. The carbon copies were put in as well. She felt any changes he made on the original drafts he would want to repeat on the carbons.

Shortly after she found a compartment, she left the train to buy a newspaper and a bottle of Evian water. There was a delay before it was due to take off. She killed time by walking up and down the platform. When she heard the conductor call, 'All aboard!' she re-embarked.

When she got to her compartment she saw, to her horror, that the valise was gone. She called the conductor. The train was searched but it was nowhere to be found. The thief was probably unable to read English. It was likely he destroyed it as a worthless haul. Why not? It 'only' contained paper.[14]

When Hadley met Hemingway at Lausanne, she was so upset she found it difficult to speak. Her silence caused his imagination to work overtime. What could be so terrible? Had she fallen in love with somebody else?[15] When she eventually told him what happened, he said he forgave her.

He told her it would be good discipline for him to start afresh. His critics would now have a harder time tracing his development.[16]

He wrote of the lost novel in later years: 'I was glad it was gone because I could see already, as you begin to see clearly over the water when a rainstorm lifts on the ocean as the wind carries it out to sea, that I could write a better one.'

Inside himself, however, he seethed. He got someone to cover for him at the conference and went back to Paris to see if anything had been left behind. Sadly, he drew a blank.

As he opened the door of the cupboard in the apartment, he wrote:

> I felt almost as though I could not breathe when I saw that there were no folders with the originals. Then I locked the door and went into the next room, which was the bedroom, and lay down on the bed. I put a pillow between my legs and my arms around another pillow and lay there very quietly. I was in despair. I never had despair before, true despair, nor have I ever had it since. My forehead lay against the Persian shawl that covered the bed. The bed cover was dusty. I smelt the dust and lay there and the pillows were my only comfort.[17]

An hour later, he went downstairs to talk to the concierge. She was almost as shocked as he was. He put his arms around her. Then they started drinking.

A novel Paula McLain wrote about Hemingway's time in Paris, *The Paris Wife*, captured how he must have felt the moment he learned the writings were gone:

> He puts his hand on the knob and pulls the door open and then he knows everything. There isn't a page left in the cupboard. Not a note or a scrap. He looks and looks, standing there wrenched out and hollow. As desolate as the cupboard is, that's how he is too because the pages belong to him and are him. It's like someone has taken a broom to his insides and swept them out until everything is clean and bright and hard and empty.[18]

4

Forging a Style

Hemingway claimed he lost a total of eleven stories as well as an unfinished Nick Adams novel that day. His friend Bill Bird called it 'The Great Train Robbery'. The stories that survived—'My Old Man', 'Out of Season', and 'Up in Michigan'—show he was at the height of his literary powers at this time. Some critics have suggested Hadley lost them deliberately. They argue that she was feeling depressed about the fact that he was starting to concentrate more on his writing than on her at this time, that she was afraid he might drift away from her more if fame came his way.[1] This is a ludicrous theory in view of how traumatised she felt.

That said, Hemingway's wound was very raw. He underplayed it, not wanting to make her feel worse than she already was, but he could never feel the same about her afterwards. Despite what he said to friends, losing his work was like losing a child. To pursue this line of thinking, Hadley stopped using precautions when they made love afterwards in hopes of giving him an actual one. She fell pregnant within the month but delayed telling him; she feared he might not be pleased.

He wrote to Ezra Pound to tell him about the lost manuscripts. Pound tried to console him by advising him to rewrite everything from memory. 'Memory is the best critic,' he said, 'If the thing wobbles & wont reform, it never wd. have been right.'[2] Hemingway told him all that remained of his writings were the stories he sent out to editors and 'three pencil drafts of a bum poem'.

'Up in Michigan' was the one he thought most of. It had been described by Gertrude Stein as *inaccrochable*. This was a term applied to a painting that had to be removed from art galleries because of its moral offensiveness. It survived because it was stuffed in a drawer away from all his other writings. 'My Old Man' had been sent out to an editor. It was rejected (thankfully) and made its way back to him. Apart from these, all the stories he slaved over for months were gone.

He continued to downplay the loss to friends in the same way as he did to Hadley. 'Poor Hadley was so broken up about it,' he said to one of them, 'I actually felt worse for her than for myself. She hadn't been hired as a manuscript custodian. What she had been hired for—wifeing—she was damn good at.'[3]

He wrote about the incident in a different manner in *The Garden of Eden*, a posthumously published book. In the course of it a character burns her husband's writings. She does so for sadistic reasons. He describes the loss as being 'like coming around a curve on a mountain road and the road not being there and only a gulf ahead'.

The trauma of the lost manuscripts went into abeyance when Hadley finally revealed that she was pregnant. Hemingway's reaction, as she feared, was negative. He knew a child would cut in on his lifestyle. It would disrupt his concentration when he was writing and stop Hadley being able to accompany him on trips when he was between books. In a panic, he ran to Gertrude Stein. 'I'm too young to be a father,' he grieved.

Ezra Pound told him the baby would change his life irrevocably. Pound had a bias against children. He doubted writers should have any.[4] After his mistress had a daughter some time beforehand, he persuaded her to give her to a peasant woman in the maternity ward whose daughter had died.

Hadley played tennis and other vigorous sports during her pregnancy. Her doctors disapproved. Hemingway said nothing. Perhaps he wanted her to miscarry. Hadley herself was overjoyed to be pregnant. 'I discovered what I was born for,' she declared, 'It was very good for my ego.'

Pound now introduced Hemingway to Robert McAlmon, another American living in Paris. He had a small printing press. It had just published the first of Pound's *Cantos*. Hemingway had mixed feelings about these. 'There's quite a lot of crap in them,' he denounced, 'but there's also some Christwonderful poetry that no one can do better.'[5]

McAlmon was aware of Hemingway's talent. Disappointed to hear he lost so much of his material at the train station in Paris, he privately published his first book, *Three Stories and Ten Poems*, in August 1923. It had a mere fifty-eight pages in it.

Only 300 copies were printed, but it left a mark on the public. Already the Hemingway stamp was there, albeit writ small. Edmund Wilson was lavish in his praise of it. For Hemingway it was a precious book because it could so easily not have come about. He had a special affection for the three stories that survived the Gare de Lyon débâcle.

'Up in Michigan' was the most sexually daring vignette of his early career, 'My Old Man', his alleged debt to Sherwood Anderson, also resounded, as did 'Out of Season'. He referred to these stories as 'Das Kapital' with a grim sense of irony, meaning they were his sole literary capital now.

His family was angered by 'Up in Michigan'. The names he used in it were those of real people from Oak Park. According to Marcelline, they were close family friends. She was shocked that her brother would do that, even if there was very little chance of them seeing it.[6]

The book was slight. When he saw a galley of it, he asked for blank pages to be inserted at both ends to flesh it out. It was well received but only reached a limited readership.

An editor called Edward O'Brien now asked him if he could use 'My Old Man' in an anthology he was compiling called *Best Short Stories of 1923*. Hemingway was flattered when O'Brien wrote to him saying, 'Dear Hemenway [*sic*], I want to dedicate the book to you. May I?' Hemingway wrote back, 'Yes you may, and to show you how much I appreciate it I will make a very solemn vow to you and God never to think about anything but you and God when writing stories all the rest of my life.' The misspelling of his name, unfortunately, also appeared on the story itself. As a result, Hemingway complained, 'No one believed I wrote it.'[7]

He always hated it when people misspelled his name. A terrible speller himself, all his life he put an extra vowel into words like 'liveing', 'hopeing', and 'haveing'. Scott Fitzgerald had a habit of spelling his name with two Ms. Hemingway told him he was glad to discover that someone in the world was an even worse speller than himself. He once told Sunny that bad spelling never bothered him: one could always hire someone to fix it.[8]

He brought Hadley to Spain with him for the San Fermin festival in Pamplona that summer. It was just what he needed to take his mind off her pregnancy. There was five days of bullfighting and non-stop dancing on the streets. Thus began his love affair with Pamplona. Hadley could take or leave it. She spent most of her time at the bullfights knitting clothes for her forthcoming baby, 'embroidering in the presence of all that brutality'.

Money became a concern now. He needed a steady job to support his soon-to-be born child. Hadley encouraged him to move back to Toronto before the end of the year to work for *The Star* again. She thought there would be better post-natal care in Canada than in the US.

Hemingway hated Canada. It had no culture for him. There was nothing anything to do between work shifts. Neither were the people friendly. 'Hadley and myself are the two nicest individuals in the country,' he bragged.

His boss was a man called Harry Hindmarsh. Seeing Hemingway as cocky, he resisted few opportunities to pull him down to size. 'He says I think I know more about the assignments he gives me than he does,' Hemingway wrote to John Bone towards the end of 1923, 'but I have given him no cause to think this. I cannot be accused of every thot [*sic*] that his inferiority complex suggests to him.'[9]

Hindmarsh threw menial chores at him, like writing obituary notices. Hemingway was outraged. He wanted to be at the cutting edge of current affairs. One day he sent him 600 miles away to investigate a mining problem.

Hindmarsh was the son-in-law of *The Star*'s owners. As a result of this, he was in prime position to do what he wanted. Hemingway wrote to Gertrude Stein, saying, 'I have understood for the first time how men can commit suicide simply because of too many things in business piling up ahead of them that they can't get through.' This was a dramatic overreaction to his workload and an early reference to a preoccupation that plagued him during every crisis of his life—the temptation to end it.

Hindmarsh was jealous of him.[10] He gave him not only an endless litany of graveyard shifts, but also a range of dead-end commissions guaranteed to ensure geographical inconvenience. As envious of Hemingway's journalistic expertise as he was resentful of his self-confidence, he did his utmost to destroy both qualities by his bullyboy tactics. After a few months, Hemingway realised he was going nowhere in his career. His boss was blunting his creativity. He said he wanted to kill him.[11]

Hindmarsh sent him on an assignment to New York shortly before the baby was due. From there he went to Canada to interview David Lloyd George, the British statesman. His child was born while he was away. It was a boy. They named him John Nicanor after the bullfighter Nicanor Villalta. He was nicknamed Bumby because of his bulky appearance. Jack became a more familiar term of address in later years.

Hemingway did his best to play the father figure but had a hard time doing so. 'The baby has taken to squalling and is a fine nuisance,' he wrote to Clarence, 'I suppose he'll yell his head off for the next two or three years. It seems his only form of entertainment.' To Hadley he pronounced, 'To be a successful father, there's one absolute rule. When you have a kid, don't look at it for the first two years.'[12]

He frequently fled the house to do his writing when Bumby was noisy. Bringing his notebook and pencil to nearby cafes, he sought out the proper atmosphere to get 'the juice' flowing.

When his writing was finished, he played with Bumby, sometimes engaging in mock-bullfights with him. 'He's becoming a *torero* now,' he wrote to his parents when the boy was hardly out of the cradle, 'Chances are he'll be able to support us in years to come.'

Paris was on his radar again now. He gave his notice to *The Star* in November of that year. After that it was back to Oak Park for a brief pre-Christmas trip. Clarence had offered to pay for round-trip tickets for Hadley and himself but Hadley chose not to go. She thought it would disrupt Bumby's nursing.

Hemingway brought a few copies of *Three Stories and Ten Poems* with him. They were intended for various members of the family as presents but a row about the book broke out shortly after he arrived. He realised nobody wanted it.

He slipped a copy of it quietly to Marcelline. She was unimpressed with it, especially after reading 'Up in Michigan', a story she found sordid. It was a good thing, she said, that the book would only go on limited release. 'Up in Michigan' features a scene of what would be called 'date rape' today. This has often been used as a stick to beat Hemingway. Some critics say it exposes him as sexist but we should remember that the story is written from the point of view of the woman. He argued with Marcelline about it, imagining her to be jealous of him.

He was back with Hadley for Christmas to play Santa for Bumby. The following day, they started packing their things to return to Paris, doing so stealthily to avoid their landlord finding out they were breaking their lease.

They got to the city in January 1924, taking up residence in a modest apartment at 113 Rue Notre Dame des Champs. It had no electricity or hot water, not even a bathtub. At night they read by gas lamp. It was situated above a sawmill owned by their landlord. Sawdust often came in through the windows. It got into Hemingway's lungs, giving him some of the sore throats he was plagued with throughout his life.

'You're conscious all the time,' he said, 'of a very gentle buzzing noise and always the smell of fresh cut wood.' He wrote to Ezra Pound: 'Dear Prometheus, We have *trouved* an apt.'[13]

They lived on Hadley's income. Hemingway sweated on his stories and also busied himself working as sub-editor of *The Transatlantic Review* under Ford. There was no fee for this. He wrote to Pound, 'I'm going to have to quit writing because we haven't any money. I will never have a book published. I feel cheerful as hell.'[14] Hadley wrote to his parents, 'The sawdust flies down below and Ernest keeps the keys on his Corona flying above.'

In March, his second book, *In Our Time*, was published by a small company, Three Mountains Press. Little more than a selection of vignettes, it nonetheless capitalised on the attention he received from his previous work, tapping into the penchant for private press publishing that was in vogue in Paris at the time.

It was proudly displayed in the window of the famous Shakespeare and Company bookshop. Sylvia Beach, its owner, sold as many copies as she could, but the publishers failed to supplement her supplies quickly enough for Hemingway. 'She orders 12,' he complained, 'but they only send her 6. She sells them in a day and then has to cable for more.' Beach was almost as great a friend to Hemingway as she was to James Joyce, for whom she was a benefactress. She went to bicycle races with Hemingway and Hadley, and even boxing matches. 'No one I ever knew,' Hemingway commended, 'was nicer to me.' After Bumby was born, he wrote to her, 'If he'd been a girl we would have named her Sylvia. Being a boy, we couldn't call him Shakespeare.'[15]

He brought Hadley with him to the Austrian ski resort of Schruns in the winter of that year. They sub-let their apartment. While they were there, Hemingway received news that his next book had been accepted. It was the same name as his previous one.

In Our Time was published by a company called Boni & Liveright. It was Hemingway's first title with a commercial publishing firm. While the advance of £200 was hardly a princely sum, he was over the moon with it.

Gertrude Stein refused to review it. She preferred to wait for him to write a novel before putting pen to paper about him. If she was on the record as boosting him for his stories and he fell on his face with a novel, she told him, she would feel embarrassed. He found it difficult to understand that attitude, thinking that every publication should have been evaluated on its merits.

The book confirmed the fact that a striking new voice had arrived on the literary scene. A compilation of material from his two previous books, it encapsulated his work to date and gave him a window to a wider reading public than had been his lot up to now. The title was derived from the chant in the Common Prayer Book, 'Give us peace in our time, o Lord.' This was ironic considering so much of the material was anything but peaceful.

It hit readers in the solar plexus right from the first sentence. 'The strange thing,' he wrote, 'was how they screamed every night at midnight.' The violence jars with Hemingway's nonchalant tone.

He makes no attempt to explain who 'he' or 'they' are. We plunge into the story without any of what J. D. Salinger called 'that David Copperfield crap'. This would become a feature of all his work in time.

These are stories that shout at us with their mouths shut. Many of them lack a development of plot or character. People communicate with one another in cryptic monosyllables.

'Any part you make will represent the whole if it's made truly,' he maintained.[16] In previous eras, readers had been spoon-fed extraneous details, flowery adjectives, spidery subordinate clauses. Hemingway's brief was indeed brief. It was life without the appendages.

Nonchalant on the surface, these early stories contain any number of incendiary devices that explode more in the reader's head than they do on the page. The readers join the dots where characterisations remain incomplete.

The approach is continued in 'Indian Camp'. Here a man slits his throat after he sees a doctor delivering a stillborn baby from the womb of his screaming wife without an anaesthetic. This is the story that introduces us to Nick Adams. He will be Hemingway's *doppelgänger* for many years, a conduit through which he will filter muted shock.

Nick has witnessed death beside his father. He feels numb. His father is 'terribly sorry' he had to see it. Hemingway ends the story with Nick being 'quite sure' he himself will never die. The 'quite sure' is unusually laconic considering what we've just witnessed. Hemingway is undercutting the violence by ironic asides. They intensify its effect.

He deleted the first few pages of the original version of the story. These had Adams fearing being alone in the woods at night. Was this an exemplification of the trauma of Hemingway's war wound? It was easier to project it onto a fictional character than speak about it to people he knew. He told Lillian Ross he avoided writing about 'the first war [*sic*]' for ten years after it happened.[17]

'Soldier's Home' is a story about a war hero, Krebs, who finds it difficult to adapt to civilian life after he comes home. There are also biographical parallels here. Krebs' mother castigates him for his post-war lassitude.

We see an indication of Hemingway's closeness to one of his sisters in the flirtation that goes on between him and the girl depicted as his fictional sister, Helen, in the story. I suspect Ursula to be the likelier candidate, though Sunny insisted it was her rather than Ursula in a memoir she wrote about growing up with Hemingway.

Krebs tries to console himself that things are 'fine'. This is like the 'quite sure' of 'Indian Camp'. He immerses himself in trivia to deflect attention from his depression. The mind-numbing boredom of the backwater in which he lives is brilliantly evoked.

The story is a closer inspection of Oak Park than we get anywhere else in Hemingway's work. Domestic friction becomes the subtext of his pain. The glow of having excelled in military combat has worn off for Krebs as it had for Hemingway. The future has to be got on with now; Krebs looks for places to start. Watching Helen playing indoor basketball is hardly the ideal place.

In 'The End of Something', we get another theme that figures largely in Hemingway's output: the break-up of a romance. For Nick, being with his girlfriend Margie 'isn't fun' any more. He refuses to talk about it. The story ends in mid-air, like many of Hemingway's early stories, making us wonder if a page is missing. Again we have to fill in the blanks.

The following story, 'The Three-Day Blow', picks up where 'The End of Something' left off. The tone is disarmingly low-key. We get two-thirds of the way through it before we realise why Bill and Nick are getting drunk. This is another theme that figures strongly in Hemingway's work, the idea of alcohol as a palliative.

'The Three-Day Blow' gives us the beginning of a negative view of marriage that runs through Hemingway's work. Bill says married people get 'this sort of fat married look' that makes them 'done for'.

'A Very Short Story' is ominous in a different way. It has, in miniature, a depiction of the relationship between Hemingway and Agnes, something that will become expanded out of all proportion in *A Farewell to Arms*.

This is also the story that, more than any other in the collection, was responsible for Clarence's disgust at the book. How could he be expected to accept his son writing about people who contracted gonorrhoea in taxis? That happens to 'Luz' at the end. She was originally called 'Ag'. Hemingway changed it due to fear of a libel action.[18] Having Agnes suffer from gonorrhoea was seen as revenge for her having jilted him.

Another one of the stories, 'My Old Man', as mentioned, survived Hadley's Gare de Lyon travesty. Hemingway told Clarence not to think of it as being about him. An impressionistic porthole into the relationship between a jockey and his father, its main interest comes from the fact that the reader realises at a certain point that he knows more about the 'old man' than his son does. It reminded Edmund Wilson of the race-track stories of Sherwood Anderson. Hemingway said that while the subject matter may have been the same, the treatment was his.

'Mr and Mrs Elliott' employs the satirical style he would soon use in *The Torrents of Spring*. Even from the humorous names of the characters

(Hubert and Cornelia), one is being prepared for what follows. The idea of trying hard to have a baby, and crying when things go wrong, becomes the stuff of farce. The fact that Mrs Elliot is 'quite' happy at the end is about as convincing as the fact that Nick Adams is 'quite' sure he will never die at the end of 'Indian Camp'.

The story drew an angry response from an acquaintance of Hemingway's called Chard Powers Smith. Claiming he recognised himself in it, he wrote to Hemingway to tell him how contemptible he found him for satirising him. Hemingway wrote back to say he would greatly enjoy knocking Smith down a few times if he ever saw him.

The story is a good example of his 'necklace' style of writing. Each sentence has a hook word that leads into the next one. This is what Madox Ford meant when he used the word 'tessellation' to describe it. In the first sentence we see two chains of the necklace, 'Mrs Elliott' and 'tried'. These are repeated in the second one. 'Tried' is repeated in the third. Here a new element of the chain is introduced: 'boat'. This gets repeated in the next sentence. Now 'sick' becomes the new hook. And so on. Hemingway is using a simple but effective manner of creating a mesmeric effect with little effort—or at least little apparent effort.

People talk often about Hemingway's use of repetition. This is an inadequate term to describe what he does. Every time he repeats a term, he adds something new beside it. This gives him ammunition for an extrapolation of it. His sentences cascade down upon one another in marginally varying form like in those notebooks where children draw slightly different pictures and then flap the pages to create the illusion of movement. Hemingway practises the same sleight-of-hand with words.

'Big Two-Hearted River' is the story that closes the collection. Many critics were intrigued by it. Again, it features Adams.

The references to the war, or whatever other crises Nick is undergoing, are too flimsy to make an impact. One finds it difficult to care what, if anything, they mean. As Gertrude Stein once said, 'Remarks are not literature.'

If Hemingway took the trouble to inject more human interest into the story, it would have worked better. As it is, it never really becomes more than a serviceable piece of narration. Nick's 'other needs' go for nothing. The descriptions we get would have fared better in a novel where the characters were already established. Scott Fitzgerald remarked that the story had no tail in it, 'no sudden change of pace at the end to throw into relief what has gone before'. He was right.

This story has been taken far too seriously by people who analyse it for its Fisher King undertones. Critics also harp on about its perceived neo-modernist nods to the likes of T. S. Eliot. Hemingway was pleased with the fact that the war gets no mention in it. He prided himself on his 'iceberg' style of writing. This meant that six-sevenths of the meaning was usually hidden below the surface.[19] Such a ploy lacks its usual potency here.

The presence of Adams in the stories became almost ubiquitous in time. He reminds us of Mr Junior America, a young man both outdoorsy and resourceful. Combined with this is his vulnerability. Somebody once said of Marlon Brando that he brought doubt into the locker room. Adams, in the same way, undercuts the Jock stereotype by embodying many of the characteristics of the existential hero. What we get is Huckleberry Finn crossed with J.D. Salinger's Holden Caulfield.

Slotted in between the stories of *In Our Time* are a series of italicised vignettes. Nearly all of them focus on violence, a subject that fascinated Hemingway all his life. He saw them as 'interchapters', comparing the effect to that of watching a coastline from a ship—first with the naked eye and then with binoculars. 'After each story comes a bang' was the way he put it.

His cross-cutting techniques owed as much to the cinematic montage of Eisenstein as they did to the collages of Miro and Cezanne. He loved abstract painting and tried to reprise its chaotic structure on the page.

The negative tone of the book affected his parents. Their insular upbringings taught them never to wash dirty linen in public. There were wonderful things in the world, they pointed out to their son, and he should go looking for them. Hemingway's answer was that he did but he could rarely find them.

Writers like Hemingway were too edgy for Oak Park tastes. As he made headway in Paris, his parents began to worry about him more. His father still wanted him to go to college. That was hardly possible now. Maybe it never had been. His 'college' was the forest, the feria, the green hills of Africa.

When his father wrote to him telling him he disapproved of the sordidness of his stories, he replied by saying that in trying to grapple with life in all its parameters he had to describe not only the beautiful but the ugly as well, 'because if it is all beautiful you can't believe in it. Things aren't that way. It is only by showing both sides—3 dimensions and if possible 4—that you can write the way I want to.' He explained what he meant by this: 'It comes close to a man's soul. That's the most difficult thing there is to do. I'd rather not take the easy shots if I stand a chance to make a hard one.'

His explanation for all the bloodletting in the collection was interesting: 'I have been working for a precision of language and to get it I've had to treat of things where simple actions occurred. The simplest, and what I had seen the most of, was one form and another of killing.'

This was not what his father wanted to hear. The book was more a source of embarrassment to him than a cause for celebration. Losing his temper, he decided to return all the copies of it that had been dispatched complimentarily to him.

Surprisingly enough, it was Grace rather than Clarence who wanted to keep a souvenir copy. It may be worth remembering that this was the woman who, when Ernest was in seventh grade at school, protested to his English teacher that *The Call of the Wild* was far too violent a text to impose upon his tender mind.

Hemingway was by now a taboo subject in Oak Park. His father said he would prefer him to be dead than notorious. From now on, stories of his that were serialised in magazines had to be smuggled into the Hemingway household by his siblings.

His mother wrote to him saying she knew one day he would write a book that appealed to people's better instincts. In doing this she was only egging him on to further explorations of the dark corners of the psyche.

He told Grace he thought she was only willing to love him on her terms. That was no love at all as far as he was concerned. His resentment with her grew as time went on and his books became racier. This one served warning to the reading public that he was here to stay. He was getting a grip on the literary totem pole.

'Almost every American writer in Paris sought Ernest out,' Hadley proclaimed.

He had arrived.

5

Climbing the Literary Ladder

Hemingway attacked life. He worked hard and played hard. He out-talked people, out-drank them, out-hunted them, out-fished them. When they were ready for bed, he was often just warming up. On the mornings after binges, he went into his study and typed up all the thoughts that had gone into his mind the night before. 'When I work,' he told Harvey Breit once, 'I work so hard I nearly work myself to death. If I'm not tired I know I haven't worked as hard as I should have. But I always stop when I'm going good and know what's going to happen next in what I'm working on. That way you can always go on the next day.'

How did he find time for bullfights, skiing holidays, and bicycle races? There always seemed to be more than twenty-four hours in his days.

Events impacted on his senses to an intense degree. He took in ten times what an average person would have from an experience—its sights, sounds, smells, touches, tastes. Shooting game or fishing was the same to him as sitting at a typewriter sculpting words from his brain. As well as being a sensualist, he had an incredible memory. When we combine that with his combination of machismo and sensitivity, we have the formula for someone who had to become a writer.

Anybody as gifted as he was would have risen to the top of the literary tree without having his path smoothed by the people he encountered in Paris. They admired him as much for his personality as for his way of writing.

Chief among these was F. Scott Fitzgerald. When Fitzgerald first became aware of Hemingway, he was a famous author. He had written *The Beautiful and the Damned* and *This Side of Paradise* and was about to publish *The Great Gatsby*. All Hemingway had to his credit were the published stories and limited-edition books.

Such was Fitzgerald's reverence for Hemingway that he almost looked upon himself as the apprentice and Hemingway the established writer when they met. He told Maxwell Perkins, his Scribner's editor, that he was going to be the next big thing. He thought it was only a matter of time before everybody would be talking about him.

Fitzgerald first became alerted to Hemingway's talent as the result of an Edmund Wilson article in *The Dial*. It inspired him to seek out his work. When he read it, he was blown away. He now made it his business to seek out the man himself.

They met for the first time in 1925 in the Dingo bar on Rue Delambre off the boulevard de Montparnasse on the Left Bank. Fitzgerald had just published *The Great Gatsby* and was very proud of it. He was bowled over by Hemingway's personality. Hemingway thought Fitzgerald effeminate. 'He had a long-lipped Irish mouth,' he sneered, 'that on a girl would have been the mouth of a beauty. It worried you until you knew him. Then it worried you more.'

Fitzgerald found it difficult to hold his drink. In his excitement at meeting Hemingway, he started glugging champagne. He became giddy with it. Such giddiness emboldened him to ask Hemingway if he slept with Hadley before marrying her. Hemingway ignored the question. Fitzgerald passed out a few minutes later. He had to be brought home in a taxi.

Hadley read *The Great Gatsby* that night and raved about it.[1] Hemingway was slow to read it. He thought Fitzgerald was over-enamoured of it. But when he read it, he agreed with Hadley that it was finely written.

Fitzgerald advised Hemingway to stop selling his stories to 'cuckoo' magazines for peanuts when he could be working for Scribner's. Hemingway cocked his ear at this. He was more interested in what Fitzgerald could do for his career than he was in forming a friendship with him.

The two men could hardly have been more different. Hemingway was a controlling person who had his writing life enhanced by Hadley. Fitzgerald had married a selfish woman, Zelda, who short-circuited his creative powers.

Fitzgerald wanted to be in the heat of battles like Hemingway. When he told him he had a fantasy about fighting in a war, Hemingway told him he would probably be shot for cowardice.[2]

Fitzgerald took insults like this on the chin. So enamoured was he of Hemingway, he told him he thought his work was on a par with the Bible's 'Let there be light.' Hemingway was more amused than flattered by his obsequiousness.

They argued about literary principle. Fitzgerald said he was happy writing high-paying stories for glossy magazines to help tide him over financially when his novels were going through lean sales patches. Hemingway believed that to go down this road was a kamikaze act. It was capitulation to market forces.

At this point Hemingway had just finished a novel, *The Torrents of Spring*. It was a satire of *Dark Laughter*, a book of Sherwood Anderson's that he hated. Anderson had done him a favour with his letters of introduction, but Hemingway had a short memory for things like this. When he saw weakness in a writer, he pointed it out, regardless of what that person might have done for him.

Hemingway had submitted *The Torrents of Spring* to Boni & Liveright. He expected them to reject it because of their loyalty to Anderson. He was one of their chief writers. If and when they rejected it, he could then submit it to Scribner's, thereby paving the way to join their stable. Maxwell Perkins' suggestion that he might be able to publish it, Hemingway was aware, could become a contract-breaker for him with Boni & Liveright. It would open the door for him to join the bigger company.

He wrote to Horace Liveright at the end of 1925 saying he was aware the book might offend him because of its satire of Anderson. He asked for an advance of $500 in the event of acceptance. 'That is the smallest guarantee I can have,' he said, 'that it will be pushed.' This was like a gun to Liveright's head. $500 was a lot of money at the time.

'It falls below your usual standard,' Liveright wrote back. It was the reply Hemingway was waiting for. Contractually bound to Boni & Liveright as a result of their publication of *In Our Time*, he would be free to go where he wished if they rejected *The Torrents of Spring*.

The fact that he repaid Anderson's kindness by lampooning him was a cruel act by Hemingway. He added insult to injury by writing to Anderson and saying there was 'nothing personal' in it.

This was ridiculous. If not personal, what was it? If he felt so strongly about the decline in Anderson's talent, was there not a gentler way to tell him? He was more honest when he wrote to Anderson, 'You were always swell to me and helped like the devil on *In Our Time*. Now it looks like I had an irresistible need to punch you in the face with true writer's gratitude.'

Hemingway's hunger to get a deal from Scribner's can be traced back to the fact that Perkins had accepted *In Our Time* at the same time as Liveright had shortly before. Due to a delay in the post the letter failed to reach him until after he committed himself to Liveright. He was now putting that glitch to rights, albeit in an underhand way.

When submitting *The Torrents of Spring* to Liveright, he tried to cover himself *vis-à-vis* Anderson by saying, 'In the golden age of the English novel Fielding wrote his satirical novels as an answer to the novels of Richardson. In this way *Joseph Andrews* was written as a parody on Richardson's *Pamela*. Now they're both classics.' This was a non-sequitur. He knew neither *Dark Laughter* nor *The Torrents of Spring* would come within a mile of being called classics.

He never liked Liveright personally. Their relationship was formal. He always addressed him as 'Mr Liveright'. Liveright addressed him as 'Mr Hemingway'.[3]

Hemingway thought Liveright was lax in his promotion of *In Our Time* so he felt he owed him nothing. He was confident that the clause obliging him to send his next book to his company could now be broken. He assured Fitzgerald that Liveright 'could not and would not' be able to publish *Torrents*, 'as it makes a bum out of their best-selling writer'.[4] 'I did not,' he added, 'have that in mind in any way when I wrote it.' This last comment one finds very difficult to believe.

Fitzgerald sent Liveright a letter saying he thought *Torrents of Spring* was 'about the best comic book ever written by an American.' He added ominously, 'I hope you won't like it as I'm something of a ballyhoo man for Scribner's and I'd like to see people I admire rounded up in the same coop.'[5]

A letter from Hemingway to Anderson in May 1926 tried to justify his behaviour. In it he contended that authors had to keep up standards: 'When a man like yourself, who can write great things, writes something that seems to me rotten, I ought to tell you so.' Fair enough, but did he have to publicise it to the nation in the form of an under-the-belt broadside?

It smacked of biting the hand that fed. 'Outside of personal feelings,' he added, 'nothing that's any good can be hurt by satire.' This was irrelevant since he was just after telling Anderson *Dark Laughter* was poor. That was why he lampooned it. Nobody ever lampooned a quality book.

'You've changed since you went to Paris,' Anderson replied. When Hemingway was in America, he sat at Anderson's knee and drooled over everything he said. Now he was speaking to him like a master to a pupil. Anderson was more upset by Hemingway's attempt to wriggle out of the problem than he was by the book. 'Damn it, man,' he remonstrated, 'You're so patronising.'[6]

Perkins thought *The Torrents of Spring* was just an average book but he knew he had to take it to 'get' Hemingway. He accepted it because the book Hemingway was now working on, *The Sun Also Rises*, came with it and he dearly wanted that.

Liveright met Hemingway for a drink as the situation came to a head. In the relaxed atmosphere of the bar, he tried to soften him up by addressing him as Ernest. He asked him if he would still give him *The Sun Also Rises* even if he refused *Torrents*. Hemingway roared, 'Absolutely not!' With these words the matter was closed.

'I'm loose,' he beamed when the rejection finally came.[7] He wrote to Liveright to tell him he now had no option but to release him from his company. Hemingway was always very forthright in situations like this. The sensitive story writer had a very hard business head when he needed it.

Liveright came to regret his decision not to accept *Torrents*. Anderson's star fell as Hemingway's rose. His company lost money in the following years and he did too. Eventually he even lost his house. He took to drink and died of alcoholism at the age of forty-six. For Hemingway, it was the end of a 'dismal' life.[8]

His own fortunes were on the upturn now. He knew he was onto something good with *The Sun Also Rises*. He worked tirelessly at it in various places—Madrid, San Sebastian, and Hendaye in France. There were nights when he stayed up until 3 or 4 a.m. pumping it out. 'Then he would fall asleep,' one of his biographers wrote, 'only to jump awake again a few hours later with the words already stringing themselves into sentences, clamouring to be set down.'

Perkins thought he was a much more incisive writer than Fitzgerald. In his view he was 'up there' with James Jones and Thomas Wolfe, the two other main writers he was publishing at the time.

The Torrents of Spring was a one-joke book. Part of the joke reverberated on Hemingway himself as it displayed elements of his own literary style. In a sense he was sending himself up as well as Anderson. He once told his friend Aaron Hotchner that satires were 'the last refuge of the frustrated writer'. The greater the work of literature, he believed, the easier the satire. 'A step up from writing parodies,' he said, 'would be writing on the wall of the urinal.'

He was drifting away from Hadley as he wrote *The Torrents of Spring*. There were signs that she was tiring of the pace at which they lived. She wanted a quieter life. That was never going to be on the cards with this man. Money had also started to come his way with the Scribner's contract. This meant he was no longer dependent on her financially.

Hadley fulfilled a great function for him in exorcising the ghost of Agnes but Hemingway was a different person now. Confidence oozed out of him. He was hungry for life. The last thing he wanted was a woman who tied him down. Domesticity was death to him.

Hadley had started to look matronly after Bumby was born. To use an expression of William Congreve's from *Way of the World*, she had 'dwindled into a wife'. Many men showed a wandering eye when their wives give birth. Hemingway was no exception.

He became interested in a woman called Duff Twysden, a titled British lady. Born Mary Smurthwaite, she was the daughter of a wineshop manager. This gave her an early exposure to the alcohol she loved so much. She married a baronet called Roger Twysden in 1917 but had a 'knee-trembler' with the best man on her wedding day. The marriage went ahead but, hardly surprisingly, soon faltered.

She was a free spirit. As one writer put it, 'She wore the scent of opium like a perfume.' She had an androgynous appearance, wearing her brown hair cut short like a man's. This intrigued Hemingway. He flirted with her frequently in front of Hadley, often reducing her to tears.

He was always impressed by titled women. This one had it over most of them in that she knew how to enjoy a good time. She could drink and swear like any man. This was Hemingway's favourite type of woman.

In the summer of 1925, he attended a fiesta in Pamplona with Hadley and some friends. Twysden was among them. The others were George O'Neil, John Dos Passos, Robert McAlmon, Bill and Sally Bird, Bill Smith, Donald Ogden Stewart, Twysden's Scottish cousin Pat Guthrie, and the Jewish novelist Harold Loeb. The fiesta not only gave him a book but also his fame.

He set out with Hadley in late June, meeting up with Smith a week later. Afterwards the others joined them. Twysden and Loeb had just spent a weekend together despite the fact that she was living with Guthrie at the time.

Hemingway loved being at the fiesta. Every morning he showed off by doing 'veronicas' in the amateur ring with young bulls whose horns were padded. A veronica, as most aficionados know, is a pass made with the cape in both hands. The term was derived from the image of St Veronica. She wiped the face of Jesus with a napkin on the hill of Calvary.

He taunted the bulls with his cape until they charged at him. Then he grabbed their horns and wrestled them to the ground. O'Neil filmed an incident where both himself and Stewart were thrown into the air by a charging bull. He was bruised in the stomach. Stewart broke two ribs.[9] The story made the papers in Madrid.

Hemingway went fishing and hiking some days. At night he drank and exchanged banter with his coterie of friends, basking in the aura of machismo his actions invited. When he was away from them, he was writing about them.

Hadley was lonely for Bumby. They left him with friends in Paris. Hemingway was too immersed in the thrill of the fiesta to think too much about him.

She was late with her period at one point of the holiday. Hemingway started to worry that she might be pregnant again. He expressed his fear to Sally Bird. 'I'm not ready for another child,' he told her. 'Stop acting like a cry baby,' she scolded, 'You're responsible too. Either do something about not having it or have it.' Somebody needed to say that to him. It was as if birth control was solely Hadley's responsibility.

The Sun Also Rises is interesting because of its reversal of the traditional male/female roles. 'Lady' Brett Ashley, who was modelled on Twysden, is promiscuous. Robert Cohn is her love interest. He becomes the book's least attractive character as it goes on. The hero, or rather anti-hero, is Jake Barnes. Barnes is impotent as the result of a war wound that has deprived him of his manhood.

Hemingway told Leicester he got this idea from a genito-urinary hospital ward in Italy where they put him after he was wounded in Fossalta. It was there he saw 'all these poor bastards who had everything blown off'.[10]

The first draft of the book, written both in Paris and Valencia, only took him forty-eight days. He edited it in Austria and New York. It has a wide array of characters in it. We get a cocktail of bartenders, prostitutes, matadors, lowlifes, gin-sodden pedants. The tight-lipped banter is compulsive, edged as it is with a bleak dismay. One writer described it as encapsulating the 'glamorous disaffectedness' that characterised the Lost Generation.[11]

Romero is a bullfighter who forms a fulcrum to the action. He comes across as the only person who emerges with his dignity intact, despite being somewhat boring.

The original version of the book started with the words: 'This is a novel about a lady. Her name is Lady Ashley. When the story begins she is living in Paris and it is spring.' Scott Fitzgerald prevailed upon Hemingway to delete this chapter. The book is much more effective because of that.

It was before its time with its crew of laidback malcontents. Such characters would become common currency in the novels of the future. At this time, they were unusual.

Hemingway knew readers were tiring of Scott Fitzgerald's Jazz Age euphoria. They wanted something more existential: the heady undercurrents of self-obsessed souls.

His characters act as if they suffer at a more profound level than other mortals. They manage to conceal their angst under a plethora of jokes, at least while the wine is flowing and the bulls running and the love is going good. They often seem to be on the verge of some revelatory pronouncement that fails to make it to their lips. Instead they speak in measured tones undercut with gallows humour. Their code precludes emotional honesty. One must not break down under the weight of all that navel-gazing. You can always have another glass of absinthe to anaesthetise the pain. And the feria will be 'swell'.

These people live in a kind of air pocket of the emotions. They come at us without histories. Drink gives them oblivion. The party goes on endlessly, shot through with their smart-alecky epithets. They champion the now.

The search for instant gratification is particularly the case with Jake. Having been close to death, he wants to snatch at what life has to offer without any compunctions. As he puts it at one stage, 'I did not care what it was all about. All I wanted to know was how to live in it. Maybe if you found out how to live in it you learned from that what it was all about.' The inside-out philosophy is as close to an epiphany as this motley crew of *soi disant* misfits is going to come.

The impossibility of a relationship developing between Brett and Jake is typical Hemingway. In most of the books he will write from this point on, we see the dynamics of love and fulfilment summarily scuppered by emasculation, incompatibility, hatred, death, suicide, or murder.

Brett is tired of men who want her for her body. The chemistry between herself and Jake works from this point of view because of his inability to express his attraction for her in a physical way. The parallels with Hemingway are clear. He wanted Twysden but was blocked from her by the presence of Hadley. Harold Loeb got her instead. After a while at the siesta, Loeb became bored by the bulls. Hemingway gave out to him for this. The giving out was tinged with jealousy. He had the woman Hemingway was lusting after.

Hadley was disappointed that she was nowhere to be found in the book. Was her husband writing her out of his life before taking her out of it for real? He once told his friend Howell Jenkins, 'She's the best guy on a trip you ever saw.'[12] He felt differently now. She was too quiet to be a part of the hellraising that went on in Pamplona.

Hadley had an admirer in the bullfighter Cayetano Ordonez. She played on it to make her husband aware she was still desirable as a woman.

Hemingway, meanwhile, was making a play for Twysden. She visited the sawmill apartment many times in Paris. Hadley knew her well. Hemingway often flirted with her in front of Hadley. He did this as with many women throughout his life. Triangular situations seemed to turn him on. This one brought Hadley to the point of tears.

Twysden was flirtatious. Loeb she picked up and dropped at will. She admitted being attracted to Hemingway but refrained from doing anything about it because of Hadley. Hemingway envied Loeb's freedom to indulge himself with her.

Brett is one of the most fascinating female characters Hemingway ever created. Her dialogue is refreshingly spiky. Pillow talk in Hemingway's novels is often mushy. Here it has an edge to it. He keeps her credible because of her being neither angel nor bitch, the plight of many of his subsequent heroines and anti-heroines.

Dashiell Hammett once said, 'Hemingway has never been able to write a woman. He only puts them in books to admire them.'[13] Women often act as spoilsports in his work, as interlopers on male bonding sprees.

Just as Aunt Sally was a killjoy for Huckleberry Finn and Hemingway's mother for his own early roistering, so do many of his female characters attempt to put the brakes on male fun. They do this either through jealousy or a pragmatic edge. Brett is the exception to this.

The Sun Also Rises is arguably Hemingway's most realistic novel. No 'big themes' enmesh it as in his future ones. Jake is far from being a Hemingway trope. He becomes part of the book's overall mosaic rather than the omniscient narrator he may appear to be at the beginning.

The other characters also go about their days without appearing to be under the guiding hand of an intrusive author pulling the strings. They cajole one another to desensitise themselves to their angst. Bullfights serve a similar function for them and so does sex. The cult of sensation is their holy grail.

The Sun Also Rises is as much a satire of the expatriate culture as a celebration of it. Hemingway was annoyed that many critics failed to appreciate this. He was angered by the ones who lambasted the book because it featured characters they deemed unsavoury. Surely, he mused, the pages of literary history were littered with such disreputable people, all the way from the Bible to Henry Fielding.

Conrad Aiken was closer to the point. The characters may have been unattractive, he remarked, but Hemingway's narration made them dignified. Christopher Morley said the book reminded him more of Greenwich Village than the Left Bank of Paris.

Other critics busied themselves trying to find out who was who. Barnes was Hemingway, it was assumed, and Cohn was Loeb—or 'Low Ebb' as Hemingway called him. His negative feelings about him are given free rein in the book.

Loeb rescued *In Our Time* from the slush pile at Boni & Liveright. His 'reward' was to be lampooned ferociously. Sherwood Anderson's largesse had been rewarded by a similar sideswipe not long before. It was as if Hemingway resented being under a compliment to anyone. 'If you give him a helping hand,' Robert Coates blasted, 'You're dead.' Another possibility was that he portrayed Loeb negatively as a result of anti-Semitism.

The most ridiculous theory mooted about his satirical portrayal of Loeb was that it came about because he was upset that Loeb was a better tennis player than he was. Hemingway was weak at tennis for many reasons: poor coordination, a trick knee (the heritage of Fossalta), and his bad eyesight. What he lacked in expertise he did his best to make up for with an almost childish delight over his occasional good shots.

He told his friend Peter Viertel he was anything but an anti-Semite.[14] Viertel's wife, Jigee, had previously been married to Budd Schulberg, a Hollywood screenwriter. Viertel was a screenwriter too. Hemingway became close to both of them. If such a quality was present in his book, he argued, it was from his characters rather than himself. He merely compiled a document of the time.

Loeb was so disgusted by his portrayal that he sent a message to Hemingway one day telling him he wanted to shoot him. Hemingway replied that he would be in Lipp's brasserie from two to four on Saturday and Sunday afternoons. Anyone who wished to shoot him should come at that hour and 'for Christ's sake stop talking about it'.

Loeb denied making the threat. He cut off all connections with Hemingway after the book came out. It was also untrue, he stressed, that he developed an ulcer after reading it. Or that it led to him having to spend a decade 'on a shrink's couch'.

Hadley tried to convince him that he was a composite character. He found it difficult to believe her. She told him he was originally supposed to be the book's hero. If that was the case, he wondered, why did Hemingway change his mind? He surmised that it was because he went off with Twysden.

The Sun Also Rises was one of the most influential books Hemingway ever wrote. When it hit the stands, suddenly the world seemed to be overcome with characters acting disgruntled with life even though they were born with silver spoons in their mouths. These were the precursors of the teenagers of the fifties, the Me Generation, mouthing quasi-philosophical one-liners through clenched teeth while ordering another daiquiri from the bar.

It went on to sell 7,000 copies in the first two months, thereby making Hemingway into a household name. Suddenly, the people who spurned him up to now were searching him out. *Vanity Fair*, which had turned down one of his stories in the past, said it wanted to interview him. James Joyce recommended him to his German publishers.

The book's popularity with the outer world failed to make his parents like it any more than his previous one. His father abhorred excessive drinking and smoking. He would have been the last man in the world to look at another woman besides his wife so he could hardly be expected to empathise with the louche characters presented here. Grace felt the same. After thumbing through the book, she enquired of her son if he had other words in his vocabulary besides 'damn' and 'bitch'. She despaired at his treatment of 'so degraded a strata [sic] of humanity'.[15] 'Honestly, Marce,' she huffed to Marcelline after she finished it, 'With the whole world full of beauty, why does he have to pick out thoughts and words from the gutter?'

The book was reprinted seven times in the next ten months. Nobody was in any doubt that Hemingway was now eclipsing Fitzgerald as Scribner's most valuable asset. He was able to name his price for future works. Gone were the days of nervously submitting short stories to *This Quarter* and *The Transatlantic Review*. The Hemingway *lingua* was now part of the global culture.

Archibald MacLeish wrote:

> Veteran of the war before he was twenty;
> Famous at twenty five; at thirty a master.
> He whittled a style for his time from a walnut stick
> In a carpenter's loft in a street of that April city.[16]

6

The Perils of Pauline

Twysden was the first serious threat to Hemingway's marriage. Hadley never asked him if he slept with her. She hoped her suspicions about this were unfounded. But in the summer of 1926, she watched him falling for someone who was an even bigger threat than Twysden. Her name was Pauline Pfeiffer.

When Hemingway first met Pauline, she was with her sister, Jinny. He was more attractred to Jinny at first.[1]

Pauline thought Hemingway was scruffy. He wore a baggy tweed suit that was patched at the elbows. The pockets were torn from having notebooks jammed into them too often. These were the notebooks where he jotted down all his observations.[2]

She was a fashion reporter for *Vanity Fair.* Intelligent as well as debonair, she might have been Scott Fitzgerald's Daisy Buchanan come to life. She was older than Hemingway by four years and a day.

Pauline was like a flapper girl with her bobbed hair and jaunty manner. Though not especially beautiful in a chocolate box sense, she exuded vitality. Hadley was more composed. Such a quality had suited Hemingway a few years before. Now he wanted something different—a woman to carry him to his next phase.

Pauline won a major brownie point with him when she encouraged him to publish *The Torrents of Spring.*[3] Hadley was upset about the fact that it betrayed Anderson. Pauline felt anyone was fair game for satire, even a friend. She also found the book funny. Hadley had reservations about Hemingway's facility with comedy. *Torrents* was never going to be her favourite book even apart from the mean motive behind it.

An old saying has it that a man owes his success to his first wife and his second wife to his success. When Hemingway met Hadley, he was a nobody. He was about to become famous when he met Pauline.

She had a lot in common with Hadley. Not only was she older than Hemingway but she came from St. Louis as well. And she had a Trust Fund.

Her father practically owned the town of Piggott in Arkansas. He made his fortune as a commodity broker in St. Louis, afterwards investing his profits in cotton and timber enterprises. His brother, Gus, was equally wealthy. He owned companies called Hudnut Perfumes, Sloan's Liniment, and Warner Pharmaceuticals. 'If one is perpetually doomed to marry people from St. Louis,' Hemingway once joked to Hadley, 'it's best to marry them from the very best families.'[4] Gus never married. He treated Pauline and Jinny like daughters and was supremely generous to them.

It was widely believed that Pauline had gone to Europe to find a husband.[5] Her relationship with Hemingway began platonically. She was an equal friend to both Hadley and him at the beginning. She became so close to the pair of them, one morning she even slipped into bed with them while they were having breakfast.

She went on bicycle races with them. She played bridge with them. She went skinny-dipping with them. Pauline was a better swimmer than Hadley and also enjoyed sunbathing more. Hadley's fair skin had a tendency to burn.

Hemingway was physically attracted to Pauline, especially when she swam in the nude. She had a good figure and liked showing it off to him. Hadley's weight had been growing since giving birth to Bumby so hers had disimproved.

The scene was set for Pauline to 'steal' Hemingway from Hadley. She had an added advantage over her in that she was adept at literary banter. Hemingway loved hearing her yarns about working at *Vanity Fair*.

When she got to know Hemingway and Hadley first, Pauline held herself back from Hemingway. She watched and waited, plotting her move like a military campaign. She felt sure that, in time, Hemingway would have a problem resisting her. This all happened without Hadley knowing anything was going on between them. She was too trusting to suspect an ulterior motive even when it was staring her in the face.

Pauline accompanied Hemingway and Hadley to Schruns ski resort in the winter of 1925. Her friend, Kitty Cannell, who introduced her to Hemingway, was surprised at this. She passed her on a Paris street one day as she was carrying her skis. 'I never associated you with ski-ing,' she said to Pauline. Pauline just laughed, which made Cannell wonder if something was 'cooking' between herself and Hemingway.

Their romance blossomed in Schruns. Hemingway slept with her as Hadley minded Bumby. Pauline was willing to go against her Catholic conscience to get her man. When she felt she had him, she went back to Paris. Hemingway was lonely in her absence. The atmosphere with Hadley was tense for the rest of the holiday.

Pauline often told Hadley she had more affection for her than she had for Hemingway. She probably said this to lull her into a false sense of security. 'She didn't go straight for my husband,' Hadley said, 'but once she made up her mind he was what she wanted she spent a lot of violent energy on him.'[6]

Pauline saw Hemingway as impractical. What he needed to advance his career, she felt, was a wife who could double as a business manager and PR person. She believed she was qualified for both roles.

It was Pauline's personality rather than her looks that Hemingway mainly fell for. And her sense of style. Hadley could never hope to compete with her wardrobe. This was more Hemingway's fault than hers. He was more inclined to buy her the occasional luxurious gift, like Miro's painting *The Farm*, than anything to wear.

'You can either buy clothes or pictures,' Gertrude Stein advised, 'It's that simple. No one who is not very rich can do both.'[7] Kitty Cannell disagreed. 'Why does he buy paintings by Miro,' she chided, 'when Hadley is going around in last year's clothes? They're falling off her. And it's *her* money.' Cannell brought Hadley shopping for jewellery one day. Hemingway resented the usurping of his marital authority. He got his revenge on her by lampooning her in *The Sun Also Rises*.

Hadley became depressed when she saw Hemingway spending more and more time with Pauline. The penny slowly dropped that she was losing him. It disappointed her, as she thought he had more character than that. Of course, half of the enthusiasm was coming from Pauline. 'Ernest,' she said, 'was weak in the sense that if someone wanted him very much he was tremendously touched by it.' She had already seen this happening with Twysden.

Hemingway seemed content to string both Hadley and Pauline along together indefinitely. He refused to acknowledge his attraction to Pauline because of the fear of giving Hadley up. His dilemma appeared in an unpublished extract from *A Moveable Feast*:

> To truly love two women at the same time is the most destructive and terrible thing that can happen to a man. When you are with one you love her and with the other you love her too and together you love them both. You break all promises and do everything you said you would never do.

> You lie and hate it and it destroys you and every day is more dangerous and your work harder but you live day to day as in a war and the strange part is that you are happy.[8]

Hemingway's physical courage was never in question, but he lacked the gumption to square up to Hadley and tell her how much he was falling for Pauline.

Pauline was aware of his tendency towards vacillation. She knew he was capable of casting her in the mould of 'the other woman' until his infatuation with her spun itself out. With this in mind, she did all in her power to advertise the situation between them to Hadley. It was the opposite to her previous behaviour. Up to now, she understated it.

She kept their intimacy a secret in the early stages. Its illicit nature had been half the thrill for Hemingway. But it was now time to say to him, 'Who is it going to be—Hadley or me?' Her ultimatum had to be timed until it was too late for him to want to run back to his wife.

Hadley accepted the fact that she was dim-witted at the outset. 'I was too dumb,' she admitted, 'to see Pauline had fallen like a ton of bricks for Ernest.'[9] When she did, she went to Jinny. She asked her if she thought Pauline was in love with her husband. Jinny replied, 'I think they are very fond of each other.' Hadley now went to Hemingway and confronted him with the situation.

He sat on the fence.

'Why can't we go on the way we are?' he pleaded. When she said she knew Pauline was in love with him, he grew annoyed, telling her that she was upsetting their cosy threesome. 'What he seemed to be saying to me,' Hadley pondered, 'was that it was my fault for forcing the issue. Now that I had broken the spell, our love was no longer safe.'[10]

Pauline seized the moment, expressing a wish to have a talk with Hadley. Hadley demurred, fearing she would be no match for her in a showdown. 'I thought she'd best me in any conversation,' she said, 'She was very quick. I wished I was that smart.'[11]

The next time she talked to Hemingway she knew the writing was on the wall. The atmosphere between them was cold. She knew he was going to leave her.

The woman who had overseen *In Our Time*, *The Torrents of Spring*, and the first draft of *The Sun Also Rises*—not to mention all the stories where he cut his literary teeth—was soon to be out of his life for good. Her 'parfit, gentil knight'—as she dubbed him after reading Chaucer's Prologue to *The Canterbury Tales*—was about to divorce her.

Hadley now demanded of Hemingway and Pauline that they spend a hundred days away from one another. They acceded to this. Hadley hoped that the time lapse would make him realise he loved her more than Pauline.

That was never going to happen. The ploy only served to throw them closer together. Forbidden fruit is generally a balm to a relationship. This one was no exception. Hemingway was more prone to loneliness than we might imagine. It ate away at him like a disease. He even confided to Pauline at one point that suicide might be the only option for him. Hadley came to recognise in time that she might have been better off to encourage him to 'take Pauline off somewhere and burn out the sex appeal they had for one another'.

He communicated with Pauline by letters at this time just as he had with Hadley at the beginning of their relationship. Most of these were written with passion. Hadley was unaware of them. Pauline wrote so many that she eventually became embarrassed going to the post office with them.

When Hadley discovered that they were communicating with one another she attacked Pauline, telling her it was a betrayal of her promise to her. How could it be a separation when they were in almost daily contact? Pauline accepted this point, agreeing to begin the 'hundred days' again if Hadley wanted her to.

Hemingway was against this course of action. In one of his letters to Pauline, he wrote dramatically: 'You see Pfife I think that when two people love each other terribly much and need each other in every way and then go away from each other it works almost as bad as an abortion.'

Hadley freed Hemingway from his isolation shortly before the hundred days expired. Hemingway had made her feel like a tyrant. 'I might have been the Emperor Tiberius,' she remarked. She realised the velvet glove would probably have been a more beneficial approach to the crisis than the iron fist.

Hemingway became excited when Hadley wrote to him to tell him that the three months' separation clause (what he later referred to as 'The Hundred Days' War') was officially over. He replied by offering her all the royalties from *The Sun Also Rises*. He also drew up a will that made Bumby the chief beneficiary of any income he received from his books. He ended the letter by saying, 'I won't tell you how I admire your straight thinking, your head, your heart and your lovely hands. I pray to God that he will make up to you the very great hurt that I have done you who are the best and truest and loveliest person that I have ever known.'[12]

Hadley accepted the situation. 'Our love ran its course,' she said philosophically.

After Hemingway's parents heard the 'awful rumours' of his impending divorce, they wrote to him saying they hoped they were false. 'I'm sure all the gossip is bunk,' Clarence speculated. Grace astoundingly remarked that most marriages ended up 'on the rocks'. She held 'modern and heretical' views on marriage but had always kept them under her hat, at least until now.

Hemingway told them he was now living apart from Hadley. A wealthy friend of his called Gerald Murphy offered him a studio he had at Montparnasse as a temporary accommodation for him. Hemingway would go on to form a strong attachment to Murphy and his wife, Sara. They were an expatriate couple from America who were very generous with their money.

Hadley kept Bumby. She baulked at the idea of going back to the sawmill apartment, taking rooms at a small hotel instead. Here she cried bitter tears at what had happened. The fact that it was situated across the street from the café where Hemingway did most of his writing compounded her agony. She later found an apartment for herself and Bumby. Hemingway brought her anything she wanted from the apartment—her silver, her Dresden plates, the Miro painting he gave her for her birthday the year before.

Clarence sent him a letter. 'I hope,' he wrote, 'that you may in some way reclaim your dear Hadley and Bumby.' He exhorted him to 'put on the armour of God and shun evil companions'. His letter ended with the words, 'Remember—What doth it profit a man if he gain the whole world and lose his soul.'[13]

Divorce had always been a dirty word in Oak Park. Even if married couples abhorred one another, they stuck together for the sake of respectability. It was the same with any other problem. The whited sepulchres of the neighbourhood had always shone brightly in the past. Now the son of one of its most respected denizens was casting a pall on that tradition. He had already done so with his 'pornographic' books. Divorce was an even worse curse.

Hadley appreciated his gesture about the royalties. Of course, without her there may not have been a book in the first place. Her dignified attitude exacerbated Hemingway's guilt. If she swore at him or hit him, it would have made things easier for him. Neither of these reactions were in her nature. She bore the situation with fortitude like a Hemingway hero. Her dignified attitude made his shame worse. Asked why he was leaving her, he replied, 'Because I am a son-of-a-bitch.' He said to Hadley herself, 'I wish I died before I loved anyone but you.'

In order to make his marriage to Pauline acceptable to the Church, he had to render the one to Hadley null and void. This was ironic considering she was the love of his life.

His first exposure to Catholicism was when he received the Last Rites from a priest after his Fossalta wound. As he lay bleeding on a stretcher, he claimed he was baptised by him. This is questionable. A baptismal certificate was never found.[14]

Gravitating towards Catholicism was more of a pragmatic move for Hemingway than anything else. He was aligning himself to what Nick Adams had called a 'fake ideal' to get away from Hadley. He admitted as much when he said, 'Hell, any man could become a Catholic for a million bucks.' Having said that, he threw himself into Catholicism with as much enthusiasm as he could muster, wearing a scapular and going to Mass and even making the sign of the cross when he went swimming.[15]

Catholicism appealed to the romantic in him. It was a colourful religion and also had its share of poets and alcoholics. These were his favourite kinds of people. Pauline saw his conversion a different way. 'The outlet of confession will be good for him,' she smirked.[16]

The literary set of Paris was devastated at the news that he was splitting from Hadley. John Dos Passos wrote to him saying 'I'd like to knock both your and Hadley's heads together.'[17] Up to now, they seemed like the happiest married couple Hemingway's fellow writers knew. Gertrude Stein and Scott Fitzgerald had trouble-strewn relationships and so had Ford Madox Ford. Sally Bowen, who lived in a *menage* with Ford and his mistress, Jean Rhys, for a time, wrote: 'It was quite all right to be dirty, drunk, a pervert and a thief provided you had a lively and honest mind, and the courage of your instincts.'

Hemingway's friends 'flaunted their promiscuity and joked about their abortions and venereal diseases'. Hemingway and Hadley, in contrast, looked for all the world like an idyllic pair. 'Even at parties,' Harold Loeb noted of Hemingway, 'he seemed uninterested in other women.'

He may have missed something. There were rumours that Hemingway had been intimate with Katy Smith while he was dating Hadley. It was also alleged that he threw himself at a woman called Irene Goldstein after meeting her in the Smith's apartment one night. Apparently she resisted his advances. Hemingway was said to have backed away from her with the words, 'I've never yet raped a virgin.'

Pauline's parents were opposed to their daughter marrying Hemingway because of his having been married before. There were also murmurings about the fact that he was a drunk and a ne'er-do-well. Her Uncle Gus disabused them of such notions after meeting him. His positive appraisal of him led Pauline's mother, Mary, to warm to him as well. She conveyed such warmth in a letter to him: 'My dear Ernest, if you are all that those who know you best believe you to be, we are glad to give our heart's treasure into your keeping.'

He went on to form a strong friendship with her. They had the same sense of humour and shared a fondness for alcohol. He was a little stiffer with her husband, Paul.

Like Gerald and Sara Murphy, the Pfeiffers seemed almost bored by their wealth. They did their best to share it with those less fortunate than themselves. When people lost their jobs during the Depression, Paul performed many generous actions to help ease the blow. One of them was asking out-of-work locals to paint his house even though it had recently been painted. He thought this was better than giving them hand-outs that would have dented their pride. By the end of the Depression, it was said, his house had over forty coats of paint on it.[18]

Hemingway and Pauline were married in France in May 1927. They had a civil service and also a religious one. Hemingway's banker, a man called Mike Ward, was best man. Jinny was maid of honour. It was thought she looked sad on the day. Was she carrying a torch for Hemingway? It was possible. She was prettier than Pauline. His initial interest in her could well have been reciprocated.

Archibald MacLeish and his wife, Ada, disapproved of the wedding. They attended a luncheon with Hemingway and Pauline after the nuptials but left early. Ada remarked acerbically, 'To see this farce being solemnized by the Catholic Church was more than we could take.'[19]

The Pfeiffers were generous with their wedding gifts. Both of Pauline's parents gave cheques of $1,000 and so did Gus and another uncle. Such largesse meant the newly-weds could continue their luxurious lifestyle for an undetermined period of time even if Hemingway's earnings from his writings were low.

They honeymooned in both France and Spain. The Murphys congratulated Pauline on rescuing Hemingway from a 'destructive' relationship with Hadley. They always felt she was 'miscast' as his wife.[20]

Hadley started seeing a man called Paul Mowrer now. They became close quickly. Mowrer knew Hemingway. In fact, he invited him to dinner one night after he heard he was having problems with Hadley. He asked him if it was true that his marriage was over. Hemingway told him it was.

Mowrer was the foreign editor of *The Chicago Daily News*. He was the first recipient of the Pulitzer Prize for foreign correspondence. Though he was a lover of poetry and the outdoors, there any comparison with Hemingway ended. Their personalities were poles apart.

Mowrer was married when he met Hadley, but the marriage had been dead for years. He only stayed with his wife, Winifred, for the sake of their children. This fact made getting close to him easier for Hadley. She could never have stolen a man from his wife as Pauline did.

Mowrer proved to be a good stepfather to Bumby. In the early days of their relationship, Hadley was closer to Bumby than she was to him. She described him as 'the sweetest, dearest, naughtiest, handsomest boy in the Kingdom. My time with him is full even if my life isn't.'

She was very possessive of him, but as time went on, she became comfortable releasing him into Pauline's care for visits. Bumby enjoyed being with both women. In fact, he came to regard having two mothers as normal. Those with only one he saw as being 'underprivileged'.

Hadley's affection for Mowrer grew as she got to know him better. Living with Hemingway, she said, had been like living over the San Andreas fault. Bumby believed she would have died young if they stayed together. Such was the pace of their life. Mowrer sometimes became bored when she recalled anecdotes from their time together. He would sometimes say, 'Enough is enough' if she did this too often.

They postponed getting married until they knew they were right for one another, choosing to just live together instead. Winifred was fine about this arrangement. 'It's lots of fun having an affair,' she opined to Hadley once, 'but once you're married it's just a bunch of troubles.' Hadley was more conventional. She wanted to formalise their union. It was strange for her to be 'the other woman' in a love triangle after just getting out of one where she was in the opposite position.

Hemingway wrote to Scott Fitzgerald later that year to say Hadley had divorced him. It was a misleading phrase, one of his familiar half-truths. He promised to refrain 'from any half-turnings on of the gas or slitting of the wrists with sterilised razor blades'.[21] The self-pitying tone was typical of him. He was the one, after all, who had called the shots.

He told his father, 'I would have gone back to Hadley if she wanted me. She said things were better as they were.' If she said this, which is unlikely, it would have been merely to ease his conscience. Mowrer was a convenient excuse for him to do what he was going to do anyway.

The fact that he was giving Hadley the royalties from *The Sun Also Rises* meant he was, as he put it, 'poorer than any time since I was fourteen, with an earning capacity of what stories I sell to Scribner's. The only thing in life I've ever had any luck being decent about is money.' His situation was ironic. He spent most of his life thus far dreaming of a book that would make him rich. Now that it was here, the royalties were going to someone else.

He went through a period of being uneasy in his new situation. Hadley and Bumby were gone and with them all his old routines. He loved Pauline but maybe not quite as much as when that love was hidden and returning to Hadley still an option. What was his future going to be like? Would he carry a sense of 'Paradise Lost' with him always?

He tried to act happy, but there seemed to be two people inside him, both wanting different things. Sometimes that confusion came out in anger, anger even at the woman he felt guilty for leaving.

He went into a bar one night with Pauline. They spotted Hadley across the way. He was drunk. In a stupor, he told her that their marriage was illusory because of the ceremony not being performed by a priest. Hadley was disgusted with him. She snapped, 'If that's the case, Bumby is mine.'

Hemingway responded to this by telling her he wanted Bumby to become a Catholic. Hadley dug in her heels at this, saying he was an Episcopalian and an Episcopalian he would stay, at least until he was eighteen. Then he could be 'as many Catholics as he wants'.

His denial of the validity of his marriage to Hadley in the eyes of the church in effect made Bumby illegitimate. It galled Hadley to see Hemingway using religion to create this state of affairs.

Hemingway gave Aaron Hotchner a different reason for why he embraced Catholicism. After divorcing Hadley, he told Hotchner, he found it difficult to make love to Pauline. 'Don't know if it was auto-suggestion from *The Sun Also Rises*,' he speculated. To try and alleviate the problem, he went to a mystic. The mystic advised him to fasten electrodes to his hands and feet. When this failed to work, Pauline suggested prayer. Hemingway went into a church two blocks away and then made his way back to bed. Afterwards he made love to Pauline 'like we invented it'.

'We never had any trouble that way again,' he told Hotchner, 'and that's how I became a Catholic.'[22]

7

King of the Fiction Racket

Gerald Murphy's studio was Hemingway's home for much of 1927 when he was working on his next book. It was another collection of stories, *Men Without Women*. 'It will probably have a large sale,' he predicted, 'among fairies and old Vassar girls.'[1]

He usually scoured the Bible for his book titles. It let him down in this instance, despite hours of rummaging. The one he chose instead was hardly applicable to his circumstances. He wrote it while he was cavorting between Hadley and Pauline.

The inapplicable title apart, it contains some of the greatest stories he ever wrote.

'In Another Country' was one of his favourites and we can easily see why. Set against the backdrop of a man's physiotherapy sessions at the Ospedale Maggiore after being wounded in the war, its main emphasis is a war veteran, a major who has just lost his wife.

His loneliness for her, subdued under the Hemingway canon of harnessing one's emotions, gives the story its poignancy. Becoming dependent on a person means leaving oneself open to pain. In the lottery of life, these are the kinds of stakes we play for in war and peace alike.

'In the fall,' Hemingway wrote in the first line of the story, 'the war was always there, but we did not go to it any more.'[2] This is a sentence that begs many questions. What war, for instance? And where is 'there'? Who, for that matter, is 'we'? And what does 'any more' mean? Sentences like this, stripped of context, whet the appetite for more. This is language pruned almost to nothing but still stylised. Scott Fitzgerald said it was the most beautiful sentence he had ever read. Assonance contributes to its musicality.

Hemingway is extending the possibilities of language here. All those supposedly flat sentences are pregnant with meaning, always hinting at something beyond them.

The 'go to it' phrase suggests war is like a show. That was the term he used for it as an eighteen-year-old. In the later stages of the story, we find ourselves back in the traumatised world of Krebs from 'Soldier's Home'.

The most well-known story in the book is probably 'The Killers'. This is an ostensibly straightforward parable about an ex-heavyweight boxer awaiting the arrival of two hitmen from Chicago. Even though it only runs for thirteen pages, it was made into a full-length film. This is a testament to its richness. The idea of a man with nowhere to run is engaging. Hemingway delivers it in his familiar hard-boiled language, refusing to ink in the details of his plight. We end as wisely as we began.

Much the same could be said of 'Hills Like White Elephants'. This is another story where the language is stripped to the bone. Hemingway presents us with a man and his girlfriend as they sit together outside a railway station. He wants her to have an abortion against her wishes. Her reluctance to 'let the air in' makes him nag at her. She takes it for a while but towards the end she explodes with, 'Would you please please please please please please please stop talking?'[3]

Nowhere in the story is the word 'abortion' mentioned. We get it all by innuendo. This is something anyone familiar with Hemingway will be expecting. 'Hills Like White Elephants' is one of his simplest stories and also one of his most reverberative ones.

The word 'it' occurs a dozen times to signify the abortion. Such a subject disturbs the woman greatly. The emptiness of her relationship with the man is captured in the terseness of their dialogue. When she says 'I feel fine' at the end, we know she is anything but that. One is reminded of Mrs Elliot feeling 'quite happy' at the end of 'Mr and Mrs Elliot'.

Hemingway wrote the story while he was on honeymoon with Pauline. It may have been inspired by him listening to a couple arguing on a train on which they were travelling in the course of it, but it could equally have been from his own experience. He was so distraught when Hadley became pregnant with Bumby he considered asking her to abort it at one point.

'The good parts of a book,' he remarked once, 'may be something a writer is lucky enough to overhear or it may be the wreck of his whole damn life.' The abortion theme made it unpublishable in America as a story. It first appeared in a European magazine called *Transition*.

'Now I Lay Me' was Scott Fitzgerald's favourite story from the collection. It was one Hemingway's mother could never forgive. He comes out forcibly against her in it. It includes a mention of her burning all of Clarence's beloved tools and arrowheads in one section. This is a rare example of him choosing a real-life incident to amplify his feelings of scepticism about the long-term viability of marriage.

His disenchantment with other kinds of relationships can be seen in many of the other stories, from 'Cat in the Rain' to 'Cross Country Snow' and 'A Canary For One' to 'Homage to Switzerland'. In the same way as he silenced those who accused him of copying Sherwood Anderson by writing *The Torrents of Spring*, here he tried to addle those who thought he aped the style of Ring Lardner in stories like 'Fifty Grand'.

The Lardner label had haunted him throughout most of his early writing career. In his teens, he was dubbed 'our Ring Lardner Junior' by *Trapeze*, one of the magazines he wrote for. The analogy was ill-founded. Lardner was primarily a comic writer. Hemingway was anything but that. His humour, on the odd occasions that he employed it—as in *The Torrents of Spring*—was usually barbed.

Reviews of the book ranged from those who saw him as the pioneering voice of a new era to those who disparaged his 'sordid little catastrophes'. He became annoyed when critics labelled the stories as reportage. It reduced him to the level of a journalist posing as a fiction writer.

The New York Herald Tribune suggested that his talent lay in contracting rather than expanding. Virginia Woolf claimed his characters were 'the people one may have seen showing off at some cafe, talking a rapid, high-pitched slang because slang is the speech of the herd'. They seemed to be relaxed, she wrote, 'but if we look at them a little from the shadow they're not at their ease at all. It would seem that the thing that's faked is character. Mr Hemingway leans against the flanks of that particular bull after the horns have passed.'

Wyndham Lewis wrote the most scathing review of all, accusing Hemingway of invoking a 'dull-witted, bovine, monosyllabic simpleton, a lethargic and stuttering dummy, a super-innocent, queerly sensitive village idiot of few words and fewer ideas'.[4]

He was dismissed as a documenter of facts rather than someone who used his imagination to create scenarios. If this was the case, he sputtered to Scott Fitzgerald, 'What a life I must have led.' His view of writing was that it was more real than reality. Life was unbelievable. It was the duty of fiction to make it credible.

The negative publicity the book received was contradicted by its sales. Published in October, by Christmas it had sold 13,000 copies. So much for critics—though Archibald MacLeish gushed about it.

'A fine, cool, clean piece of work,' he wrote, 'Sure as leather and hard and swell. Ten things said for every word written. Overtones like the bells at Chartres. All the stuff you can't describe but only do—and only you can do it.'

Hemingway had a series of accidents around this time. When he was skiing in Switzerland before Christmas, he had a fall that could have been dangerous. His goggles broke as he went down but thankfully no damage was done to his eyes. He had a further mishap the following month at Montreux after another skiing expedition. He was lifting Bumby up to bring him to the toilet when the boy put a fingernail into his eye. 'The child was more dangerous than the mountain,' he joked. His nail cut a half moon into Hemingway's pupil, causing him excruciating pain. He was practically blind for a week. 'Now I know what agony you go through,' he wrote to James Joyce. (Joyce had been plagued with iritis all his life.) He had to have a cocaine wash to relieve the pain.

Three months later, he was involved in yet another accident. It happened in the bathroom of an apartment he was renting with Pauline in Paris. He had gone out to the toilet in the middle of the night after a drinking spree. When he reached for the chain to flush it, his hand instead connected with a cord attached to a skylight window above him. It crashed down on his head and gave him a severe gash. Pauline had her work cut out trying to stanch the flow of blood. It took her 'thirty thicknesses of toilet roll' to do so. The wound was badly stitched in the hospital he attended, leaving him with a C-shaped scar that lasted for the rest of his life.[5] It faded somewhat with time but was often airbrushed out of photographs of him to make him more handsome.

Hemingway and Pauline, who was now pregnant, left Paris shortly after this incident, going back to America in March 1928. Pauline wanted to have her child there, being wary about the quality of European medical care. The baby was due in June. Her physician advised her not to leave it later than March before crossing the ocean.

The question now became where they were going to live. They discussed various options before John Dos Passos recommended the island of Key West to them. Dos Passos had visited it in 1924 during a walking tour through Florida. It sounded more interesting to them than anywhere else they were considering.

It was only 1.5 miles wide and 4.5 miles long. Hemingway saw it as an offshoot of America, a part of it and yet not really so. Its main attraction for him was the thought of the fishing he could do on the Gulf Stream. It was also accessible both to Cuba and the hunting grounds of Wyoming.

They left for Havana on a ship called the *Orita*. Afterwards they took a boat to Key West. A car was waiting for them there, a gift from Pauline's Uncle Gus. They could have done with a more practical one. There was no road connecting Key West to the mainland at that time, only some car ferries to Havana.

They spent most of the next two years there. Hemingway described it as 'The St. Tropez of the poor.' It became their permanent address in January 1930. It was another year before they bought a house there.

Hemingway's parents were having financial problems at this time. They visited Florida in the spring of 1928 to view some properties in which they had invested. To their shock, they discovered their value had dipped dramatically. The realtor told them to hang on, that it had to be only a matter of time before the prices went up again.

They went to Cuba for a holiday afterwards. When they came back to Key West, they met Hemingway. It was their first time seeing him since he left Hadley. He took them to his home to meet Pauline. Their friendliness relieved her. She was worried they might be cool with her.

Clarence's nerves started to trouble him when he got back to Oak Park. He worried more and more about the Florida properties. His health was also a problem. He suffered from angina pectoris. There was even a suggestion of diabetes. Laboratory tests confirmed he had indeed 'a touch of the sugar'.

He distanced himself more from Grace as the year went on. At one stage, he even locked his bureau drawers to prevent her going through them. This was because he kept a gun in one of them. He became close to Leicester at this time. In the absence of Ernest, he leaned on him for support, being the only other male in the house.[6]

Pauline went to Piggott in May. She wanted to be near her family as the birth of her child drew near. Hemingway joined her there at the end of the month. He hated it. In some ways, it reminded him of Oak Park. The people were confused by him and he by them. They were mainly WASPs. The temperature was also too humid for him. 'What a christ offal place,' he wrote to Maxwell Perkins, using one of his familiar puns.[7]

He walked around the town in shorts. This was frowned on. It was almost tantamount to indecent exposure for the town's old-fashioned residents. The editor of the local paper referred to him as a 'queer duck'. Parents warned their children away from him. They were attracted to this strange creature who gave them nickels for shinnying up drainpipes.[8]

Pauline gave birth in June. It was a boy. They called him Patrick. Hemingway nicknamed him 'Mouse'.

He was delivered by Caesarean section. This had been expected because of Pauline's narrow hips. Her life was in danger at one point because of the umbilical cord. Hemingway told his friends, 'They had to open her up like a picador's horse to lift Patrick out.'[9] The doctor advised her not to get pregnant again for another three years if she wanted to avoid becoming a cripple—or a corpse.[10]

Maxwell Perkins had five daughters and wanted a son. Hemingway wrote grimly to him, 'I wish the boy had been one of your girls.'[11]

Patrick screamed as much as Bumby had after he was born. Hemingway was never able for this kind of thing. He took off for Wyoming to get away from him.

Pauline wrote to him shortly after he arrived. 'With you away,' she said, 'it seems as though I was just a mother, which is certainly not very gripping, but in three weeks I'll begin to get ready to go to Wyoming where I shall be just a wife.' Hadley had been too devoted to Bumby after he was born. It led to problems between herself and Hemingway. Pauline was determined not to make the same mistake with Patrick.

She wrote to Grace after bringing him home:

> My dear Mother Hemingway, here we are at last, father, mother and son home from the hospital. Patrick and I expect to be here through August while Ernest goes on a fishing trip out west with a friend and finishes up his book. I hope they have a glorious trip, for I don't think Ernest has had much fun for the last month.[12]

Her remarks are astounding. She nearly died after carrying Patrick for nine months, but Hemingway was the one who deserved the sympathy for not having had 'much fun' because he was busy finishing his book. (She was referring to *A Farewell to Arms*.)

Grace wrote to Hemingway the following month to tell him Clarence was demented with worry about the Florida properties. His brother, George, had advised him to get rid of them. He thought they were dead weight.

Even though they were losing money, there was still tax to be paid on them. Clarence forgot to pay it. He was penalised as a result, which meant that his tax bill for 1929 was twice as much as it was the year before. Hemingway told him not to worry, that he could send him the difference. 'If I have some luck with my book,' he vowed, 'Everything will be easy.'

He had been working on *A Farewell to Arms* for some time now, as Pauline alluded to in her letter to Grace. It was the story of a love affair between a soldier, Frederic Henry, and a nurse, Catherine. Henry deserts the army during the course of it to engage in what becomes an ultimately tragic romance with Catherine.

Pauline was typing it up for him, but it was getting to be too much for her. Hemingway wrote to Sunny to ask her if she could leave her job—she was working as a dental assistant—to help her. He offered to match whatever money her boss was giving her if she did this. Sunny was delighted to facilitate him. She was bored at her job.

Hemingway picked her up at Piggott and drove her to Jacksonville, Florida. Pauline met them there with Patrick. She then went to Key West with Pauline by train. Hemingway drove there on his own.

The chemistry between Sunny and Pauline was bad. Sunny felt she was treated poorly on the train journey. Pauline deserted her at one stage to have a drink with a stranger in the club car while she minded Patrick.

Things got worse when they reached Key West. She was instructed in the care and feeding of Patrick. His bed was put in her bedroom so she could tend him if he woke during the night. Hemingway's typewriter was also put in her room. It looked like she was going to be doing most of the work on the book and being a babysitter to boot.

She became cool with Pauline. There were times she felt her supposed secretarial tasks were a cover for her being a nurse to Patrick so that Hemingway and Pauline, who were still at the 'honeymoon' stage of their marriage, could go out together at night.

John Dos Passos called one evening during her visit. Hemingway had told her how nice a guy he was. He tried to 'fix' Sunny up with him, but she had no interest in him. 'I was shocked,' she said, 'to see a bald man with nervous, jumpy movements. Ernie had neglected to give me a physical picture of his friend, who was nine years older than I.'[13] There was some consolation for Dos Passos, however, as Katy Smith was also in the house that night. They found they had a bond together and went on to marry one another in later years. Jinny Pfeiffer had been interested in him as well but marriage always seemed to pass Jinny by.

Each time Hemingway finished a chapter of the book, he totted up the page tally. Sometimes he disclosed it to Pauline. He wrote with painstaking slowness at first. Then he got into a rhythm that enabled him to work faster. 'Am now on Page 486,' he wrote to his parents enthusiastically as he got towards the end of it.

He wrote to Waldo Peirce on 9 August, 'I've written 548 pages.'[14] Three days later, he wrote to a woman called Isabel Godolphin, 'Am on page 574.'[15] That was nearly thirty pages in a few days. He cut the letter short. All the 'juice' had to go into the book.

He was with Pauline in Wyoming now. They went to Piggott in September. Every time he talked to her about it, she became more and more intrigued.

Catherine dies in childbirth at the end, her baby becoming strangled by the umbilical cord. The incident was inspired by Pauline's problems with Patrick. Its romantic elements were more reminiscent of Hemingway and Agnes. Hemingway neglected to tell Pauline about this aspect of his past. Catherine's death, however, upset her. It was very close to her own experience. She was spared the knowledge of how close she came to dying that way herself when giving birth to Patrick but now she could imagine it.

Hemingway paid a visit home in October. His father had declined. The life was gone out of his eyes. Sometimes they welled up with tears for no reason. His hair was greying as well.

He told Grace she needed to take better care of him. Grace paid little attention to his words, talking more about her paintings than her husband. It was almost as if they had become a substitute for him. She asked Hemingway to try and get them into galleries in Paris. He promised to see what he could do.

Clarence began to get cantankerous with everyone. He even refused to allow people in his car with him, fearing he could crash if he got an angina attack at the wheel.

A levy for the Florida properties was due in December. He had no money to pay it so he asked George for help. 'Don't throw good money after bad,' George cautioned. It was advice Clarence should have taken but he failed to do so. His head was too muddled.

His nerves got worse as the year neared its end. By the morning of 6 December, they reached their nadir. After coming home from a call, he went up to his room. He sat on the bed. The problems of the past few months tumbled around in his head, coupled with other more mundane ones, like the fact that Grace had been nagging at him all morning and Leicester was unhappy at school.

He decided to end his life. What was the point in going on? His health was in bits, and he was facing bankruptcy. He worked hard all his life to be able to afford a comfortable retirement, but his plans had come to nothing.

He took a Smith & Wesson revolver out of his bedside locker and put it to his head. He pulled the trigger. A man who spent all his life saving other people's was now ending his own one. It was that absurd.

The bullet hit its target. He fell onto the bed.

Hemingway became numb when he heard the news, numb like one of the characters in his stories when they were confronted with a crisis. He was on a train between New York and Arkansas when he got the telegram telling him what had happened. He got off at the next stop, linking up with a different train to get back to Chicago.

Police were swarming around the house when he got there. 'It wasn't like our house anymore,' Leicester recalled. His sisters were crying. Grace was placed under sedation, as was Sunny. Carol had been summoned home from school.

They all tried to make sense of what happened. Grace took them through the sequence of events leading up to the tragedy. Clarence had woken with a pain in his leg that morning. He feared it might be gangrene caused by neglecting his diabetes. If it was, his foot would have to be amputated. He had a patient who lost one that way.[16]

He mentioned it to Grace but only casually. Afterwards, he burned some documents in a furnace. Then he did his calls. When he came home, he told Grace he was going to lie down until lunchtime. He made his way slowly upstairs, hanging onto the banister in pain.

Leicester had been left home from school that day with a cold. He was sleeping as his father went upstairs. The gunshot woke him. He ran up to Clarence's room and saw him lying dead on his bed. He had the Smith & Wesson in his hand. Leicester would write about the incident years later in a novel, *The Sound of the Trumpet*.[17]

Hemingway thought he should have seen it coming. On his last visit home, his father's cavalcade of health problems were screamingly obvious. As well as angina and the threat of diabetes, he had blinding headaches and high blood pressure.

It was his financial worries, however, that were uppermost in his mind when he died. He had invested heavily in the Florida properties but they started to drop in value almost as soon as his signature was dry on the purchase document. Some strange circumstances were responsible for this. A freighter capsized the year after he made his first instalment. It sank off the coast of Miami. The harbour was blocked for over a month, preventing imports from coming through.[18] Neither did a couple of hurricanes that took place at the time help matters.

He remortgaged Oak Park to raise the money for his investments. If he withdrew his money in time, as George suggested, he might have been able to cut his losses. Failing to do that meant he was always chasing them. His medical practice, the main source of revenue in the past, was also slackening off by now. And there were still some children in the house that had to be educated.

His own father had died in 1926. In a letter to Hemingway, he told him he slipped away with no pain. At the end of the letter, he wrote, 'The day before, he'd paid all his bills.' The necessity of squaring one's accounts was huge for him.

The final financial blow for him was the fact that Grace was losing some of her musical pupils now. They preferred the more sophisticated academies that were springing up in the area. She had extravagant tastes. Clarence believed that by killing himself he was giving her the ability to indulge them. The children could also be kept in school. His insurance policy would see to that.

Before his depression overcame him, he was making plans to retire to Florida. If he did, he would have been a neighbour of Ernest's in Key West. He was looking forward to fishing the Gulf Stream with him. He intended to practice medicine there as well, having applied for a licence and getting the application approved.

Marcelline said he changed his personality in his last year, becoming agitated for little or no reason and retiring to his room at every opportunity. Everything was kept under lock and key there. He was communicating only vaguely with his wife and children at this point. One day he was up, the next down. 'Gracie will be able to paint her pictures,' he would say on his 'up' days, 'and I'll grow oranges.' But then the dark moods would arrive, making him doubt any of this was going to happen.

When Nick Adams asks his father why the Indian killed himself in 'Indian Camp', he replies, 'I don't know, Nick. He couldn't stand things, I guess.'[19] Hemingway pondered the line in the aftermath of his father's death. What was the main reason behind it, he wondered. Was it caused by Grace's domination of him or the more obvious fear of bankruptcy? Not long before he pulled the trigger, he went to George for a loan and George refused him. His attitude was, 'You got yourself into this mess. Get yourself out of it.'[20] George had invested money in Florida real estate too. His investments had worked out better. Clarence lacked his savvy.

George tried to play Clarence's money problems down at the funeral. 'His financial affairs were in order on the day he died,' he insisted. This was a lie. He told it to preserve his social standing in Oak Park, to stave off any possible broadsides from Hemingway or the rest of the family.

Clarence had written to Hemingway some time before to ask him if he was interested in accompanying him on a trip to the Smoky Mountains in North Carolina. He replied that he was too busy writing to entertain the idea.

Hemingway was unaware of the depth of Clarence's depression. 'What a private hell he must have endured in his last years,' he ventured. Grace trivialized his health problems just as George had trivialised his financial ones. 'She misread his behaviour,' Hemingway complained. She would never be forgiven for this.

He often changed his theories about why his father killed himself over the years. Under the influence of drink, he told people that 'the All-American bitch' (i.e. his mother) was responsible. In 1929, however, he wrote in a letter to Grace that George had 'done more than anyone to kill Dad'.

He told Leicester not to cry at the funeral.[21] Above all, one had to show dignity at times like this. 'We have to be strong,' he said, 'when others are weak.' What bothered him most, he said to him, was the fact that shortly before he died, Clarence had written him a letter asking him for money. Hemingway had replied immediately with a cheque. It arrived on the very day of his suicide but according to Hemingway the envelope lay unopened on his cabinet. He believed that if Clarence saw the cheque he might have decided to battle on.

This is an interesting story, but it may not be true. If it was, why did he not keep his father's letter asking him for the money? He kept every other letter he sent him. And where was his own letter with the cheque in it? Neither of these have surfaced—if they existed at all.[22]

In both *For Whom the Bell Tolls* and *Green Hills of Africa*, Hemingway refers to his father as a coward for killing himself. His anger at him for doing so hints at a fear that he could go down this road himself one day. He often talked about suicide as an escape from his problems. He had been doing it as early as when his marriage with Hadley was breaking up, when he was forced to spend time away from Pauline during the infamous 'Hundred Days' War'.

He made an eerie prediction to Sunny at the funeral, telling her, 'I'll probably go the same way.'[23] In his Paris notebooks, he speculated about various ways of killing himself. He spent so much time flirting with the idea of suicide over the years that his father's action must have posed, as Archibald MacLeish put it, 'almost a personal threat'.

The residents of Oak Park saw his death as a scandal in the same way as they had Hemingway's divorce. People became more aware of mental health problems in later generations than they were then.

Hemingway now became the 'man of the house'. He was in charge of Clarence's financial affairs and the disbursement of his assets. This meant he could finally assert himself over his mother in a way he always wanted to.

It was difficult for Grace to have to take orders from someone she once branded as being a sponger before ordering him out of Windemere. He was a man of means now and she faced an uncertain financial future. The boot was on the other foot. He who paid the piper was calling the tune. Pressure under Grace was very definitely a thing of the past, whatever about grace under pressure.[24]

Her assets comprised the summer cottage, the dead Florida property, the home residence in Oak Park—which still had an outstanding mortgage—and an insurance policy Clarence left. It was hardly the scenario she envisaged as a young woman intent on conquering the world when she went up the aisle with him.

She was no better a manager of money than her husband. Hemingway had given her some loans in recent times which she sorely needed. She once told him he overdrew on his emotional bank account. She was now over-drawing on her actual one.

He told her if she refused to adapt her lifestyle to improve her situation, his cheques to her would stop. 'Never threaten me with what to do,' she wrote to him after he advised her to take in boarders, 'Your father tried that once when we were married and he lived to regret it.'

It was outrageous of her to imagine she could still bargain with a man who now held the purse-strings. His reply to her was crisp: 'I am a very different man from my father and I never threaten anyone. I only make promises. If I say that if you do not do certain sound things I will no longer contribute to your support it means factually and exactly that.' She never wrote him an aggressive letter again.

Even though Hemingway despised Grace, he set up a trust fund for her with $30,000 of his own money borrowed from future royalties. In return for his generosity, Grace asked him if there was anything he wanted. He told her the idea of owning Windemere Cottage appealed to him so she deeded it to him. She said she hoped he would bring Bumby back to it so he could experience the kind of childhood experiences he had himself.

Some people believe Hemingway asked Grace to send him the gun his father used to shoot himself. He denied doing so, telling people she sent it to him unsolicited.[25] It had been seized by the coroner's office but was released after much form-filling. When Hemingway received it, he threw it into a lake. It was a kind of ritualistic cleansing for him, an exorcism. 'He saw it go down,' he wrote in a story featuring a character in a similar predicament, 'making bubbles until it was just as big as a watch charm in that clear water. Then it was out of sight.'

After he got home from the funeral, he resumed work on *A Farewell to Arms*. Writing always carried him through the distressing periods of his life, but it failed to do so now. He felt a mixture of guilt and sadness as he sat at his desk trying to get the words to come out. It had been so easy up to now. The irony was that it was because he was so immersed in writing *A Farewell to Arms* that he turned down Clarence's invitation to join him for the trip to the mountains he wanted to take with him.

He wrote it anywhere he found himself—Wyoming, Key West, Kansas. He thought shifting locations as much as he could would summon his muse. He wrote to Guy Hickok, 'I'm working like a bastard to get it finished by the end of January.' That didn't happen.

His concentration was further disrupted when, at the beginning of February, he received a telegram from Maxwell Perkins to say Twentieth Century Fox wanted to make a film from his story 'The Killers'. He was hoping to get well paid for it, needing the money to help his mother. She had to pay a tax bill for the Florida lots and was also behind on the mortgage repayments for Oak Park. He told her not to worry, that he would take care of everything.

A Farewell to Arms was published in August. He dedicated it to Pauline's Uncle Gus. Gus had been especially supportive to him in the aftermath of his father's death and also very generous to himself and Pauline with money. He said he would have given any amount to Clarence too if he knew how badly off he was. 'Alas,' he wrote to Hemingway in a letter, 'the opportunity is gone now.'[26]

The book showed the influence of both Joyce and Stein in the stream-of-consciousness passages. The style was like a repudiation of the 'cablese' that he used it his journalism and shorter fiction. He was going for the bigger stage now. It was time to trade in spareness for the epic sweep.

The title was ambiguous. It carried a double edge to it, suggesting the book was going to be a renunciation of both love and war.

He started it, as he started everything he wrote, as a short story. If his novels have urgency—few would deny they have—this is probably the reason. Such urgency gave them a sharpness that kept one's eye from wandering. The tightness of construction made every word count. It opens beautifully:

> In the late summer of that year we lived in a house in a village that looked across the river and the plain to the mountains. In the bed of the river there were pebbles and boulders, dry and white in the sun, and the water was clear and swiftly moving and blue in the channels. Troops went by the house and down the road and the dust they raised powdered the leaves of the trees. The trunks of the trees too were dusty and the leaves fell early that year and we saw the troops marching along the road and the dust rising and leaves, stirred by the breeze, falling and the soldiers marching and afterward the road bare and white except for the leaves.[27]

This became a much-quoted paragraph. People often wondered where its power came from. Perhaps it was due to the repetition of the word 'and'. Hemingway repeated it over and over in the same way as, he contended, Johann Bach repeated notes in music, as a kind of counterpoint.[28]

He was glad to see *A Farewell to Arms* on a shelf. Many people he knew had written books about the war by now and he was beginning to worry about not having done so himself: 'Like the last girl on the block who hasn't been married, I felt my time to write a war book had come.'[29] Already we see the competitive urge, the sense of writing as an activity like boxing where nobody remembered the guy who came second.

Though there are autobiographical references in the book, it was primarily a work of the imagination. He was nowhere near Caporetto, the scene of a famous retreat by the American army and one of the most talked-about chapters in it, but so faithfully did he record it that the fascist government banned the novel from publication in Italy until after World War II. 'All good books,' Hemingway said once, 'have one thing in common—they're truer than if they had really happened, and after you've read one of them you will feel that all that happened, happened to you and afterwards it all belongs to you, the good and the bad, the ecstacy, the remorse and sorrow, the people and the places and how the weather was.'[30]

He once told a group of writers, 'If you invent successfully, it is more true than if you try to remember it. A big lie is more plausible than the truth. People who write fiction, if they had not taken it up, might have become very successful liars.'[31]

A Farewell to Arms was one of the few war novels that was read as much by women as men. Hemingway turned a casual fling with a nurse into a work that became a benchmark for his age. It became one of the most powerful anti-war statements of modern times, couched as it was in a love story.

Indeed, that was one of its problems, especially in the pages were there are lengthy stretches of dialogue. Frederic and Catherine speak to one another sometimes in a kind of formalised diction that suggests the pair of them are on a first date together rather than in the throes of passion. This is in stark contrast to Hemingway's proficiency with dialogue in the stories where less is very definitely more.

As well as the famous opening paragraph, the book contained another oft-quoted passage, the one where he gives us an exemplification of what will become his trademark fatalism: 'The world breaks every one and afterwards many are strong at the broken places. But those that will not break it kills. It kills the very good and the very gentle and the very brave impartially. If you are none of these you can be sure it will kill you too but there will be no special hurry.'[32] The last line is beautifully sardonic, a magnanimous concession from the fates that hover over his characters dispensing their rough justice. Catherine has to die because it breaks the Hemingway code to have people who love each other live happily ever after.

His creative powers were often activated by 'the sense of an ending', either the ache of regret or the dying of love. Or dying, period. His code dictates that such pain be borne quietly and with dignity. It becomes apparent not in what his characters say as in what they fail to say. He believed writers should welcome tragedy 'because serious writers have to be hurt really terribly before they can write seriously'.

An air of ominousness hangs over the book. We see it in the impending violence, in the retreating armies, in the tragic ending when Catherine dies in childbirth as Henry leaves the hospital and walks back to his hotel in the rain. This is a character who has decided to deal with life on its own brutal terms.

Some chapters earlier, Henry has reflected that abstract words like glory, honour, and courage were meaningless beside the human tragedies that unfolded daily in the rigours of war: 'There were many words that you could not stand to hear and finally only the names of places had dignity.'

Henry becomes even more traumatised than the Jake Barnes of *The Sun Also Rises* but is equally stoical about it, realising through clenched teeth that winners take nothing in a war. Hemingway delivers this message to us in language that stuns us with its reserve. The reader is left to us to fill in the spaces of his emotional deadness. Having lost the war of the head, Henry also loses that of the heart. Maybe Catherine is the lucky one to have shuffled off the mortal coil.

'The more things in life that we love,' he reflects, 'the more things there are to die.' The best survival tactic is to burn the need out of oneself, as Hemingway did with Agnes. Catherine's death may be seen as an example of him vicariously punishing Agnes for jilting him. Marcelline always thought such a jilting was the springboard for the book.

He claimed he rewrote the ending a staggering thirty-nine times.[33] Marcelline put the figure closer to fifty.[34] He was still searching for that 'one true sentence'. He was prepared to go to enormous lengths to find it.

Patrick asked him to edit a short story he wrote one day. Hemingway read it. After he returned it to him, Patrick looked at it with a shocked expression on his face. 'But Papa,' he said, 'you only changed one word.'

Hemingway replied, 'If it's the right word, that's a lot.'[35] The 'Papa' moniker went back to his days in Paris when Bumby used to say, 'La vie est beau avec Papa.'[36]

There were problems with the credibility of some parts of *A Farewell to Arms*. The main one was the over-romanticisation of Catherine. As she lies dying at the end, she thinks not of herself but of Henry. 'Poor darling,' she says to him, as if he is the person fatally ill in the hospital bed. How angelic is this?

Catherine has often been seen by critics as being unconvincing because of her submissiveness. Hemingway defended this by saying she was based on Hadley. The meek heroine is as much a staple in his fiction as the wounded hero. How curious it is that these tropes are based on fact and yet often seem implausible whereas some of his weirder characters, created out of his imagination, come across as highly credible.

The idea that the love scenes with Catherine emanated from his experiences with Agnes was false. His romance with her went no further than 'brief hand-holding under cover of her taking his temperature', according to Henry Villard, another hospital patient of that time.

Hemingway was always able to make capital out of small incidents. We see this in the odyssey from Agnes to Catherine. It also happened in his evocation of the Caporetto retreat. If he fought at Caporetto and consummated his fling with Agnes, *A Farewell to Arms* might have been a lesser book.

Agnes was embarrassed by the fact that people mistook her for Catherine. She saw herself coming off badly in the comparison. 'I wasn't that type of girl,' she insisted, referring to the fact that Catherine was sexually free with Henry. Catherine, she suggested, was his wish fulfilment, the woman he wanted her to be.

Neither, she claimed, was Hemingway like Henry. He arrived into the hospital as a shy young man. Confidence came with all the attention he received. Afterwards he became boorish. In this she saw the seeds of the self-serving mythmaker of the fifties. Fossalta had a lot to answer for.

Hemingway was inspired by his rejection of Agnes to write a fantasy of what he wanted to happen. He used his experiences with Hadley and Pauline to help him along his way. Catherine was a composite character in the same way as Harold Loeb was in *The Sun Also Rises*. He used Agnes and Hadley to create her.

The death scene at the end came from Pauline's problems in having children. She may not have died giving birth but, as we saw, was warned if she got pregnant again, she could be in danger of doing so. Hemingway combined these things into a situation that had all the stuff of grand passion acted out against the backdrop of the war.

All Quiet on the Western Front was the only novel that came near *A Farewell to Arms* on the best seller list that year. The Wall Street crash, amazingly, had no effect on its sales. By 24 October 1929, the very day of the crash, it had sold 28,000 copies. By December, that figure increased to 30,000. Dos Passos chirped to Hemingway, 'Do you realise you're the king of the fiction racket?'

Fan mail arrived from everywhere. Hemingway wrote to Hugh Walpole, 'I've answered them all—and have done nothing else.' He asked Walpole, 'Do they become angry if you don't answer and go around raking up your past life and getting you indicted? Or do they get sullen and never buy another one of your books?' When *The Sun Also Rises* came out, he recalled, 'There were only letters from a few old ladies who wanted to make a home for me.' Some of them told him not to worry about Jake Barnes's 'disability'.[37]

Later that month he was shocked when his friend, Harry Crosby, a promising poet and publisher, shot both himself and his mistress in a murder/suicide. No reasons were given. It was an eerie footnote to the decade. Crosby had been married to a good friend of Hemingway's, Caresse Crosby.

There was worse to come. One day he was driving near Yellowstone Park with Dos Passos and another friend, Floyd Allington, on the way to do some elk hunting when he had a car accident. He was blinded by the lights of an oncoming car and swerved to avoid it.

The car turned upside down and went into a ditch. Dos Passos escaped unhurt but Hemingway was badly injured. At first it was thought his legs were broken. This was later discounted. The main damage turned out to be to his arm. It had been pinned back by the top of the windshield and broken between the arm and shoulder. A bone stuck out of the muscle.

'The inside,' he croaked, 'looked like the part of an elk you have to throw away as unfit for human consumption when you butcher it out.'[38] He kept it clamped between his knees on an agonising 40-mile drive to a hospital in Billings, Montana.

Two ends of the bone in his elbow had been sheared off. A few attempts to set it failed. A doctor eventually operated, boring a hole through one side of the arm and tying it together with kangaroo tendons. Hemingway was frustrated having to lie around for long periods with his arm in a sling. He spent a month in the hospital, growing a beard to save himself the trouble of shaving.

One day a local reporter came in to visit him and they started to talk. In the course of their conversation, the reporter said he heard Hemingway had been castrated in the war. Hemingway replied, 'I see you've read *The Sun Also Rises*. You think I'm Jake Barnes.' He flipped the bedsheet over and displayed his 'fully intact' male member. 'Now are you satisfied?' he asked, exploding with laughter. The reporter went off with his tail between his legs.

Like many hyperactive people, Hemingway was a poor patient. When he was wounded in 1918, he had friends smuggle drink in to him. He did the same here, hiding it under the mattress to prevent the nurses seeing it. They found him to be a difficult patient. He was in bad form for a lot of the time. When Archibald MacLeish visited, he turned on him. 'You've just come here to see me die,' he taunted.[39]

He went to Piggott to convalesce. The weather was freezing but he often stayed out in it. Otherwise he got cabin fever. One day as he was about to enter the Pfeiffer's house after a walk, he was pelted with snowballs from children. They thought he was a hobo with his long beard and unkempt clothing. It was suspected he was breaking into the house.

He wrote a letter to Maxwell Perkins. Scribner's, he suggested, could save a lot of money by insuring him against accidents and illness. Since signing with them, he suffered an anthrax infection, the cut in his eyeball from Bumby putting his fingernail into it, the skylight wound, a forehead gash from the branch of a tree, congestion of the kidney, a sliced index finger, and a torn chin. 'On the credit side,' he allowed, 'during that whole period I never had constipation.' There was also, of course, the Fossalta wounding. His friends joked that he spent more time in bed than any action hero in history.

He was now working on a book about bullfighting, the one that would become *Death in the Afternoon*. Pauline offered to type it up for him. He declined the offer as he felt it would take away its spontaneity. The words had to be born on the page. 'I'll learn to write with my left hand,' he vowed, 'or my big toe. I'll still out-write anyone who thinks it's good news I'm laid up.' He said he had no problem dictating letters to her but not books.

He was grumpy away from the typewriter. His mood lifted when Paramount bought the film rights to *A Farewell to Arms* for $80,000. He was always sniffy about Hollywood, but the money came at a good time.

He spent the winter of 1930 and the spring of 1931 in Key West. One day he heard through the grapevine that Jinny told people he was a burden on the Pfeiffer family during his convalescence from the car accident.

Never a man to let any criticism of him go unanswered, he wrote the following words to her mother Mary: 'Can't promise not to go in the ditch again but next time will try to see the car is one of the kind that kills you when it turns over on you instead of merely making you a nuisance to friends and relatives.'[40] The dig was mainly at Jinny. Mary laughed it off, understanding Hemingway's defensive nature like few others did.

8

Frightened Angel

The '30s was a good decade for Hemingway but a disastrous one for F. Scott Fitzgerald. Sales of his books slumped dramatically, causing him to descend into a pit of self-doubt. Hemingway tried to talk him out of it but without much success.

'He takes pride in his defeat,' he said. He thought he wore it like a badge of honour. 'He has the sloppy Irishman's love of failure,' he snarled, 'He would quit at the drop of a hat, and even borrow someone else's hat to drop.' Hemingway was the opposite. He had to win at any activity in which he engaged.

That principle applied to boxing as much as writing. The manner in which he overreacted to being bested in a boxing match with Morley Callaghan in 1929 shows just how true that was. Fitzgerald was the timekeeper. Callaghan started to do well in one of the rounds. Hemingway thought Fitzgerald let it go on too long.

After Callaghan drew blood from him during its later stages, Hemingway spat in his face. It was probably due to frustration. Hemingway refused to admit that. He told Callaghan it was a tradition among bullfighters.

He never forgave Fitzgerald for being remiss in his time-keeping duties, bringing it up in innumerable conversations (and even letters) over the years. The story changed many times. Each time he told it, he made Fitzgerald's lapse worse. The round eventually became a thirteen-minute one.

He wrote to Fitzgerald that year telling him to pull himself together and stop complaining about his creative problems. He advised him to stop writing stories for the high-priced magazines and embark on another novel. It might not pay as much as the stories, he conceded, but would help him preserve his dignity.

Fitzgerald said there was no way he could give up the stories. He had too many expenses. It cost him approximately $30,000 a year to live. Such a figure was largely caused by Zelda's extravagances. He was only averaging a sixth of that from book royalties.

Both Scott and Zelda, in Hemingway's view, fed off 'the festival conception of life'. Not for them the dullness of a dawn rise to get a paragraph right. They were too busy tripping the light fantastic—and passing out on people's lawns.

The Princeton educator Christian Gauss compared Hemingway to an infra-red heater. Fitzgerald he saw as being more akin to an ultra-violet one. Fitzgerald felt he came off worse in the comparison.

As the years went on, Fitzgerald saw Hemingway writing the kinds of books he wanted to. He only earned $31 in book royalties in 1929. Hemingway made $30,000 that year from *A Farewell to Arms* alone.

He distanced himself from Fitzgerald as their fortunes changed. 'Ernest will always give a helping hand to the man on a higher rung of the ladder than him,' Fitzgerald charged. He was entitled to say this. Hemingway had used him to get into Scribner's. Now he was deserting him.

Hemingway denied this. He maintained the distancing was because of Fitzgerald's increasingly erratic behaviour, especially when he was drunk—which was most of the time. Fitzgerald's definition of sobriety was to 'only' take beer, not hard liquor.[1] Hemingway said he embarrassed him too much over the years with drink. He sometimes called to him at four in the morning when Bumby was young.[2] 'We didn't appreciate it very much,' Hadley said. She wondered how he found time to write.[3] He did things like throwing toilet rolls down the stairs, unravelling them all the way down.[4] He introduced himself to people with the words, 'I'm F. Scott Fitzgerald, the well known alcoholic.'[5]

'First you take a drink,' he said, 'Then the drink takes you.'[6] After becoming a victim of the habit, he let it dictate the pattern of his indulgences. As Sylvia Beach put it, 'Poor Scott was earning so much money from his books, he and Zelda had to drink a great deal of champagne to get rid of it.'[7] As they began to disgrace themselves at parties, a familiar groan was, 'Here come the Fitzgeralds.'[8]

Anita Loos remembered a night when she was bombarded with Scott and Zelda firing enormous candelabras and a metal wine cooler at her.[9] Scott was also said to have driven his car into a lake after a party. Another time he went into the offices of the *Paris Tribune* and started ripping up pages of news copy.[10] He described this time of his life as '1000 parties and no work'.[11]

The relationship between Hemingway and Fitzgerald continued to deteriorate throughout the '30s. It turned into farce when Hemingway started to treat Fitzgerald like an idiot. 'Don't worry about money,' he wrote to him once, 'Chink [Dorman-Smith] says he'll leave you Bellamont Forest. Pauline says you can have her job in *Vogue*. I've written Scribner to send all my royalty cheques to you.'

They differed radically in their attitude to wealth. Hemingway enjoyed the company of rich people but not, he insisted, *because* they were rich. Fitzgerald, he thought, had excessive awe for the trappings of wealth in and of themselves. When Fitzgerald put it to Hemingway, 'The rich are different from you and me,' Hemingway famously replied, 'Yes, they have more money.' He later adapted that comment to, 'They think money alone confers distinction.'[12]

The rich people Fitzgerald and Hemingway fraternised most with over the years were Gerald and Sara Murphy, the American couple previously mentioned who relocated to the French Riviera. Gerald was from a New York family that owned a chain of leather goods stores. Sara was the daughter of a Cincinnati ink manufacturer. Bored by people like themselves, they sought out the company of writers instead. Gerald was an architect by profession. After he got to Paris, he decided he would prefer to be an artist.

Hemingway soon became part of their circle. At first admonishing them for their lifestyle, he subsequently came to embrace it, blithely accepting their invitations to stay with them in their villa on the French Riviera and to partake of the blandishments they offered. If they were capitalists, he noted, they were extremely likeable ones. Hemingway accepted the money they gave him but—conveniently—retained an intellectual superiority over them.

The Murphys had known Fitzgerald before Hemingway. They too distanced themselves from him when his career faltered. Hemingway's one, by contrast, rose meteorically at this time. He sometimes read his work to them. They were entranced by it, especially Sara. Gerald was overwhelmed by his personality but still fascinated by him.

He became closer to Sara than Gerald over time. In her eyes, he could do no wrong. She even blamed Hadley for confronting him about Pauline when he was vacillating between the two women. It was as if it was her fault for bringing up the infidelity rather than Hemingway's for engaging in it.

Bumby noticed Sara's negative attitude to Hadley when he was a child. 'She thought my mother was from a lower class of people,' he recalled, 'She wasn't high falutin' enough for her.' Sara thought Hadley was 'plain' and 'not very quick-witted'. Neither description was true. She took less care of her appearance as the years went on, but she never lost her beauty. As for not being quick-witted, few could compete with the banter that went back and forth with Hemingway and his friends when they were on a night out. Hadley had a deeper intelligence. She was uninterested in such exchanges.

Hemingway brought the Murphys to Pamplona with him one year. Gerald was reluctant to go, but when he got there, he did his best to fall in with Hemingway. He knew he was expected to. 'When Ernest suggested something,' he said, 'You didn't say no.' He had the knack of persuading people something was a good idea simply because he wanted to do it.

The more time Hemingway spent with the Murphys, the less he saw of Fitzgerald. 'I always had a very stupid feeling of superiority about Scott,' he told Maxwell Perkins, 'like a tough little boy sneering at a delicate but talented one.'

Such superiority made him sarcastic. When he was writing *The Sun Also Rises*, he told Fitzgerald the plot went as follows:

> The heroine is a girl called Sophie Irene Loeb, who kills her mother. The scene in which she gives birth to twins in the death house at Sing Sing where she is waiting to be electrocuted for the murder of the father and sister of her as then unborn children I got from Dreiser. The title of the book comes from Sophie's statement as she's strapped into the chair as the current mounts.

Hemingway's relationship to Zelda was more complicated. If he had a tendency towards misogyny, it was more than indulged by this pampered Southern belle. They took a dislike to one another from the moment they met. Hemingway was impervious to her beauty. The ugliness he saw in her personality negated it.

He thought she did everything in her power to destroy her husband's creativity. This, he believed, was done by plying him with drink so his writing would deteriorate.

Hemingway saw her as a controlling woman like his mother. As well as being fanatically jealous of Scott, he believed she was an 18-carat bitch who was only able to enjoy herself when other people were suffering. He thought Fitzgerald could have been one of the greatest writers in the world if he never met her.

'She's crazy,' he attested, 'There's no other word for her.' There had to be something wrong with a woman who believed Al Jolson was greater than Jesus. She startled Gerald Murphy with this 'revelation' one night.[13]

Her behaviour became crazier as she aged. One night when Scott was talking to Isadora Duncan, she leaped across a table and down a stairwell. He thought she was dead. There was blood all over her. On other occasions she hoisted her dress up over her waist and started dancing madly. One night when Scott was driving on a cliff road near Monte Carlo, she pulled the steering wheel from him and nearly killed both of them.[14]

Zelda castigated Hemingway for, as she put it, wearing 'false hair on his chest'. The first person to accuse him of this was Max Eastman.[15] Fitzgerald was disappointed in her attitude. He wanted her to like him as much as he did.

Hemingway saw Zelda as a metaphorical castrator of her husband. His negative feelings towards her rubbed off on Hadley. She came to dread their visits, especially the morning ones when they were still drunk after being up all night. On one of these, Zelda said to Hadley, 'I notice that in the Hemingway family you do what Ernest wants.'[16] Hadley knew that in the Fitzgerald family, Scott also did what Zelda wanted.

Hemingway was angered by Fitzgerald allowing a woman rule his life. 'I never had any respect for him,' he wrote in *A Moveable Feast*, 'expect for his lovely, golden, wasted talent.' In a letter to Maxwell Perkins, he said he was 'a rummy and a liar and dishonest about money with the inbred talent of a dishonest and easily frightened angel'.[17]

Success was like a bucking bronco to him. He milked it for a time before the decline set in. 'There are no second acts in American lives,' Fitzgerald once pronounced. How true it was for him. When his first one ended, all he could do was reminisce about 'the good gone times when still we believed in summer hotels and the philosophies of popular songs'.

'All Scott ever got out of writing,' Hemingway concluded, 'was a few bottles of whiskey and a few hotel rooms.'[18] The basic problem was selling himself short for movies and money, a practice he referred to as 'whoring'.

'If you start writing phoney stuff for the pulps,' he asserted, 'Chances are you'll never learn how to write anything else. I've known a lot of pulp writers who thought they'd keep on until they'd saved enough money to live on and then write good stuff but it never works that way. The talent is gone by then.'[19] Integrity in a writer, he asserted, was like virginity in a woman. Once lost, it could never be recovered.[20]

Hemingway claimed he was once offered $25,000 for *A Farewell to Arms* by a publisher he had no respect for. He was broke at the time but still resisted the temptation to take it.[21] He doubted Fitzgerald would have been able to make a decision like that. Even if he wanted to, Zelda would have forced him into it.

Fitzgerald knew Hemingway was right about him letting his talent go. To try and get it back he started writing like Hemingway. He found himself mimicking his cadences when he ran into cul-de-sacs. In the end, he had to stop reading him for fear of replicating his style by a process of infiltration.[22]

9

New Pastures

Uncle Gus bought Hemingway and Pauline a house in Key West at the beginning of 1931. By now he was almost like a Santa Claus figure to them. They spent most of the '30s there. A two-storey French neo-colonial house with an address at 907 Whitehead Street, it had been built in 1851. They moved into it that April, thereby making it their first permanent home in the US. It cost $8,000, a phenomenal sum at the time. Even at that, it needed a lot of work done on it. The paint was peeling off some of the walls and the plumbing in severe need of repair.

Hemingway's sister, Carol, was on vacation from college when they moved in. Hemingway asked her if she could help them renovate it. She said she would. She worked on it with Jinny. They had it re-wired and extended. Pauline put cheesecloth on the ceiling of the children's room to stop the plaster falling on the cots of her two sons. She installed a pine floor in Hemingway's study. As it was in the process of completion, his writing chair was precariously balanced between slats and in danger of toppling over.[1]

He became frustrated with the disruption to his work. Not a man to relish performing domestic tasks like interior decoration, Pauline gave him a free pass in this regard. She knew he had to get on with his 'important work'. When inspiration proved elusive, he took off anywhere that took his fancy. She later installed a swimming pool in the grounds of the house to try and entice him to stay home more. It was the only pool on the island but hardly served to curb his wanderlust. He went ballistic when he heard what she paid for it ($20,000) even though Gus was footing the bill.[2]

His controlling behaviour continued. He was forever making plans for outdoor pursuits. Pauline did her best to fall in with them. He brought her on hunting trips to Wyoming in the summer. The winters they generally spent in Key West. It was difficult for her having to rough it with her fragile frame, especially when she became pregnant again. Hemingway was furious when this happened. He had been practising *coitus interruptus* because of the danger of pregnancy. Her Catholic conscience precluded any other form of contraception besides 'the rhythm method'. Or as Hemingway dubbed it, 'Vatican roulette'.

The two of them were invited to a costume party one night. Hemingway wanted to do some writing before they went, but he lost the key to the door of his studio. Never the most patient of men, his reaction on this occasion was extreme even by his standards. He shot the lock off the door with a pistol.[3] Pauline fled to the party to get away from him. When he arrived at it later in the night, he found her dancing with another man. Being Hemingway, he punched him out.

When Sinclair Lewis won the Nobel Prize for Literature that year, he exploded with a different kind of anger. How, he wondered, could such a mediocre writer be chosen for the award instead of Joyce or Ezra Pound?

He went to Spain in May, arriving just in time for the bullfighting season. Pauline travelled to France on a separate ship. She joined him in mid-June. They visited Patrick and Bumby together in Hendaye.

Hemingway's mind was on the forthcoming birth. 'I want a girl very much,' he wrote to Waldo Pierce, 'but so far have never had a legitimate nor illegit daughter so don't know how to go about it.'

On their way back to America on the *Île de France*, he was introduced to a woman called Jane Mason. She became a large part of his life over the next few years. Mason had film star good looks and a personality to match. Calvin Coolidge's wife referred to her as 'the prettiest girl who ever entered the White House' after she attended a party there.

She was married to a man called Grant, an executive of Pan American Airlines in Cuba. Hemingway kept seeing her regardless. Grant allowed him to. Both he and Jane lived separate lives. Hemingway referred to Grant as 'a wealthy twerp'. He bored Jane. Before Hemingway, she had many other extramarital flings to indulge her restless spirit.

She was unable to have children but adopted two. They fulfilled her for a time. Then the allure wore off. When it did, she left them to the care of a nanny. Hemingway went on to become a godfather to the older one. Mason, meanwhile, continued her quest for diversion with activities like sculpture. She also opened a craft shop specialising in the work of Cuban artists.

This was a busy time for Hemingway. A dramatised version of *A Farewell to Arms* opened in Berlin that year. Two months later, his second son was born. It was another Caesarean birth. 'They took nearly half an hour to start him breathing,' he wrote to Maxwell Perkins, 'I hope he never regrets the decision.'

They called him Gregory. Hemingway said he was named 'after any number of bad Popes'. Was this crack an attempt to get revenge on the church's ban on contraception? 'If a sovereign pontiff bore children,' he wrote to Pauline's mother Mary, 'he might write a bull of exceptions.'

The name actually came from his maternal grandfather. He wrote cruelly to Mary, 'We would have called him Max but it seemed bad luck. You can call him Max if you like.' A son of hers called Max had died. At times like this, he seemed bereft of empathy.

Pauline celebrated Thanksgiving in hospital. The following week Hemingway went to Piggott for some quail hunting with her brother, Karl. After he arrived, he found a note from Pauline in his suitcase. The heroine of *A Farewell to Arms* may have died in childbirth, she wrote, but she survived. She added that she loved her husband more than ever. Not all mothers of recently born children would have been as understanding of their husbands going off hunting so soon after a birth.

Hemingway reached Piggott a day before Karl. He had no luck hunting on his own. Things improved when Karl arrived. He had two bird dogs with him. On the second day, with the dogs' help, they shot twenty quail within an hour.

Death in the Afternoon was published now. A new departure for Hemingway, it was the first book in which he appeared without the mask of the novelist. There was no Jake Barnes or Frederic Henry to impart his manifestos about life, so he invented a new character, one called Ernest Hemingway.

Such a character annoyed as many readers as he entertained. Anthony Burgess wrote about 'the foliage of nonsense, the bar-room metaphysics and the pompous *longueurs*'. The socialist writer Max Eastman published a critique of it called 'Bull in the Afternoon'. An outraged Hemingway wrestled him to the ground in Scribner's office in retaliation.

It has the kind of gently hectoring tone he adopted all his life on practically every subject he ever tackled, from the best place to have a meal in Montmartre to how many leopards you had to kill to reach safari heaven. Just as Hemingway knew the best writers to learn from and the best way to hunt and make love, so he also knew everything worth knowing about the feria and its convoluted parabolas. He was only twenty-nine when he wrote *Death in the Afternoon* but was already speaking to us like the paternalistic seer of his later career.

John Dos Passos read the book before its publication. He visited Hemingway on Whitehead Street when he and Katy were *en route* to Mexico. 'It's absolutely the best thing on bullfighting,' he said to Hemingway during the visit. He was less impressed by the passages where 'old Hem straps on the long white beard' and pontificates. This was a fair point. Hemingway took it in good part, whittling the text down as a result.

He was less happy when he received the proofs. Plastered across the top of each page were the words, 'Hemingway's Death'. He wrote to Maxwell Perkins to tell him he wanted to break the neck of the 'punk' responsible for this. For someone who was superstitious to start with, it was 'a hell of a damn dirty business to stare at those two words a thousand times' while reading the proofs. If he died while in the process of checking them, he propounded, it would be the 'punk' who was responsible.

Bullfighting was just a springboard for Hemingway in the book, allowing him to sound off on various topics. His mind was too jumpy to confine itself to any one of them for too long. He needed a licence to ramble. But the bullfight ritual was an ideal metaphor for him to express his grace-under-pressure thesis. The fact that it was a duel to the death crystallised everything he felt about man's struggle against the world of nature.

Here was a microcosm of all our lives acted out in bald terms on the grit of an arena where a man with a studded costume and a red cape confronted a bull. The bull charged and the bullfighter evaded the charge or fell prey to it. He had nowhere to run and nobody to make excuses to. He was quintessentially honest, unlike those in other walks of life. The only creature he attempted to deceive was the bull. At the end of two hours, either the bullfighter was left standing or the bull. There was no more to it than that, no more except the elegance of the veronica, or bringing the bull to its knees.

Many people condemned bullfighting as barbaric. They argued that it was an unfair fight because the bull had no chance. Hemingway preferred to see it as theatre, an exemplification of gallantry. As he watched the bulls being killed—or, occasionally, killing—he felt the Shakespearean emotions of pity and fear. He became both elated and sad at the spectacle. Killing for him was a Christian sin but a pagan virtue. His primary loyalty always lay with pagans.

'This is not being written as an apology for bullfights,' he wrote in one part of the book, but that was precisely what it was. How could he justify it as a 'sport'? It may have carried an element of danger for the bullfighter, but it meant certain death for the bull.

He wrote about brave bulls and cowardly ones, about graceful toreros and manipulative ones, about people who 'show their contempt for death on a hot day in their own town square'. There was nothing for them to gain, he wrote, except the inner satisfaction of having been in the ring with the bull. But like being in Paris in the '20s, it was something that, 'Once you have done it, it stays with you forever.'

The 'minor aspects' of the contest, he wrote, 'are not important except as they relate to the whole'. This caveat absolves him of the problem of how to deal with the agony of the horses when they were killed, or the gratuitous bloodletting that troubled most members of the public. What the torero seeks is honesty, he argued, not tricked emotion but the purity of the execution.

This is a kind of ideological totalitarianism, the gospel according to Hemingway. We were informed that bullfighting was more than a question of putting spears into the necks of brutes. It was a spectator sport of sub-Homeric proportions, a cathartic ritual where one had to kill cleanly and beautifully without subterfuge or a failure of nerve.

Was this how he really felt? A letter he wrote to Bill Horne in 1923 probably better exemplifies why he spent so much time at the corrida: 'It's like having a ringside seat at the war with nothing going to happen to you.'

Bullfighting for him was like a staged war where soldiers were dressed not in uniforms but in suits of lights. It was where they set their own terms. They could kill or be killed with more dignity than on the average battlefield. No guts meant no glory. Immortality could be theirs if they went in close above the horns and avoided a *cornada*.

Death in the Afternoon failed to pull up any trees in the sales department. This was mainly because of the Depression. Neither was the subject high on the priority list of American readers, though Hemingway opened his country's eyes to another way of viewing the blood sport.

He published another short story collection the following year. It was called *Winner Take Nothing*. There was little warmth in the book.[4] It was transcribed in the same stripped-down style as its predecessors, the cumulative effect of his crude, unforgiving sentences giving readers so many linguistic kicks in the groin.

'Fathers and Sons' touches upon his father's suicide. In 'The Mother of a Queen', he issues a broadside at his mother by writing about a man who stops paying the rent on her grave, thus causing her remains to be dumped on a public heap. Grace also features in the 'The Light of the World' in thinly disguised form. If we wish we can see this story as a whinge on

Hemingway's part for having to send a monthly cheque to a woman he abhors. 'Capital of the World' is transcribed in the same tight-lipped argot as 'Hills Like White Elephants' but lacks its edge.

Winner Take Nothing had Hemingway on his familiar hobbyhorses of death, decay, corruption, alienation, and despair. The stories gained little from these themes. If anything, they were hurt by them. For some readers he was beginning to become repetitive. The shocking was no way as shocking as it used to be. Not only were the characters numbed at this point, the readers were in danger of becoming so as well. Hemingway seemed to be approaching auto-pilot mode.

With one exception. This was the story called 'A Clean, Well-Lighted Place'. It was always his favourite. Here he writes about an old man who goes to a café at night. All these years later it still stands up as the most darkly beautiful story he ever wrote, a bittersweet paean to anyone the world over who ever had trouble making it through the night. 'A Clean, Well-Lighted Place' is a delicate descent into the lean grey wolves of the subconscious, delivered with his customary nonchalance.

All the desperado poets and lonely souls need a light for the night. Finally, at sun-up, they will go to sleep—or maybe not. You can put a plaster over the wound of your depression, but clean, well-lighted places are only there for a while. Afterwards you have to negotiate your own mind without waiters or bodegas or youth or brandy or nieces. You can attempt suicide, perhaps, and afterwards be cut down, but what dignity is there in that?

The café provides the old man with a brief respite from his demons. After it closes, they return with a vengeance. When one of the waiters asks a colleague what his problem is, he gets the answer 'Nothing.' In actual fact, nothing *is* his problem—or, more specifically, *nada*.

Pier Francesco Pasolini called the story 'a Magna Carta of nihilism'.[5] Rarely has Hemingway been so grimly poetic. He gives us a piquant dirge to loneliness. Is it possible that the old waiter in the story is himself? He too needed clean, well-lighted places after his wounding at Fossalta. And Oak Park's 'lousiest Catholic', as he once described himself, would be no stranger to a prayer that began 'Our nada who art in heaven.'

A Farewell to Arms was made into a film in 1932. It starred Gary Cooper and Helen Hayes and was directed by Frank Borzage. The studio issued a publicity puff of Hemingway focusing on his wartime achievements. He poured cold water on this, writing to Maxwell Perkins to say the only reason he went to Italy during the war was because there was less chance of dying there than there would have been in France. This must have come as a surprise to people who watched him building up a heroic persona over the years. Now that it was established, he was free to chip away at his legend. The irony was that if anyone else but himself had suggested he went to Italy to avoid being killed in France, they might well have got a punch in the jaw.

The film was produced by David O. Selznick. He took the assignment on reluctantly, having heard stories about Hemingway's belligerent personality. His fears were well-founded. Hemingway argued with him about almost every frame of it. He wondered how anyone would go out to buy his book after seeing anything this trite.[6] It was not just bad, he snorted, it was preposterous. The reason Cooper deserted the army, as the film saw it, was because his girlfriend stopped writing him love letters.[7]

Borzage shot two endings to it. Hayes lived in one of them. Hemingway was incandescent with rage when he heard about this. When he made it manifest, Borzage decided to print the one where she died. Even so, the film ends on a kind of triumphal tone. This was far too upbeat for Hemingway. He had written a grim finale to the book in which Henry expels the nurses from the ward where Catherine lies dying so he can be alone with her. 'After I got them out,' he wrote, 'I shut the door and turned off the light. But it wasn't any good. It was like saying goodbye to a statue. After a while I left the hospital and walked back to the hotel in the rain.'

The film was so jingoistic he found himself wondering if Borzage might have liked to have Catherine giving birth to the American flag in the final reel.[8] One sees his point. Hollywood sanitised war in the same way as Oak Park sanitised life.

He grudgingly agreed to attend the premiere but changed his mind after hearing two women giving out about the fact that its showing meant *Tarzan the Ape Man* was being taken off the local marquee board in Piggott to make way for it. They wanted the escapism of a man swinging between trees to ease their Depression jitters rather than an angst-ridden war deserter losing his wife. Hemingway got drunk to console himself.

The film performed well with the public but not as well as it might have if Borzage was allowed to pump up its tearjerker element. Hemingway's books seem like film-makers' dreams because of their big themes and the crispness of the dialogue but their subtle elements are better suited to the page than the stage. Aldous Huxley was aware of this fact when he turned down the challenge of adapting one of his novels for the screen. 'What Hemingway has to say,' he stated, 'is in the white spaces between the lines.'

After the disappointment of the film, he went back to doing the things he loved best: hunting and fishing. He was dividing his time between various places at this point: Florida, Wyoming, Piggott, and Key West. Paris had become almost a thing of the past for him now. He dropped into it now and then when he was passing but gone were the days when he worked there, or met fellow writers. Most of the people he befriended there during his time as a fledgling scribe were no more than memories—Scott and Zelda, the Murphys, the MacLeishes, Duff Twysden, even John and Katy Dos Passos. The city would always be beautiful and a necessary part of a writer's education, but it was like a mistress for Hemingway now, with 'other lovers'.[9]

In 1934, he bought a boat which he called the *Pilar*. 'Pilar' was his code name for Pauline when he was courting her. It would also become the name of a character in *For Whom the Bell Tolls*.

It was 38 feet long and built, he said, for 'fishing, not pleasure boating'. He spent so much on the engines and what he called the 'fighting chair', there was little money left over to make it comfortable.[10] Not that he wanted this, though in time it became a home from home to him.

It cost $7,500. Nearly half of the amount was advanced to him from Arnold Gingrich, the editor of *Esquire* magazine, for articles he was commissioned to write for it. 'The boat is marvellous,' he wrote to Gingrich after it was delivered to him, 'It fishes well. Sleeps six in the cabin and two in the cockpit. Can turn on its own tail.'

He spent a lot of his time on it, too much as far as Pauline was concerned. She wanted him home more with his sons.

He was an undependable father. At times he appeared to dote on his children and at other times to ignore them. When he was with them he gave them the best of himself, but he was frequently absent.

Neither was Pauline a hands-on mother. Gregory never felt he got enough love from her in childhood. 'Gig,' she admitted to him once, 'I just don't have much of what's called a maternal instinct. I can't stand horrid little children until they're five or six. They're pretty awful then [as well] but at least I can communicate with them on a semi-rational level. That's why Ada always took care of you.'[11] She was referring to Ada Stern, her governess. One is reminded of Hemingway's joke about the best way to be a father being not to look at one's child for the first two years. Gregory once said of Pauline, 'I hated the bitch. She never showed any affection towards me. She never kissed me once in my life that I know of. She never held me.'[12]

The Pauline who appeared so sweet when she was replacing Hadley in his affections showed some unsavoury qualities to both Hemingway and their sons as the marriage went on. Stern looked after Gregory when she was otherwise engaged, or when she was on one of her many trips away from home with Hemingway.

Stern was well named. 'Any infraction of her rules,' Gregory taunted, 'would cause her to fly into a screaming fit.' She usually ignored him when he cried. 'When I was an infant,' he recalled, 'there was a theory that you should ignore a baby when he cried as crying would develop his lungs.' Stern adhered to this policy religiously.[13]

Hemingway and Pauline went to Africa on safari when Gregory was only three. He was left to Stern's tender mercies for nine whole months, which caused him severe distress.

In later years, he became dependent on her, seeking from her the love he felt was denied him by his absent parents. She sometimes used bribery to make him behave himself, saying she would go away too if he acted up. Her reply would be something along the lines of, 'All right I'll stay, you little shitsky. But if you misbehave one more time…' It was a nasty trick to play on such a troubled child.[14]

Bumby and Patrick were more independent than Gregory but Patrick hated her too. He prayed for her to burn in hell.[15] Bumby used to bribe her with liquor to get his way with her. Stern had a drink problem, so this usually worked.

Though Hemingway was glad to have Pauline with him on his travels, the more time they spent together the more they seemed to get on one another's nerves. In time he found himself becoming angry with her for little or nothing. In any comparison with Hadley, she came off second best.

When they came home from their travels, he started to spend more time away from her. He would be on the *Pilar* or in hotel rooms in Key West. Whenever she went to Piggott he scooted off to Cuba.

He also spent a lot of time in Sloppy Joe's, his local tavern. It looked more like a cave than a bar. Its tomb-like aura was just what he needed to escape the world outside.

He soon became friends with its owner, Joe Russell. For a time, he was even a co-owner of the bar. Russell and himself organised gambling competitions in the back of it which involved dice-throwing. These were illegal in Florida. Eventually the police got wind of them. They closed the operation down after a practice of crooked throwing was discovered.[16]

Hemingway afterwards turned his attention to cockfights and boxing matches. He even tried to get a bullfight arena erected in Cuba at one stage but this, like so many of his plans over the years, came to nothing.

10
Green Hills of Africa

Going on safari became one of Hemingway's great passions in the '30s. Everyone knew he enjoyed killing animals. He had no more sentiment for lions than bulls, though he pointed out that one should only shoot at a lion when close enough to smell its halitosis.

He liked being photographed beside whatever game he disposed of. The lions of Kenya became trophies to him just like the marlins he exhibited on Havana harbour. He stood proudly beside them, usually with a broad smile on his face. His pose attested to a victory over nature. It was a cause for celebration like a sexual conquest. 'Africa and the sea are the two loveliest whores I know,' he declaimed.[1]

His first safari lasted from December 1933 to March 1934. It bequeathed him a so-so book and two stunning short stories. The book was *Green Hills of Africa.* His main ambition in writing it was to compose something that, as well as being a journalistic treatise, could also cut it as a work of the imagination. Many critics thought it failed on both counts.

Edmund Wilson said of the animals featured in it, 'Almost the only thing we learn about them is that Hemingway wants to kill them.'[2] We were vouchsafed a much richer treatment of bulls in *Death in the Afternoon.*

He ranted on about killing cleanly and well in a similar manner as he had in the earlier book but there was a depth missing from this one that was in its predecessor. It also had a more cavalier attitude to violence. This undermined the respect he purported to show for his beasts of prey.

As was the case with *Death in the Afternoon*, his sermonizing was at variance with the reticence we were familiar with from the fiction. He declaimed on every issue that crossed his mind with garrulous excess.

To find the real richness of his safari experience we have to turn to *The Snows of Kilimanjaro* and *The Short Happy Life of Francis Macomber*, two stories he wrote at this time. They concern men who feel guilty of selling out to their wives' richness and power. Both manage to reclaim some semblance of dignity before they die. The women in the stories, the 'rich bitches' who hover over them, remain stagnant.

Hemingway's heroines tend to be either idealised on the one hand or demonised on the other, except perhaps for Brett Ashley. Here we see the demons. Both of the men, on the contrary, are richly realised.

Each of them has a catharsis in the course of the stories. Harry Walden, the central character in *The Snows of Kilimanjaro*, reaches his as a terminal disease eats into him. Macomber becomes purified by conquering his fear of lions at a seminal moment.

The Snows of Kilimanjaro deals with a man who scapegoats his wife for his various compromises. Tenuously modelled on Tolstoy's 'The Death of Ivan Ilych', Hemingway grafted a neo-modern slant onto it. He included enough material in it, he bragged, to fill three novels.[3]

Walden has gangrene. It feels absurd to him because of it being caused by an ostensibly negligible scratch from a thorn. His wife, Helen, is with him. She shows little concern for him as they wait for a plane to airlift him to hospital.

Helen bears certain resemblances to Zelda Fitzgerald, but is more obviously modelled on Pauline. Hemingway's problems with Pauline were reaching crisis point at the time he wrote the story. 'She was a fine woman,' he writes, 'marvellous really.' The truth is that she is a viper who witnesses Walden's descent into physical and artistic destruction without batting an eyelid. Walden refrains from blaming her. 'If it had not been she,' he surmises, 'it would have been another.'

The story gets most of its power from the intensity of his reminiscences. Rarely have Hemingway's powers of narration been as strong as here. A lifetime is condensed into a small number of pages. Walden's cerebral memories oscillate with the banality of his exchanges with his wife.

Sentences like 'Death had come and rested its head on the foot of the cot and he could smell its breath' sit alongside small talk about whiskey soda.

'The marvellous thing is that it's painless,' he says of Walden's impending death, 'That's how you know when it starts.'[4] This is the first sentence of the story. From here on in, the downward spiral is tortuous. 'So this was the way it ended,' he writes, 'bickering over a drink.' Helen badgers him as his life drains away.

She professes to be 'awfully sorry' about the odour. The way they speak to one another, they might as well be playing bowls on the lawn. Death for

Walden is 'a pleasant surrender' to the inevitable. He has been dead inside himself for many years anyway because of having 'fat on the soul'.

The same is true of 'Poor Scott', a reference to Scott Fitzgerald. Hemingway cruelly maligns Fitzgerald in the story as having been wrecked by his reverence for the rich.

The Snows of Kilimanjaro and *The Short Happy Life of Francis Macomber* are written in a laconic style that inversely emphasizes the desperation of their characters. Macomber experiences his moment of truth by shooting at a lion as he finally decides to impress his wife, Margot. It may be too late to save his marriage—or his life—but he still redeems himself by it. He is 'destroyed but not defeated', as Hemingway might say.

Margot then shoots him. Is she aiming for the lion or her husband? This is the central conundrum of the story.

Hemingway claimed to be ignorant of Margot's intentions.[5] 'I could find out if I asked myself,' he teased, 'because I invented it. The only hint I could give you is that it is my belief that the incidence of husbands shot accidentally by wives who are bitches and really work at it is very low.'[6]

On another occasion he contradicted that, saying Margot hated her husband because he was a coward, 'but when he gets his guts back she fears him so much she has to kill him'.

The story can be seen as a metaphor for the relationship between Scott and Zelda Fitzgerald. If Scott got his courage up, would Zelda have hated him as much as Margot Macomber hated her husband before she shot him? Hemingway probably thought she would. He often talked about how Zelda hated Scott when he stopped drinking and was able to write the books she was jealous of.

A more common belief is that Margot was based on Jane Mason. Though she has loathsome qualities, Mason was flattered when people suggested this to her.[7] She took care to tell them she was very different in character from Margot but was still glad to be in a book.

In *The Snows of Kilimanjaro*, Hemingway writes very well of a writer who has lost his ability to write. It can be read as an exemplification of his fear that he too would die without having realised his potential, having sold out to, if not money, a life of action and hell-raising that cut in on his craft.

We can also read it as an *exposé* of how things had deteriorated with Pauline. He refused to acknowledge this. Instead he pedalled the story that it concerned what might have happened if he gave in to a rich woman who offered to pay for an expensive African safari for him.

In both *The Snows of Kilimanjaro* and *The Short Happy life of Francis Macomber*, he conveys his distaste for the kind of woman who would marry for money, conveniently ignoring the fact that his own first two wives had trust funds that enabled him to live in a manner he would have struggled to with his writing alone. He may not have married them for their money—but it helped.

Hemingway started to sleep with Mason at this time. She radiated a large sexual charge for him. Sex with Pauline had become increasingly problematic for him by now because of his fears of her becoming pregnant.

She was never in any doubt about the threat Mason posed to her marriage. Her trips to Piggott followed by Hemingway's to Cuba were too coincidental for her to imagine anything else.[8] Was she losing her attraction for him? Were the events of a decade ago between herself and Hadley coming back to haunt her? At one stage she dyed her hair blonde like Mason's to try and compete with her.

Mason often went out with Hemingway on a boat called the *Anita* to hunt for marlin. As already mentioned, it was owned by Joe Russell, the man who ran Sloppy Joe's. Hemingway often went fishing with Russell himself too. All he had to do was say, 'Let's go' and the bar would be left in the hands of his assistant.[9] That was a black man called Skinner. Hemingway liked him. Many people have accused Hemingway of racism because of the 'N' word in some of his writings, but he had lots of black friends. If Skinner ever ran into problems with a white customer he sorted them out. Skinner knew where his loyalties lay.[10]

Hemingway sometimes brought Mason to Cuba with him on the *Anita*. He had fun with her in ways he found increasingly more difficult with Pauline. Sometimes they discussed marriage. He played a game called 'Chicken' with her in her sports car. It involved driving as dangerously as one could. The chicken was the person who shouted 'Stop' first.[11]

'Ernest was always a gentleman when I won,' Mason recalled, 'but I lost many times too. He was very near-sighted and he took off his glasses to avoid hitting them off the windshield in the event of a crash. He didn't know enough to be scared half the time.'

Pauline tried to make light of their friendship while still alluding to its danger. Before joining them in Cuba once, she wrote to Hemingway, 'Am having my large nose, imperfect lips, protruding ears and warts and moles all taken off. Thought I better as Mrs Mason and those Cuban women are so lovely.'

Like Zelda Fitzgerald, Mason enjoyed the finer things of life. Also like Zelda, she had an unstable temperament, being prone to increasingly frequent bouts of depression. Hemingway would have found her too hot to handle as a wife, but he enjoyed dallying with her. He had once dallied with Pauline in the same way while Hadley tried to pretend to herself that there was nothing going on between them.

Mason sometimes used to climb through the transom of a room Hemingway had at the Ambos Mundos hotel in Key West to be with him.[12] He liked working there because of the privacy it afforded: 'The telephone and visitors are the work destroyers.'[13] He rented another room at the Sevilla-Baltimore hotel. Keeping on the move gave him the freedom to write without fear of interruption from reporters—or wives.

His fame, he said, brought to his house 'every son of a bitch I ever knew or who ever read a line I wrote. So to write I go back to the old desolation of a hotel bedroom.' 'The best way to get any work done,' he proclaimed on another occasion, was to 'tell everybody you live in one hotel and live in another. When they locate you in the other, move to the country.'[14]

He never knew what to expect from Mason. She made a bust of him once. Another time she wrote a song for him. 'I have talents too many,' she said of herself, 'but not enough of any.'

Their relationship had a hiatus in 1933 when she realised Hemingway was never going to leave Pauline for her. In June of that year, she jumped from the balcony of her house after having an argument with him. It resulted in her breaking her back. 'She fell for me,' Hemingway joked. The pun left nobody in any doubt about his feelings for her—or rather his lack of them.

She jumped into a clump of bushes so it could have been an attention-seeking action. Or she might have simply been drunk. She liked her drink. Grant denied it was a suicide attempt. 'She went off a second storey balcony,' he shrugged dismissively, 'It was an impressive altitude but not high enough to cause death.' Neither was it her first accident. Her son claimed she broke every bone in her body at some stage of her life.

The fact that it was her back that was broken this time meant she had to go to hospital. Grant put her on a ship to New York. Her berth had bars on the porthole in case she took a notion to jump out. There was even a nurse on duty. When she reached New York, she went to hospital, remaining there for five months. When she came out she had to wear a brace for a further year.

Hemingway went on another safari from August 1933 to March 1934. He continued his relationship with Mason when he came back but things were different between them now. He could have married her if he wished as she was in the process of divorcing Grant but he showed no inclination to do this. Like many men, he seemed to prefer women when they were unattainable. She later went on to marry Arnold Gingrich. Maybe Scott

Fitzgerald's comment about him only needing women when he was writing major novels held true.

Fitzgerald's literary fortunes continued to decline as the '30s went on. His novel *Tender is the Night* was published in 1934. When he asked Hemingway what he thought of it he said, 'Not much.' He saw it as being little more than his usual celebration of the high life based on a combination of the Murphys as well as himself and Zelda.

Zelda was becoming more difficult for Scott to handle by now. 'She's crazy,' Hemingway told him, 'You shouldn't have fallen in love with her. But maybe you had no choice. You're a rummy.'

Fitzgerald took every insult Hemingway hurled at him. To have him talking to him at all was almost like a favour at this stage as he was so distant from him in recent years. 'I like you so damn much,' Hemingway continued, 'but don't ever publish a book in the same year as me.' He feared that *Tender is the Night* would threaten sales of *Green Hills of Africa*.

He had little cause to worry. Fitzgerald's novel received only lukewarm reviews. It was basically a twenties book released onto a '30s market. Maybe somebody should have told Fitzgerald to put the Jazz Age champagne on ice. He seemed to have forgotten that the Depression was over. It was the era of *The Sun Also Rises*, an era that ushered in new kinds of role models for readers, ones who asked philosophical questions rather than partied gaily under klieg lights.

Fitzgerald wrote to Maxwell Perkins in 1935 to say that his friendship with Hemingway had run its course. The two men were now going their separate ways. To Hemingway he wrote, 'I wish we could meet more often. I don't feel I know you at all.'

He underwent his famous 'crack-up' between 1935 and 1937. These were years that saw his talent buried under a mound of hack work and booze. He admitted he was in a bad way, but thought Hemingway was too. The difference between them was that 'Ernest's inclination is towards megalomania and mine toward melancholy.'

The relationship between them became irreparably damaged after Hemingway maligned him in *The Snows of Kilimanjaro*. He believed he was entitled to do so considering Fitzgerald had expounded on his problems so publicly in his own writings. His motive, he claimed, was to give him a jolt, forcing him to take account of the way his life was going. This was one of Hemingway's familiar rationalizations.

Fitzgerald found it hard to believe he stooped so low. When he read the story, he tried to overdose on morphine. Hemingway, as we saw, seemed to have a need to punish anyone who'd been helpful to him in the past.

'He never forgave you if you did him a favour,' Fitzgerald accused. It was as if such actions made him feel inferior, as if he had to disavow them in some way. He had already done it to Sherwood Anderson with *Torrents of Spring* and to Harold Loeb with *The Sun Also Rises*. Now he was doing it with the man who helped him get his foot on the literary ladder in the very first instance.

'Dear Ernest,' Fitzgerald wrote to him one night, 'Please lay off me in print. If I choose to write *De Profundis* sometimes it doesn't mean I want friends praying aloud over my corpse. No doubt you meant it kindly but it cost me a night's sleep. When you incorporate the story in a book would you mind cutting my name?'[15] Hemingway did that, changing 'Scott' to 'Julian' but it was too late. The damage was done. By now most readers knew who 'Julian' really was—especially since Fitzgerald had already used the name for himself in one of his semi-autobiographical stories. The putdown gave him a 'jolt', as Hemingway predicted, but not in the way he expected. He drank more as a result and continued to misbehave when he imbibed too much.

Hemingway was also drinking to excess at this point. He differed from Fitzgerald in the sense that he was able to work off his hangovers in athletic exploits. Fitzgerald spent the mornings after the nights before undergoing bouts of self-loathing. If Hemingway drank to reward himself for work well done, Fitzgerald did so for future labours. It was like an IOU he wrote to himself. Sadly, it was one he failed to deliver on more and more as writing became a pale imitation of past glories.

After a time his soul-searching became as boring to himself as to everyone around him. 'He was a failure as a success and a success as a failure,' was the way Michael Romanoff put it.[16] His depression became all-encompassing. 'In a real dark night of the soul,' he said chillingly, 'It is always three o'clock in the morning day after day.'[17]

In 1940, his books sold only a measly seventy-two copies.[18] He was working on *The Last Tycoon* by now, a mish-mash about Irving Thalberg. Thalberg was another *wunderkind* like himself, another Beautiful Dreamer running out of time.

Hemingway had often spoken of his 'cheap Irish love of defeat'.[19] Only two events could redeem him, he claimed. Either Zelda died or he developed a stomach disorder severe enough to make him stop drinking. 'Is it true,' he wrote to him, 'that you've become blind through alcoholic poisoning and had to have your pancreas removed?'

Fitzgerald acceded to Hemingway's negative estimation of him. 'I speak with the authority of failure,' he yielded, 'and Ernest with the authority of success.'[20] They would never, he predicted, be able to sit across a table from one another again.[21]

He only met Hemingway a handful of times in the '30s. On most of these occasions, he embarrassed him with his drunken rants. 'He seems to equate growing up with growing old,' Hemingway scoffed. It was the only explanation he could give for his behaviour. Reluctant to give him his address, he preferred to meet him in the neutral territory of cafes and bars. In these places he prayed his old friend would behave himself under the influence.

Hemingway may have shown the worst side of his character in his many cruelties to Fitzgerald but, as frequently mentioned, he was a multi-layered man. He showed his best side in a letter he wrote to the Murphys after their son, Baoth, died of meningitis in 1935 at the age of sixteen. They had already lost a son, Patrick, to tuberculosis some years previously. Anyone who ever accused him of lacking feeling should appreciate the profundity of the grief he showed in the letter:

> Dear Sara and Dear Gerald, You know there is nothing you can ever say or write. If Bumby died we know how you would feel and there would be nothing you could say. Absolutely truly and coldly in the head, though, I know that anyone who dies young after a happy childhood, and no one ever made a happier childhood than you made for your children, has won a great victory. We must live life now, a day at a time, and be very careful not to hurt each other. It seems as though we were all on a boat together but we know now it will never reach port. There will be all kinds of weather, good and bad, and we are fortunate we have good people on it.

The marriage with Pauline, meanwhile, rumbled on. Their arguments increased as Gregory grew up. Both he and Patrick became very upset by these. They were also distressed by their many absences from home. 'I don't know what to make of it,' Patrick said to Ada Stern once, 'My father says he's going away for two weeks and he stays two months. My mother says she's going away for four days and she stays four weeks.'

They tried to make it up to them when they got back from their travels, but there was always an air of formality in the house. Patrick and Gregory ate their meals with Stern instead of with their parents. They rarely had playmates over because few of the people Pauline or Hemingway socialised with, like John Dos Passos, had children.

An almost sacred silence had to be observed in the house so Hemingway could concentrate on his writing. If the boys wanted to play with their toys, or with one another, they had to do so quietly. They were like 'animals caged in a zoo'.[22]

Hemingway was closer to Bumby than he was to Patrick or Gregory. One day when Bumby was misbehaving, Pauline told him he needed to be spanked. Hemingway brought him into the bathroom but instead of spanking him he took down his own trousers and started hitting himself with a hairbrush. When they came out, he advised Bumby to 'fake some loud crying' so his mother would think he slapped him.[23] He became closer to Patrick and Gregory in the mid-'30s. At the beginning of 1936, he told Pauline's mother that it was only in the past year that he got to really know them.[24]

He brought them on as many fishing trips as he could, teaching them the skills he learned from his own father when he was their age. They went riding and hunting with him on the Nordquist ranch in Wyoming.

Gregory claimed to have tied for first place in a pigeon-shooting competition once.[25] The truth was that he came fourth.[26] He wanted to impress Hemingway. 'He loved winners,' Gregory said, 'Even if you were the best axe-murderer in the world he'd give you credit. That was what counted with him more than anything—being the best.'

Hemingway's code of virility dictated that they become men before their time. One element of this involved the practice of drinking alcohol. 'I like them to have wine with their meals,' he told Pauline one day, 'but let's keep them off the hard stuff until they get into their teens.'

It was hard to know if he was joking or not when he said things like that. He told them he wanted them to live well, to write well, and to shoot well—and only to shoot animals that one intended to eat afterwards. (He broke that rule himself.)

His style of parenting, like everything else in his life, was erratic. It clashed with Pauline's more old-fashioned one. She wanted them brought up as good Catholics. Hemingway said he preferred them to be good fishermen.[27]

The virility code also entailed a parent squaring up to anyone who upset any of his family. When Ursula was visiting Hemingway in 1936, she went to a party at which the poet Wallace Stevens was present. He became drunk at it. At one stage he told Ursula that Hemingway was a 'sap', adding, 'I wish he was here now. I'd knock him out with a single punch.'

When Ursula got home, she told Hemingway what Stevens said. He immediately made his way to the party. It was ending but Stevens was still there. Hemingway told him that he was going to beat him up. Stevens prepared himself for the fray. He got the first strike in, hitting Hemingway on the jaw with what he called a 'Sunday punch', but it did more damage to him than to Hemingway, resulting in him breaking his hand in two places.[28]

Hemingway then started swinging at him. Even though Stevens was nearly as tall as him, he knocked him down three times. Stevens ended up with a black eye and a number of aching limbs. He had to stay in his room for five days with a nurse and a doctor in attendance. Ursula was afraid he was going to die at one stage. 'Ura had never seen a fight before,' Hemingway told Sara Murphy in a letter he wrote to her, 'and couldn't sleep for fear.'[29]

Stevens asked Hemingway to keep the incident quiet for fear of repercussions in his job. He worked in an insurance company. 'Tell people I fell down the stairs,' he implored. Hemingway said he would. That was a false promise as he bragged about the incident to people whenever he got the chance. He even told John Dos Passos about it.

He had no trouble with people asking him to conceal 'dirt', he informed Dos Passos, 'It goes in one ear and out my mouth.'[30]

11

The Bell Tolls for Pauline

Hemingway met the woman who was to become his third wife towards the end of 1936. She was a pretty young journalist from *Collier's* magazine called Martha Gellhorn. When she walked into Sloppy Joe's bar in the December of that year with her mother, Edna, and her brother, Alfred, he was knocked off his feet. He was about to leave the bar at the time but changed his mind after he saw her.

She was more physically alluring than Pauline. A blue-eyed blonde with an attractive mane of hair, she also had, as he put it, legs that started at her shoulders.[1] Furthermore, she was a published author with a best-selling collection of stories (*The Trouble I've Seen*) under her belt. One reviewer compared her economy of language to that of Hemingway.

He was dressed in Basque shorts and a grubby T-shirt when he met her.[2] Such a get-up failed to impress her. He had no shoes on him either. His shorts were held up by a piece of rope. When they started talking, the man tending bar compared them to the 'Beauty and the Beast'.

Martha was unsure who she was talking to at the outset. It was only when she heard his name was Hemingway that she stopped short. Was she actually in the company of 'The Great Man'?

His novels had been like Bibles to her growing up. 'God knows I think Mr Hemingway writes like the heavenly host,' she said.[3] She even used a phrase of his, 'Nothing ever happens to the brave', as an epigraph for her novel *What Mad Pursuit*. Suddenly the fact that he looked slovenly stopped bothering her.

As was the case with Hadley, Martha had more than a little in common with him in her life circumstances. Just as his father had been an obstetrician, so had hers. In fact, Hadley had attended him in St.

Louis. And her mother, like Hemingway's, had been a suffragette in her youth.

Both of them liked being the centre of attention. They also shared a wanderlust. And Martha hated her native St. Louis almost as much as Hemingway did. 'If anyone is going to sit in that dump of a city,' she drawled, 'let them stew in their own juice.'

There were even more comparisons between Martha and Hadley. Both women had attended Bryn Mawr college. Also, Hemingway met them both shortly after they lost a parent.

Hemingway became so engrossed talking to Martha that he lost all sense of time. Pauline was having their friends Charles and Lorine Thompson to dinner that night. When he showed no signs of appearing, Pauline sent Charles down to the bar to find out what was delaying him. Hemingway hardly looked at him when he came in. Charles told him Pauline was concerned about where he was. He said to tell her he was busy. They could all meet up later if they wanted.[4] It was as if Martha was his acquaintance and Charles and Lorine the strangers.

Charles went back to Pauline. She asked him what was happening in the bar. He said, 'He's talking to a beautiful blonde in a black dress.' Pauline took the news in her stride. Beautiful women frequently came up to him and engaged him in conversation.[5] The fact that Mason was out of the picture made her feel secure.

Hemingway ferried Martha around Key West in the following days. One day they spotted Pauline on the street. Instead of feeling embarrassed, he invited her to join them. She ended up being the one who felt awkward rather than him.

When Edna and Alfred went back to St. Louis, Martha stayed in Key West. Pauline was worried but she tried not to let it show. There was a surface politeness between the two women. Both of them acted casual but both knew what was going on. For Pauline it was like a *déjà vu* experience from the Christmas of 1926 in Schruns with Hadley. She was the interloper on that occasion. Now she was the victim.

Martha finally left. She later wrote Pauline a letter apologising for 'becoming a fixture, like a kudu head, in your home'.[6] She was on the move a lot now for her work. She went to Miami first and then to New York. Hemingway followed her. He gave Pauline a ham-fisted excuse about having to go there on business. She guffawed. 'I suppose you're going to help Miss Gellhorn with her writing,' she sniffed.

Martha was more politically inclined than Pauline. That suited Hemingway. When he told her he was interested in going to Spain to campaign against the Fascists because of the incendiary situation that was erupting there with Franco, she said she was too. He told Pauline they intended to go there together. It was at this point she became seriously worried about the situation.

Telegrams from various people arrived at the house over the following weeks enquiring as to when Hemingway was going. They made the problem more real to Pauline. She started to think about its ramifications. Hemingway would be alone with a pretty woman in a foreign country. She doubted they would be spending their time discussing politics.

Her nerves frayed. She had trouble sleeping. She played tennis and swam to try and keep her stress level down. Neither activity worked.

There was no word from Hemingway after he got to New York. That told a tale in itself. She wrote a letter to him that was part plea and part censure: 'Would love to be with you instead of being here with nobody and the sea. All those telegrams about Spain bring my situation of impending doom pretty near the front door where I am only used to the wolf and the stork. Goodbye, big shot. Why not start keeping me informed?'[7]

Before Martha travelled to Spain, Hemingway went there on his own. He wanted to put the finishing touches to a film he was involved with called *The Spanish Earth*. It was a documentary he narrated on the Civil War. He hoped it would raise funds for the Loyalist cause. Profits from it were being donated to ambulances to tend the wounded. The thought of this brought him back to his days as an ambulance driver in Italy.

After he got back, he stopped in Key West for a fishing trip that he intended to take with Gus. He planned to tie it in with a holiday in Bimini with Pauline and the two boys. They usually spent the spring and early summer fishing there. He made no contact with Pauline.

Gus cancelled at the last minute. Hemingway was surprised. The fact that Pauline had been left in the lurch meant nothing to him. Gus was shocked to have been given priority over his family. He started to suspect the marriage to Pauline might be in trouble. He wrote to Hemingway with a barbed undertone, saying 'I hope the happiness your return gave to Pauline and the boys was worth the trip back.'

Hemingway now travelled to New York to see Martha and edit *The Spanish Earth*. Things were hotting up in the Civil War. He described it as a dress rehearsal for the world war. How prophetic that was.

He planned to go to Spain soon. Pauline pleaded with him to take her with him. Such pleas fell on deaf ears. He saw her as trying to be another Martha. How could she ever achieve that? Any trip she took to Spain would be nothing more than a holiday to her.

By now Hemingway had finished another novel, *To Have and Have Not*. Arnold Gingrich wanted to publish sections of it in *Esquire*. It featured an unattractive character called Helene Bradley, a rich socialite based—again—on Mason. Gingrich and Maxwell Perkins, who planned to publish the text in book form with Scribner's, were worried that Mason might see herself in Bradley and sue for libel. Hemingway tried to assure them that this was unlikely. He agreed to edit any inflammatory parts of the book to assuage their fears.

Mason was still in hospital at this point with her back problem. She knew about the forthcoming novel. One day when Pauline was visiting her, she told her she was bored. She asked her if she could see the manuscript of *To Have and Have Not* as she wanted something to read. Pauline told her she needed Hemingway's permission to give it to her. She suspected Gingrich had said something to her about her similarity to the character of Bradley. By now Hemingway had removed what he saw as the more damaging passages, but there were still enough of them there for her to see herself in Bradley if she was so inclined.

Harry Morgan, the book's central character, is the owner of a cabin cruiser. He works in Havana as a fishing guide. Morgan is a realistic character who thankfully avoids falling into the barrow of the typical Hemingway hero, doing all for love and glory. As the book progresses, however, he begins to falter. This is because Hemingway places such a large socialist burden on him. Expecting him to be a peg on which he could hang a thesis was always going to be risky. Even the title of the book had socialist overtones.

Few writers impress when they become polemical. Hemingway got away with it in *Death in the Afternoon* and *Green Hills of Africa* because these books were discursive by nature. A novel should never have that label attached to it. Its cynicism saved it from the charge of mushiness, but the left-wing meanderings eventually wore it down. 'I know more about bulls than politics,' Hemingway had once confessed. Indeed.

Most of the characters in the book, Edgar Johnson wrote, 'are indeed the hollow men, wandering in despair or jerking galvanically through the mist of Hades, a grey world of doom'.

Its main problem was jaggedness. Hemingway composed it from two stories, 'One Trip Across' and 'The Tradesman's Return'. He later added a lengthy third section. The book betrays evidence of such a patchy embryology.

Did it reflect the 'yellow sere' into which his life had sunk at this point? Writing provided only vague relief from a soullessness brought on by the unfulfilling life he was living. It may lack the unifying thread of a character one can feel much for, but we should admire Hemingway for doing something the critics often accused him of not being able to do, i.e. move out of his comfort zone.

He described it as 'a teenage work devoted to adultery, sodomy, masturbation, rape, mayhem, mass murder, frigidity, alcoholism, prostitution, impotency, anarchy, rum-running, Chink-smuggling, nymphomania and abortion'.[8] Its message, i.e. that 'A man alone ain't got no bloody fucking chance', is much balder than his usual ones.

Richness is absent from the narration. This was intentional. Hemingway tried to reinvent himself with the book, to stretch himself into hitherto unexplored areas.

The most quoted passage from the book is often cited as an almost direct transcription of an argument he could have had with Pauline regarding her problems with sex. The language is unflinching as Helen turns on Harry. 'Love,' she says to him, 'is that dirty aborting horror that you took me to. Love is my insides all messed up. It's half catheters and half whirling douches. I know about love. Love always hangs up behind the bathroom door. It smells like Lysol. To hell with love.'[9]

To Have and Have Not was the only book Hemingway wrote that was set in America. Asked why he never wrote about his home country before he replied flatly, 'Because nothing ever happens there.'[10] John Dos Passos, who spent seven years working on *U.S.A.*, might have smiled at this.

It was more successful as a film than a book. This was largely due to the performances of Humphrey Bogart and Lauren Bacall in the starring roles and an in-your-face script from William Faulkner. Its most memorable line was, 'You know how to whistle, don't you? You just put your lips together and blow.' Ironically, this was neither in the book nor in Faulkner's screenplay. It came from Howard Hawks, the film's director.

Hawks secured the rights by claiming he could make a film out of Hemingway's worst work.[11] Hemingway was hurt by the slur but accepted the offer.

Bacall was unknown before she made the film. It gave her overnight success. She soon became Bogart's second wife. Despite the huge age gap between them—he was old enough to be her father—they had a happy marriage. Hemingway went on to become friends with both of them.

He was pleased with the film, more pleased in fact than with any Hollywood adaptation of his work since *The Killers*. *To Have and Have Not* was never one of his favourite books so this was probably one of the reasons.

Above: This family portrait of the Hemingway family shows the young Ernest with his parents, Clarence and Grace, and two of his sisters, (from left) Marcelline and Ursula. Marcelline was a year older than him which didn't please him. Ursula was always his favourite sibling.

Right: 'Portrait of the artist as a young man.' Hemingway as he looked before he left his Oak Park home to begin life as an author, cub reporter, and man of action.

Hemingway sits behind the wheel of a Red Cross ambulance in Italy after the First World War broke out. He couldn't be a soldier, but he was determined to see 'action' somehow—preferably at the front.

Above left: Looking every inch the soldier, but this is a Red Cross uniform.

Above right: On crutches in a Milan hospital after he was wounded one night delivering 'candy' to some soldiers. He looks unaffected by the incident but some commentators on his work see it as having influenced it more than anything else that ever happened to him.

With the first woman he loved, Agnes von Kurowsky, or perhaps infatuation would be a better word. She nursed him as he recovered from his wounds and became the template for the heroine of his much-acclaimed novel *A Farewell to Arms*.

Passport photograph of a young man who looks set to take on the world, as handsome as anyone from Central Casting.

Sitting outside his Paris apartment, *circa* 1924. 'If you are lucky enough to have lived in Paris as a young man,' he wrote, 'then wherever you go for the rest of your life it stays with you, for Paris is a moveable feast.'

Right: With Hadley Richardson, arguably the greatest love of his life, at a ski resort in Schruns, Austria.

Below: The wedding of Ernest and Hadley. Pictured with them on the left are Hemingway's sisters Carol and Marcelline, and on the right his parents and younger brother Leicester.

Enjoying himself at a sidewalk café during the San Fermin Festival in 1925 with Harold Loeb (wearing glasses), Lady Duff Twysden, Hadley, Donald Ogden Stewart, and Pat Guthrie. Most of these people would figure in some form or other in his first novel, *The Sun Also Rises*, except for Hadley.

Hemingway became something of a snappy dresser when he started shopping at Abercrombie & Fitch as a famous author. Here he is in earlier days as a fledgling author in more modest threads.

Living the simple life in Paris with Hadley and their son, Jack (aka Bumby), before things started to go wrong between them.

Left: The incredibly accident-prone Hemingway received this horseshoe-shaped gash on his forehead in Paris one night in 1928 in a toilet at 2 a.m. when he yanked a skylight chain instead of the flush box, causing the skylight to fall down on his head. It took nine stitches to sew up the wound, which left a permanent scar.

Below: Hemingway divorced Hadley for Pauline Pfeiffer, a woman whose sophistication and literary *nous* seemed more appropriate for him as he embarked on the second phase of his career. Asked why he was leaving Hadley for her, he replied, 'Because I am a bastard.'

The author beside his latest kill during his first African safari in 1933.

Proudly showing off a marlin catch in Havana harbour in 1934.

Hemingway's sometime friend and booster F. Scott Fitzgerald once said, 'Ernest needs a new wife for every book.' Hadley oversaw *The Sun Also Rises*. Pauline helped him finetune *A Farewell to Arms*. Martha Gellhorn, his third wife pictured above, was the *femme inspiratrice* behind the novel that confirmed his reputation as America's foremost scribe, *For Whom the Bell Tolls*.

Above left: The master craftsman writing one of his books, probably *For Whom the Bell Tolls*.

Above right: Hemingway photographed outside Santa Maria della Salute in Venice, 1948.

A proud father with his three sons in Cuba. From left: Patrick, 'Bumby', and Gregory. Gregory would prove to be the most problematic of the three for him as he grew up.

Sporting a moustache as he sits in a deck chair in 1946 outside the Finca Vigia, the vast Cuban domain he renovated with Martha after marrying her.

Above left: In Havana on board the *Pilar*, the boat that became a home from home to him, especially when the marriage to Martha went sour.

Above right: Hemingway broke his glasses while on board the SS *Jagiello* in 1949 so stuffed a piece of tissue at the bridge to secure them.

With his fourth wife, 'Miss' Mary Welsh, and their good friends Gary Cooper and wife Rocky. The photograph was taken in Idaho where they shot game and drank—not necessarily in that order.

Left: Aiming a rifle for a photograph to adorn a *Look* magazine profile of him in 1953.

Below: Hemingway had the unique experience of reading his own obituary. It was printed in various newspapers around the world in 1954 when he was missing—and presumed dead—after he suffered two plane crashes in the space of as many days in Africa. Here he is seen reading a report of the crashes with a member of the US military at the library of his Cuban home, the Finca Vigia.

Right: The grand old man of letters in his beloved Cuba.

Below: Traces of the 1923 scar on his forehead from the toilet accident in Paris are still visible in this shot of Hemingway as he sits on board the *Pilar* in the late '50s.

Left: Few writers loved bullfights more than Hemingway. He saw them as epitomising most of the things that made life worth living for him: honour, dignity, and 'grace under pressure'—his main mantra. Here he is with one of his favourite matadors, Antonio Ordonez, at Ordonez's Spanish ranch in 1959.

Below: This image captures the ageing author in one of the familiarly downbeat poses that characterized his final years when, as Norman Mailer put it, 'he fell through the floor of depression'.

His main grievance with it was financial. He sold the rights for a paltry $10,000. Insult was added to injury when two subsequent films based on it (*The Breaking Point* and *The Gun Runners*) netted him nothing at all.

His mind was on other matters now. The Fascist heave against the Loyalists was getting more intense in Spain. It was time for him to make his way there.

Despite her reluctance about him going, Pauline helped him pack his bags. She even flew with him to Newark to see him off. Afterwards, he boarded the *Île de France* to take him across the Atlantic, meeting Martha in Paris so they could go to Barcelona together.

Their relationship went into another dimension now. Martha saw the idealist in Hemingway rather than the shabby barfly she encountered in Sloppy Joe's. 'He really cared about the war,' she said, 'I believe I never would've gotten hooked otherwise.' Spain, she felt, was 'the place to stop Fascism. It was one of those moments in history when there was no doubt.'[12]

They started sleeping with one another in Spain. As was the case with Mason, Hemingway had no need to worry about *coitus interruptus* with her. He was in the full flush of infatuation. Combined with his political fervour, this made him feel reborn.

Their intimacy became public knowledge one night when a hotel they were staying in was bombed by a Nationalist shell. It struck a hot water tank, causing steam to fill the upper floors.[13] The rooms were evacuated. Many illicit liaisons were exposed that night as people poured from their bedrooms to seek shelter in the basement.[14] Many prostitutes emerged from the rooms of correspondents as well. Gellhorn was amused by them as they 'cried out like birds in their high voices'.

Both Gellhorn and Hemingway were covering the war for different publications. Hemingway was working for NANA, the North American Newspaper Alliance. Martha was with *Collier's*. They were as excited by the conflict as they were by one another. For Hemingway, Jose Luis Castillo-Puche wrote, it was 'an embodiment of every aspect of the myth of the bullfight, from the worship of virility to blood communion to a sort of hymn of the bridegroom at a nuptial feast'.

They went to the trenches to talk to the soldiers. They travelled across gutted country roads to bring blood to field hospitals. They dodged shells and felt flushed with pride.

Hemingway cabled Pauline to say he planned to go back to Key West in May. By now she was more hardened, having spoken to Jinny about what was happening with Martha. Jinny told her to give up on him. She decided not to go quite that far. 'If you're happy over there,' she cabled back, 'don't come back here to be unhappy. But hope you can come back and we can both be happy.'

NANA was paying him a dollar a word for his dispatches. This was a journalistic precedent.[15] Their generosity resulted from the power of his writing. He gave a view from the ground, a worm's-eye appraisal of the situation.

The heightened consciousness that was in Hemingway in Italy in 1918 was still there to be tapped. He was more famous now. His reflexes might have been slower but he was still hungry for action, still anxious to help the oppressed.

'My sympathies are always for exploited working people,' he declared, 'even if I drink with the landlords.' He put his position more bluntly when he said, 'I mix with shits, nor lose the common touch.'

The war excited him in the same way as the First World War had nineteen years before. Fossalta gave him a conduit for his energies. The guerillas of the Spanish foothills were doing so again now. Life in Key West had made him smug. It was time to get fire in his belly again, time to smell fear.

Pauline waited for him to tell her he was leaving her for Martha. In a way, she told herself, it was probably inevitable that his departure would come about sooner or later. It was as if there was a built-in obsolescence to his marriages, as if his wives outlived their relevance for him after a certain time. His mind moved so fast he needed constant change to fulfil it. A new book to write, somewhere else to live, a different woman to love.

'Ernest needs a new woman for every new big book,' Scott Fitzgerald proclaimed after Pauline took him from Hadley.[16] Hemingway admitted this himself.[17] He was writing *A Farewell to Arms* when Fitzgerald made the remark. Martha was now on hand to put him through his paces.

The novel she was mentoring would become his most ambitious yet, *For Whom the Bell Tolls*. She loved what he showed her of it, describing it as an 'absolute marvel'.[18]

He approached it with nervousness. It had been in his head for a long time before he went to Spain. During his first few weeks there he was too concentrated on staying alive to think of it. Fears of being bombed to death abated with time.

'What I have to do now is write,' he promised. 'As long as there's war you always think perhaps you will be killed so you have nothing to worry about. You worry when you live. I was not killed in Spain. Living is much more difficult and complicated than dying.'

He wrote the book in bursts, just like he had his previous ones. Never one to be humble about his gifts, pretty soon he knew it would be 'cockeyed wonderful'. All of his books came from experience. When he was passionate about something it made them easier to write.

Many critics doubted he had another major novel in him at this time. They saw him spreading his talents into so many diverse fields in the thirties. He was surprised at the words that came out of him as he sat at his typewriter. Sometimes he thought that the book was writing him rather than him writing the book. It was as if it was being given to him by some external force.

Pauline refused to read it. Her praise for *The Torrents of Spring* drew him from Hadley to her, as did her praise for *The Sun Also Rises* soon afterwards. He thought the fact that she demurred now was a 'damned shame' considering she was such a good judge of writing.[19] Her place was now being usurped by his new judge—and lover.

His fortieth birthday arrived as the book neared its completion. He was sufficiently money-conscious to be aware that the Pfeiffers were remiss in sending their usual $1,000 gift to him. Mary used to send money as well as Gus. Maybe, he thought, it would be more this year because he was reaching a milestone. Blinded by love, he was too dim to think that his problems with Pauline were responsible for their laxity.

He wrote to Mary to ask her if he could bring Patrick and Gregory to Piggott. It was an unsubtle hint that she was slow to send her cheque. It arrived by return of post, the hint received and the speed of its receipt an actual sign of it being given with a bad grace.

Undeterred, Hemingway finished his book. Afterwards he felt both exhausted and exhilarated. He felt as if he had fought in a war rather than just written a book. The final scene where Jordan gets ready to blow up a bridge pleased him most. After writing this chapter, he knew there was no way he could kill his hero off.

He wrote two final chapters after the bridge was blown but threw them away. The book ends as it began, with Jordan awaiting his fate. It was a decision that was as inspired as him cutting the first chapter from *The Sun Also Rises* all those years before, or the last one from *A Farewell to Arms*.

He got the title of the book from a John Donne poem, *Meditation XVII*. 'No man is an iland,' Donne wrote, 'intire of itself. /Any man's death diminishes me/because I am involved in mankind/Therefore never send to know/ For whom the bell tolls/It tolls for thee.'

'I think it has the magic a title has to have,' he said, 'Maybe it isn't too easy to say but maybe the book will make it easy.'

It was written in the third person, a departure from his previous novels. 'First person narration,' he attested, 'is a cinch.' The third one was more of a challenge. His hero, however, was in the classical Hemingway mould. Jordan was like another Frederic Henry.

The romantic aspects of the book fail to work as well as the adventurous ones. Jordan's love affair with Maria, one of the guerilla fighters he links up with in the mountains, is forced. Hemingway is on unsure ground—literally—when he makes the earth move for Maria and Jordan as they make love in a sleeping bag.

The shrunken time frame of the book is its best quality. Life is microscoped into seventy-two hours for Jordan. He seems to live as many years in that time. If the war in *A Farewell To Arms* was a game, here it more resembles a religion. Jordan gets the emotion that he was expected to feel when he was making his First Communion.

He exemplifies Hemingway's confusions. The Loyalists expected him to be on their side in the war, and so did the Communists, but he baulked at the idea of nailing his colours to any political mast. 'Politics I would rather not be quoted on,' he said once, 'Any contact I've had with it left me feeling as though I'd been drinking out of spittoons.'

All he told them was that he was anti-Fascist. Such nuances may not be hugely important. *For Whom the Bell Tolls* is mainly a book about struggle. Hemingway told Malcolm Cowley he put not only the Civil War into it but 'everything I'd learned about Spain for eighteen years'.

The main problem with it was the language. At times it appears to replicate peasant idioms. Elsewhere the phraseology is more a product of Hemingway's imagination than the way Castilians spoke. His formal style fails here because his own voice comes through too much.

Maria's early willingness to share Jordan's bed is another problem, being inconsistent with her shyness, especially considering her past sexual traumas.

The book is more a mosaic of set-pieces than a well-rounded novel. Each chapter seems to be a self-contained entity. Neither do the characters develop as much as they might. This is mainly true of Jordan. Over 400 pages, his internal monologues about idealism and death tend to rankle. At times they read like Frederic Henry carted off to the Iberian Peninsula and decked out in peasant garb, having traded in his army uniform for a beret. His mock-mystical philosophising gives the book a contrived edge. We feel Hemingway is pulling strings over our head. In his stories everything is more buttoned down. 'All bad writers are in love with the epic,' he said once. Maybe some great writers are too.

Another problem is the stylised expletives. One can only take so many sentences like, 'Go and obscenity in the milk of thy cowardice.' This was his way of avoiding expletives and thus censorship.[20] It was a good idea in theory, but it means readers are denied the sense of real people conversing. At times Hemingway's peasants are more like theatrical personages in a pageant than hardscrabble guerillas.

Some of the narration is over-the-top too, especially when Hemingway describes Jordan making love to Maria. This owes something to Gertrude Stein: 'To him it was a dark passage which led to nowhere, then to nowhere, then again to nowhere, once again to nowhere.'

The intensity of the love scenes in both *For Whom the Bell Tolls* and *A Farewell to Arms* results from the fact that time is short for the people involved. Death hovers near all of them. Frederic Henry has to live because of his being the narrator of the book. Robert Jordan is doomed almost from the moment Pilar—the character Hemingway named after his boat—reads his palm. The price both men pay for love is death.

Like the Frederic Henry of *A Farewell to Arms*, Jordan comes across more like a mythic hero than a flesh-and-blood character. His 'Catherine', i.e. Maria, is also too obviously a symbol of purity in the book. Her dialogue with Jordan is frequently laughable. The phrase 'Did the earth move?' entered the language after it was published. People have been using it as a stick to beat it with since.

The fact that Maria creeps into a stranger's sleeping bag so soon after being gang-raped by the Fascists is as hard to take as the fact that she has to be taught how to kiss. Hemingway tried to make her into a diamond in the rough, an earth-angel, with only partial success.

Maria is two parts Hadley and one part Martha just as Catherine was three parts Hadley, one part Pauline and one part Agnes. This is the occupational hazard of all composite characters. If the sources are too divergent, the finished product suffers.

Edmund Wilson was a severe but cogent critic of Hemingway. He thought the relationship between Jordan and Maria had 'none of the give and take that goes on between real men and women'. Instead, it was like 'the all-too-perfect felicity of a youthful erotic dream'.

At one stage, Jordan calls Maria 'rabbit' as a pet name. Hemingway ought to have known that 'rabbit' in Spanish is a term for a woman's vagina. Another possibility is that he knew full well what 'rabbit' meant in Spanish and that he was having fun sneaking the expletive past Perkins.

A major bone of contention with readers was the graphic nature of what came to be known as the 'smell of death' sequence of the book. This occurs in Chapter 19. Hemingway defended it the same way he defended the unsavoury nature of some of his early stories to his parents. To remove it, he told Perkins, would be like taking the oboe out of an orchestra. 'Oboes make an ugly noise when played alone,' he conceded, 'but in an ensemble they work.'

Statements like these are big. Hemingway felt justified in making them because of the book's epic scope. He told Arnold Gingrich that *For Whom the Bell Tolls* cost him not only a year and a half of his life but also his marriage. He thought that was a small price to pay for what he saw as his finest literary achievement. In *A Farewell to Arms* he was operating on a vast canvas. Here it was more claustrophobic. From this point of view, *For Whom the Bell Tolls* represented a bigger challenge.

Despite his misgivings about the love scenes, Edmund Wilson went on to say, 'The big game hunter, the waterside superman, the Hotel Florida Stalinist, with their constrained and fevered attitudes, have evaporated like the fantasies of alcohol. Hemingway the artist is with us again; and it is like having an old friend back.'[22]

Scott Fitzgerald was bitchy about it, castigating it for being 'a thoroughly superficial book' that had 'all the profundity of *Rebecca*'. Hemingway, he claimed outrageously, was finished as a writer.

Hemingway had sent him a copy with the inscription, 'To Scott with affection and esteem.' This was perhaps sardonic. He had little affection for his old adversary now, and even less esteem. Fitzgerald scribbled back a note of gratitude, saying, 'I envy you like hell and there is no irony in this. I envy you the time it will give you to do what you want.'[23]

The final qualification is interesting. It suggests he thought it was a potboiler. To Hemingway he said it was 'better than anybody else writing can do', but privately he grumbled, 'It's not up to his usual standards. He wrote it for the movies.'

Arturo Barea said it was 'Not so much Spain as Hemingway.' Surely this was to misunderstand its intent. It was fiction rather than social history. 'Barea,' John Teunissen remarked, 'might very well have written a review of *Moby Dick* called "Not Whaling but Melville."' But one can see his point considering Hemingway touted the book as being the ultimate Spanish tract.

Every book Hemingway wrote, one could say to Barea, was as much Hemingway as its subject. Was *Green Hills of Africa* more Hemingway than hunting? Was *Death in the Afternoon* more him than bullfighting? Stephen Spender put it more succinctly. Having him in Spain, he said, was 'like letting Edgar Allen Poe into a small cellar containing a mad cat'.

For Whom the Bell Tolls sold half a million copies within six months. It was the best-selling novel in the U.S. since *Gone with the Wind*. Hemingway's output since *A Farewell to Arms* had been fitful. This was another blockbuster with all his themes—honour, dignity, tragedy. It spelt the end of a creative burst that began in the early '20s.

His attention now shifted to Martha. She was beginning to have doubts about whether they were suitable for one another. He wrote to her in August 1940 to ask her what her intentions were. If she felt uncomfortable continuing their relationship, he told her he needed to halt the divorce proceedings that had been instituted against Pauline. If she continued it, he was going to be generous to Pauline. He intended to give her 'all of the world with a fence around it'.[24] If Martha married him, he vowed to 'fence the moon' and throw that in too. The undertone was that if she left him, he might still stay with Pauline. Martha seemed oblivious to this. She was charmed by his letter and the divorce went ahead.

Pauline broke down completely when she realised it was final. Gregory wrote in a memoir, 'I can't remember much of the divorce period, just shouting in rooms, doors slamming, Mother scurrying out of the bedroom crying—the usual "amicable" divorce.'[25]

Hemingway was more worried about money than about the emotional mess he was leaving behind him. It was the first time since he started out that he was dependent on his own finances. The Pfeiffer money was gone forever and royalties from his new novel were a while off yet. He tried not to dwell on such matters. Martha was in love with him. That was the main thing.

Pauline blamed the breakdown of the marriage on Spain. 'Don't mention that country to me,' she said to people in years to come, 'It lost me the man I loved.'

That was not strictly speaking true. By now she was past her sell-by date for Hemingway. Like the Hadley of 1926, she was a ball and chain figure for him. It was many years since she was able to share his thirst for adventure.

The marriage had lasted thirteen years. Pauline claimed only eight of these were good ones. His inability to have sex with her was the last straw in a rapidly declining relationship. 'If I hadn't been such a bloody fool practising Catholic,' she clamoured, 'I wouldn't have lost my husband.' Hemingway underlined this when he said, 'You were not beaten by Miss Martha. You were beaten by *coitus interruptus* imposed by the Church.'[26]

She got her revenge on him by demanding what he called 'blood money' from him and behaving 'wickedly' regarding custody of the children. He thought she was hellbent on destroying him financially and every other way. 'I think perhaps she is off her rocker,' he hissed, 'as women often are at such times.'[27]

Thinking about her dragged down his spirits. Martha told him to look to the future rather than the past. He said that made good sense.

She thought they should buy a house in Cuba. It would be a novelty for them. In recent months she was spending time in Hemingway's run-down room at the Ambos Mundos hotel. His 'packrat' tendencies made it difficult for her to walk around it without falling over his files—or his fishing gear.

He liked the idea of living in Cuba. He fished there for years while living in Key West. Basing himself there meant he could avoid the four-hour journey on the *Pilar*. He also loved Cuba's culture. It was the antithesis of Oak Park with its freewheeling attitude to everything. The 'festival conception of life' that he witnessed in France and Spain was writ large there.

Martha asked some real estate agents to show her the rental properties they had on their books. After viewing a few of them, she expressed interest in a rambling mansion 20 miles outside Havana. A Spanish-style structure with a 60-foot living room, it had been uninhabited for some time. Rodents and mosquitoes infested much of it. There was a swimming pool outside, but it was filled with algae. The grounds were huge but uncared for, littered with rusty tins and empty gin bottles. There were cracks all over a tennis court that made it unplayable.

Hemingway had some misgivings about it when he saw it first. Martha thought it had possibilities if it was renovated. She loved everything about it, especially a ceiba tree that had orchids sprouting from its trunk. The terraces had flowering vines. She loved listening to hummingbirds making their nests in the foliage.

Hemingway soon came to agree with her that they could make a life together there. Whenever he made up his mind about something he moved fast.

He bought it as a wedding present for her from the royalties from *For Whom the Bell Tolls*. They called it the Finca Vigia. That was Spanish for Lookout Farm. It was far enough from Havana, he remarked delightedly, to discourage visitors: 'When the guys get drunk and decide to go see Ernest, it's too long a trip.'[28]

Martha employed a crew of people to make it habitable. The algae were taken out of the swimming pool. When she swam in it, Hemingway was rivetted. He thought she looked like a mermaid.

The kitchen was modernised, and all the other rooms painted. The high-ceilinged ones were ideal for Hemingway's bullfight posters and safari trophies. The grounds were transformed from wild undergrowth to a cultivated garden providing a view of the coast that was previously obscured. With the luxuriant vegetation—mango trees, jacaranda, bougainvillea pines—it was like having Africa on their doorstep. Hemingway hung paintings by Picasso and Cezanne on the walls alongside his other artefacts.

The new living conditions made it easier to forget Pauline. In some ways, he was less tortured by what was happening with her than he was a decade before with Hadley. His guilt complex over leaving Hadley lasted right through the marriage with Pauline. The situation was different with Martha.

He was fascinated by her in a different way than he had been by Hadley or Pauline. She was the last in a long line of lovers he entertained during the bad years of the Pauline marriage. The most influential of these, of course, was Jane Mason. Martha was nearly as pretty as Mason and, more importantly, free of her emotional instability.

She was as determined as Pauline in getting what she wanted. Sometimes this involved stepping on people. Hemingway's military friend Buck Lanham alleged she was 'a bitch from start to finish, and every other member of my staff who met her—and most did—thought so too'.[29] Another military friend, Winston Guest, described her as 'a tough, mercenary bitch'.

Scott Fitzgerald speculated that it would be odd to think of Hemingway married to 'a really attractive woman. The pattern will be somewhat different than with his Pygmalion-like creations.'[30] Gertrude Stein was more droll. 'Any man who marries three women from St. Louis,' she railed, 'deserves what he gets.'

Some people thought Martha was marrying Hemingway for his money. Others suspected she was using him to advance her writing career. He joked to his sons, 'Maybe I'll retire and let her be the writer in the family.'[31]

She denied jumping on his bandwagon, pointing out that she was well established as a writer before she met him. This was true. As to the charge of being mercenary, Hemingway was never less wealthy than now. The money Martha made from her military assignments brought in more than anything he was likely to earn in the foreseeable future.

He feared Pauline was going to cripple him in court. 'She's ruthless!' he fumed. What did he expect? The marriage had been going on for thirteen years and he was now walking out on it. How could she take that lying down? He never seemed to be able to see another person's side of a story, being so fond of playing the victim. He even blamed Pauline for going to the Riviera when he was in Spain with Martha. While he was risking his life, he accused, she was sunning herself in a holiday resort.[32] Sunning herself? It was more likely she went away to try and keep her sanity.

He tried to rationalise his guilt at leaving her, telling himself it was no less than she deserved for taking him away from Hadley. Her pain was reparation for her 'sin'. Exactly how he himself should be punished he deigned to consider. Presumably there was one law for deserting husbands and another for amoral jezebels.

Many of his problems with Pauline, he claimed, had a sexual root. He once told Patrick that it was because of her difficult birth with him that their marriage broke up. Here again he was showing a pronounced disregard for the trauma this revelation could cause to his son.

Elsewhere he simply said, 'Things went to hell with Pauline.' It was the same way as they went to hell with Hadley after that marriage collapsed. Things also went to hell in Oak Park after many years of being 'cockeyed happy' there. Everything seemed to go to hell with Hemingway sooner or later. He hated making mistakes so much that when he did make one, he usually went into denial about it, scapegoating someone else instead.

His nonchalance about the imminent divorce was evident in his suggestion to Pauline that he spend the Christmas of 1939 with her and the boys. 'Absolutely not!' she huffed. She went off to New York with them instead, spending the festive season with Jinny and Gus. Hemingway went to Key West anyway. It was strange for him being on his own there. Even the servants were gone. He had to make his own meals.

He stayed nine days in the house. Part of his time he spent storing boxes of his manuscripts in Sloppy Joe's. On 26 December, he loaded his Buick with fishing gear and other personal items. He then drove onto the Key West–Havana ferry for the last time.

He was still friendly with Mary Pfeiffer. She was softer than her husband. He kept her up to speed with the details of his life in all the letters he wrote to her over the years. Many of these had humour in them.

He wrote to her to tell her how upset he was about the forthcoming divorce. The main reason for the letter was to give out about Jinny. He heard she was badmouthing him and he wanted to set the record straight. 'Virginia's version of my life and conduct is a fantastic one,' he said in the letter, 'but she spread it sufficiently and at the right time to break up my home.'[33]

Mary's reply came as a surprise to him. 'Dear Ernest,' she wrote, 'All this trouble between you and Pauline is beyond our comprehension. This is the saddest Christmas I have ever known. A broken family is a tragic thing, particularly when there are children. Sorry to send you such a message but it is the way I feel. I shall always remember you in my prayers and hope that we shall meet again in a fairer clime upon a farther shore.'[34]

Jinny told Mary she thought Hemingway married Pauline more for money than love. Such an idea had been muttered by the residents of Piggott for years. It had traction now that he was divorcing her. Another theory suggested Jinny was sexually attracted to him, an attraction that she subdued out of deference to Pauline. If she had been, she was no longer.

Jinny was mistaken in her belief that Hemingway was a gold-digger. He rarely refused the generosity of benefactors like Gus or the Murphys, but it would be unfair to brand him a free-loader. He once said in his defence on this score, 'The popular theory that I was a bum who was picked up from poverty and supported on Pfeiffer money always seemed to me a bit strange.' Anytime he got a gift from Gus, he told Patrick, 'I gave him a manuscript which was at least double the value of the present.'[35] He did this with *A Farewell to Arms* and again with *For Whom the Bell Tolls*. He objected to the image of himself as 'the little poor boy who came into the wonderful rich family and stole the spoons'.[36]

He took umbrage when Mary reminded him in a 1935 note that he had a 'fairy godfather'. He wrote back: 'When I'm writing a novel I am making nothing and am probably regarded by the family intelligence service as a loafer. On the other hand when I am through with a novel I make plenty of money.' He neglected to mention that the money he received from his 'fairy godfather' was not returned when he went from loafer to money-maker.

Hemingway married Martha in November 1940 in the dining room of the Union Pacific Railway in Wyoming. He said he was madly in love with her. The reality of the situation was that he was entering the marriage with less enthusiasm than his first or second.

Before he married her, he created a character based on her in the only play he ever wrote. This was Dorothy Bridges in *The Fifth Column*. He himself was based on the character of her husband, Philip Rawlings, a war correspondent working with Spanish counter-intelligence. Rawlings says at one stage that he made a 'colossal mistake' by marrying Bridges. Bridges is a one-dimensional version of Martha, but in her we can see the recipe for disaster the liaison with Hemingway would turn out to be.

One of the reasons for this was her workaholic nature. No sooner were they back from their honeymoon than she started eyeing up the Orient for articles she might do on it. She was commissioned to do some for *Collier's* on the Sino-Japanese War. Hemingway tried to talk her out of it, but he got nowhere. In the end, he decided to go with her. 'If you can't beat 'em,' he said resignedly, 'Join 'em.'

When he got back he faced the wrath of Pauline's lawyers. She told him she was going to take him for every penny. It was a far cry from the Hadley divorce where his generosity with *The Sun Also Rises* royalties was so appreciated. 'Boy,' he had written to Hadley in 1939, 'the more I see of all the members of your sex, the more I admire you.'[37]

Pauline was given custody of Patrick and Gregory as well as what he called 'punitive' alimony of $500 a month. This galled him considering how much wealth there was in her family between her father and Gus. He was in poor circumstances himself, he told Gus, and she was twisting the dagger. Gus tried to work out an agreement with her that softened the blow. She appeared to agree to this at first, but then went back on her word.

When Hemingway first told Pauline he was going to divorce her, she was livid. 'If you do,' she threatened, 'I'll take everything you've got.' He replied, 'If you let me go I'll be happy to give you everything.'[38] He came to regret saying this. Hell hath no fury like a woman scorned. She became determined to hit him in the pocket when there was no other way to do so.

The proceedings made him even more cynical about women than he was, which was saying something. He warned Clara Spiegel's husband never to marry a rich girl as it would turn out to be more expensive than marrying the poorest one in the world.[39]

Pauline devoted herself too much to Hemingway in their marriage. That was why she was so traumatised by the divorce. It stripped her of her identity. She tried to retrieve that now. With the money she got from him, she set up a fabric shop in Key West with Lorine Thompson, the friend she was having round to dinner the night Hemingway met Martha. She dated other men afterwards but without much conviction. Eventually, like Jinny, she started romancing other women. In both of their cases, it almost seemed like this course of action was caused by cynicism over the male of the species—in particular one male known all too well to both of them.

12

Prisoner of Fame

F. Scott Fitzgerald was in poor health by the end of the '30s. By that time there was a total lack of communication between himself and Hemingway. His behaviour had become even more desperate by now. One night he became so excited after receiving an offer from Hollywood to adapt one of his novels as a screenplay that he got extra drunk in his celebrations. He decided to have a bath so he turned on the water but he soon forgot having done so which meant it flooded the room.[1] He made various efforts to cut down on his drinking, at one stage pleading with his secretary to pour gin bottles over the side of a canyon to keep him away from them.[2] Such efforts to stay on the dry mostly proved hopeless.

The last time Hemingway saw him was at a showing of *The Spanish Earth*. He narrated it himself. Orson Welles had originally been commissioned to do it but Hemingway had a problem with the recordings he heard of his voice. The film, for him, was a simple documentary intended to apprise viewers of the reasons behind the war. He thought Welles was acting too self-importantly for that. 'Every time Orson said the word "infantry,"' he complained, 'it sounded like a cocksucker swallowing.'[3]

Welles was offended to see his contribution canned as he waived his fee for it. Hemingway turned on him with the words, 'You effeminate boys of the theatre, what do you know about real war?' He picked up a chair to hit him. Welles pretended to be afraid of him. 'Oh Mr Hemingway,' he whimpered, 'How strong and big you are!'[4] Hemingway saw the fun of the situation. The two of them ended up toasting one another over a bottle of whiskey.

Hemingway went to Hollywood for the showing. Fitzgerald was working for MGM at the time. He was nervous about seeing Hemingway as it was a long time since they last met. He was also without the dutch courage of drink. Dorothy Parker was accompanying him. 'I'm scared of Ernest,' he croaked to her, 'and I'm scared of being sober.'[5] 'Ernest still likes you a lot,' she assured him. This was hardly true.

Hemingway also had mixed feelings about Parker. He once wrote a corrosive poem about her, one of the most offensive ones he ever wrote. If she saw it, there was is no way she could have remained as friendly to him throughout her life as she did. For both of their sakes, it was a blessing it was never printed anywhere.

Hemingway threw a glass into the fireplace as soon as Fitzgerald entered the room. Fitzgerald wilted and left soon afterwards. Neither man spoke a word to one another.

Though Fitzgerald was a shadow of his former self by now, Hemingway was aware of the talent he had when he started out. He once praised it for being 'as natural as the pattern that was made by the dust on a butterfly's wings'.[6] In a crueller mood, he said, 'I never had any respect for him except for his lovely, golden, wasted talent.'[7]

He believed he could have saved himself if he divorced Zelda before she went mad. Instead, the Catholic in him clung on to the ideal of marriage. Her insanity, he thought, was related to her obsessive desire to be as successful a writer as her husband. He wondered if her insanity caused his alcoholism or his alcoholism was responsible for her madness. Maybe it was 50 per cent both.[8]

A year before he died, Fitzgerald woke up one morning unable to move. His doctor told him he was playing with fire, that the paralysis was caused by drink. It was God giving him a warning. 'What would you do if you were paralysed?' the doctor asked him. 'I'd blow my brains out,' he answered. 'Yes,' the doctor challenged, 'but who's going to hold the gun?'[9]

His drinking went totally out of control now, at one stage causing him to threaten to shoot Sheilah Graham, the woman he was living with, after she threw some of his drinking friends out of their house.[10] Another time he tried to shoot himself. She had to wrestle the gun from him.[11] It was childish behaviour. Hemingway told him once that he went 'straight from youth to senility without going through manhood'.[12]

A week before he got the heart attack that killed him in 1940, Graham showed him an article in a trade paper that described a Hollywood intellectual as 'a fugitive from the Scott Fitzgerald era'. 'You see,' she exulted, 'You're an era.' 'That means I'm a has-been,' he replied.

He was so much a creature of his environment that he almost had to assume its parameters. The Depression dragged him down in the same dramatic manner as the Jazz Age had excited him. By the end of the '20s, the party was really over for him. Though he staggered on for another decade with some vestiges of the old magic, he was really just playing out a ghostly version of his fantasies with Graham.

For a man so different from Hemingway, his message to readers was basically the same: idealists are punished, and time eventually crushes us all. Fitzgerald once emoted, 'Show me a hero and I'll write you a tragedy.'[13] He died of a massive coronary in 1940 at the age of forty-four.

Zelda was in a sanatorium at the time, having been diagnosed with schizophrenia. The last decade of her life she spent going in and out of psychiatric institutions. She died in a fire in one of these in 1948, having been locked in her room awaiting electro-convulsive therapy.

Fitzgerald's books came back into vogue after he died. Hemingway even joined the chorus of approval. '*Tender is the Night* is a most wonderful book,' he gushed in 1941, 'I don't think Scottie even realised how good he was.' Was his death the reason for his re-evaluation of it? Fitzgerald could hardly threaten him from the grave.

Literary rivalry was always huge for Hemingway. *The Great Gatsby* had been published in 1925, the same year as *In Our Time*. It received much more attention than it because Fitzgerald was more famous than Hemingway then. That year also saw the publication of Gertrude Stein's *The Making of Americans* and Sherwood Anderson's *Dark Laughter*. Hemingway would go on to rubbish these two books in later years as evidence of their authors' decline. His own one followed the publication of *For Whom the Bell Tolls*. One could argue that it burned him out.

Away from his desk, he became a public figure, an eminence who stroked his whiskers and pontificated. He came to resemble the kind of character he inveighed against in his fiction, someone like his alter ego in *The Snows of Kilimanjaro*. 'He blamed the rich who were dull and drank too much,' he wrote in that story, 'He blamed his wife who tried to make things too soft for him. And he blamed himself for trading on his talent and vitality. Now all that was coming to an end.'

People swarmed around him for autographs. Crowds formed when he went shopping in Abercrombie & Fitch. Archibald MacLeish wrote, 'Fame became of him.'[14] It had been the way even since the Paris years when, as a friend remarked, 'If he stubbed his toe it attracted attention'.[15] When his fame grew, fans sat at his feet hanging on his every word. His books had inspired a school of writing and a way of life. He was seen as an authority on everything from bullfighting to the best places to eat and drink. He grew a beard to cover skin cancers that formed on his face, thereby fortifying his paternalistic image.

'I don't want to be famous,' he explained, 'All I want to do is write, hunt, fish and be obscure.'[16] That became increasingly more unlikely with the years. Even trivial items about him sold newspapers. 'Don't believe anything you read about Mr Papa,' he warned, 'It is all shit. I never aided it but I may have abetted it by not coming out and denying it.' His legend, he lamented, had grown 'like the barnacles on the bottom of a ship'.[17]

We can take these words with a grain of salt. He enjoyed it when strangers called him 'Papa' on the street. It was difficult not to bask in the glory of being America's best-known writer.

He endorsed products. He fed gossip columnists soundbites for their columns. He became involved in pub brawls. He sounded off on rivals, friends, strangers. For a time it seemed as if his books were playing second fiddle to his life.

James Joyce died in 1941 from a perforated ulcer. Hemingway took the news badly. He saw little of 'poor, blind Jimmy' over the years, but they had a mutual respect for one another's output and a lively line in banter whenever they got drunk together.

He had many happy memories of the Irishman. One night, Joyce asked him if he felt his work was too 'suburban'. His wife, Nora, piped up, 'Jim could do with a spot of that lion-hunting.' Joyce agreed that would be fine, but with his bad eye he might not have been able to see the lions. 'Ernest could kill them,' Nora suggested, 'and afterwards you could go up and touch them and smell them. That's all you'd need.' Anytime they were threatened by violence on their nights out, Joyce retired into the background and muttered, 'Deal with him, Hemingway.'[18] 'He was the finest friend I ever had,' Hemingway rhapsodised, 'There's no one to talk to anymore about the *metier*.'

Like most people he was confused by *Finnegans Wake*, the book Joyce spent his last decade working on. If *Ulysses* was the most unread book of its time, as someone said, this was the most unreadable one. 'I wish I knew what it was about,' Hemingway admitted, 'I prefer Jim straight, with orange juice and Liffey water.'

The deaths of people like Fitzgerald and Joyce pushed Hemingway into the forefront even more. For *Life* magazine, he endorsed such items as beer and Parker pens for exorbitant sums. The idea of a writer being a personality was new to the advertising world, but he embraced it, despite his supposed aversion to 'whoring'.

The more famous he became, the more stories came out about him. Most of them were false. One alleged that he had been a professional bullfighter in the past, another that he was a professional boxer. There were other stories about how many trophies he bagged in the jungle, how many soldiers he killed in the First World War. His war wound, Malcolm Bradbury alleged, was the most famous since Philoctetes. His sleepless nights were the best-known since those of Lady Macbeth. He was a gossip columnist's delight but there was a downside. The malice with which some of his critics exploited his actions suggested they had 'the sensational value of Wordsworth's illegitimate child or Byron's love for his sister'.

He was variously described as a bully and a coward, promiscuous and impotent, effusive and taciturn, mirthful and manic, extravagant and a tightwad. What matter that the terms were contradictory? Reporters played fast and loose with his life. Had he really run away from home and earned his living by boxing? Was he a failed footballer, a mediocre student, the cello-playing son of a domineering mother and a father who lacked the gumption to put her in her place?

The distinction between his life and his art became tenuous. It was easy to see him in the heroes he created both on the page and the screen. The world recognised him in Gregory Peck stricken with gangrene on a Kilimanjaro summit, in Gary Cooper blowing a bridge behind Fascist lines in the Spanish Civil War, in Rock Hudson making his 'separate peace' with Jennifer Jones during the war. He threw his personality at the world, and it responded by taking him into its heart.

There was even a Hemingway impostor going the rounds for a while, the ultimate accolade. It stopped being funny when he left a string of bills in his name scattered across the country.

He was photogenic as well, an ideal subject to have pictured beside a buffalo or a bison even if he never wrote a word. His face sold magazines. Often his jovial features seemed at odds with the tight-lipped introverts from the stories. It was like the tail wagging the dog.

Some people wondered why he courted publicity when he would have got it anyway from the quality of his work. Had he a greed for notoriety? Maybe the years of obscurity when he lived in a carpenter's loft in Paris made him hanker for their opposite.

The more such notoriety increased, the more his writing suffered. He developed lazy habits, falling into the pit of 'putting in' the Hemingway style like icing one might apply to a cake. At times it became an affection that served more to distract from what he was trying to say than to amplify it. It attracted attention to itself to such an extent that it became decorative even in its lack of decoration. The ultimate unliterary voice became literary by default.

On the surface, his image appeared to be something that just happened. In retrospect we can see it was carefully manufactured by him. He gave so much and then drew back, dangling friends and foes alike on invisible strings, dropping them and picking them up for equally enigmatic reasons.

Apocryphal stories continued to enrage and, occasionally, entertain him. A favourite canard was one alleging he had an aluminium kneecap inserted after the Fossalta wounding. Another one suggested he was at the Caporetto retreat. He added a few of his own. One was that he bedded no less a luminary than Mata Hari. Making love to this lady would have required him to possess the gift of bi-location. He was a reporter in Kansas the year she was executed in France.

Hemingway was content to propagate such stories until they outlived their usefulness for him. By the mid-'40s, he was bored by his celebrity status. He longed for obscurity once again.

By now he was forced to use the back exits of hotels to avoid fans mobbing him. He hated people coming up to him in bars saying, 'So you're Hemingway.' They often pawed him and even the people he was with. He struggled to find ways to react to these situations. 'If you admonish them,' he griped, 'or have to clip them, it gets in the papers. Henry James wasn't faced with these problems.'

His pugilistic endeavours hit the headlines more often than accounts of how hard he worked at blackening pages. The nuances of a Hemingway short story were hardly as interesting to people as details of a punch-up in Sloppy Joe's.

Once he became famous, becoming unfamous was impossible for him. All he could become was infamous. Being a living legend meant that when he got tired of being feted there was no place for him to hide anymore.

13

Two Writers in the Family

Hemingway transferred his attention from hunting to fishing in the '40s. The proximity of the Finca Vigia to the Gulf Stream meant a lot to him. The *Pilar* was docked there. He hunted for marlin in it most days. If Paris was the quintessential city of the bohemian in the '20s, Havana fulfilled that purpose now. Paris lacked ultra-clear waters beating away at its shores all year.

His writing disappointed him at this time. Part of the problem lay with Martha. The fears he had that she could become a rival to him in the writing stakes were coming home to roost. He wanted her to gee him up for another book like *For Whom the Bell Tolls*, but that was never going to happen.

She went to Finland on a journalistic junket at the end of 1940. Hemingway tried to look on the bright side, writing to Edna, 'She's doing it to be the sort of person I admire and not the dull wife who just forms herself on me like Pauline and Hadley.' The truth of the matter was that he needed 'dull' wives to minister to him. He was more honest when he admitted he was 'stinko deadly lonely' in her absence.[1]

Martha came back from Finland the following January. She was too tired after her exertions over there to give much of herself to him. 'She's like a racehorse with just two speeds,' he remarked, 'either running away or asleep.'[2]

The marriage of the Great American Chauvinist and the Great American Feminist was always going to be problematic. Hemingway might have been better advised to just have an affair with her as he had with Mason. Sex inside marriage proved to be a much more perfunctory activity than outside it. 'I provided it to him,' Martha sighed, 'only after all excuses failed—and with the hope that it would be over quickly.' She added even more acerbically, 'Ernest needed me to run the house and to copulate on.'[3] She believed he regarded sex the same way as he did swallowing his vitamins: 'He took [*sic*] it regularly every night but gave no thought to the woman's pleasure.'[4]

The marriage was a disaster almost from the outset. Thrust into one another's arms at a time of socio-political ferment, they were united in their espousal of causes, but how could this translate into love for one another? There was also the problem of their respective achievements. Hemingway was a man who had done it all when they met. Martha still had something to prove. The fact that she wanted to prove it with one of the most famous writers in the world complicated matters. It led to rivalry.

Even when they played tennis together at the Finca, there was 'needle' in it. Martha liked her husband to 'nearly win', Hemingway told Lillian Ross, but was miserable if he actually did so.[5]

They travelled to China together in 1941. *Collier's* had assigned Martha said to report on the activities of the Japanese army there. Troops had occupied Peking in 1936, thereby starting the Sino-Japanese War. Four years later, they were in control of the whole north-east of China.

Hemingway bridled at the idea of going. Eventually he acceded. He wrote some articles for *PM* magazine when he was there without much conviction.

The trip was boring for him. It suggested to him that Martha was setting herself up as the front-runner in the marriage. For her part, instead of Hemingway's fame intimidating her, it made her desperate to cut loose on her own.

She started to outdo him as a war correspondent. Her advantage over him was that she was unlikely to be mobbed everywhere she went. Neither would she be accosted for autographs, or sidetracked into taverns by over-enthusiastic aficionados anxious to hear her latest yarn about Franco.

One day in Hong Kong as Hemingway engaged in banter with a cadre of his buddies, Martha grew bored and told him she had to be elsewhere. As she walked away from him, she heard him saying, 'M. is going take the pulse of the nation.'[6] On another occasion, he said, 'M. loves humanity but she can't stand people.'[7]

A colleague from Martha's youth gave this denunciation of her:

> She claims she loves the poor but she actually loves the rich. Whenever she came back to St. Louis to see her ageing mother she always stayed with people who had swimming pools in their back gardens. She claimed

> she was a great lover of peace but wherever there was war she rushed into the fray. She loved her mink coat and claimed it was her *entrée* into any office.

She performed somewhat better in her role as stepmother to Patrick and Gregory. 'I am now suddenly a mother of three,' she beamed, 'and I must say I love it.'[8] They enjoyed going riding and shooting with her in Sun Valley. She was 'nuts for them'.[9] They especially liked it when she came out with words like 'Fuck'. Patrick gave her the dubious honour of being 'the first attractive lady I ever heard use the "F" word'.[10] Pauline would never have done that. 'She said it so naturally it didn't sound dirty,' Jack remarked. (By now he was embarrassed to be called by his 'baby' name of Bumby.)

Gregory loved the way she tossed her hair. 'It wasn't unlike a filly in a pasture tossing her mane,' he recalled.[11] He also liked how she threw her head back and laughed. At such times she was more of a sister than a mother to him.

Martha enjoyed children more when they were beyond the baby stage. She once chuckled, 'There's no need to have a child when you can buy one. That's what I did.'[12] Hemingway chided, 'You write about them so well and so poignantly [but you] don't give a goddam about them.'[13] Books fulfilled her more than pregnancies. She said of *For Whom the Bell Tolls*, '[Ernest's] brand new book is something wonderful. Probably better than looking at a brand new child.'

Martha was annoyed by many of Hemingway's habits. He allowed foul-smelling tomcats to roam around the house—including on the tables. She finally had them neutered. He saw this as a symbolic castration of himself.[14] It was an ironic commentary on their bed-life. That soon went the way the one with Pauline had.

Her journalistic career continued to flourish as Hemingway's one went into abeyance. In time, he began to feel like an appendage to her. When he first got to know her, he said, 'I knew she collected things. She collected bric-a-brac, oriental rugs, paintings. It took me some time to realise I was part of the collection.'[15]

She became like a part-time wife to him, forever disappearing on assignments from *Collier's* to Europe and the Caribbean. 'What old Indian likes to lose his squaw with a hard winter coming on?' he asked.[16]

Martha would never be his 'squaw', as Scott Fitzgerald forewarned with his 'Pygmalion' reference. She told a journalist from *The Kansas City Times*, 'Right now I'm the war correspondent in the family.' Hemingway was incensed by the remark. During a row with her, he screamed, 'I'll show you, you conceited bitch. They'll be reading my stuff long after the worms have finished with you.'[17]

He sent her a telegram saying, 'Are you a war correspondent or my wife in bed?'[18] Following her return from a military assignment when she lay exhausted in bed, he did his best to prevent her sleeping. 'He kept waking me up,' she complained, 'to bully and mock me. My crime really was to have been at war when he hadn't.'[19]

He praised her in public but behind closed doors, she became 'The Enemy'. Patrick recalled, 'it was like the Crusades. He was Richard the Lionheart and my mother the woman left behind in the castle with the chastity belt.'

Often he was the one left behind. 'I need a wife,' he moaned, 'and preferably not in the most widely circulated magazines.'

Martha's fiction was as annoying to him as her journalism. He wanted her to publish her stories under the name Martha Hemingway. She refused. But anything she published after she married him invoked the Hemingway name somewhere in the reviews. Their marriage became like two ships passing in the night. It was like a steamer and a dinghy that wanted to be another steamer.

She stopped joining him in his pursuits. In the early days of their relationship, she used to enjoy being on the *Pilar*. That was all over now. If he brought her out on it, she became bored. As soon as he docked anywhere, she immediately hired a car to get back to the house.

One day when he was driving her home, she accused him of being drunk. She took the wheel instead. He flew into a rage, slapping her with the back of his hand. She retaliated by crashing the car into a tree. He had to walk home.

His lack of hygiene became a major bone of contention for her. She accused him of smelling as bad as the cats. He countered by saying she was trying to run the Finca like a hospital her father might have worked in.

They invited different kinds of guests to the Finca. 'Her *Time* friends,' he blasted, 'came down to play pity-pat tennis dressed in pressed flannels. My pelota friends also played, but they played rough. They used to jump into the pool without showering. They said only fairies took showers.'

She took to calling him 'Pig' when he came in from the *Pilar* smelling of fish. He sat around all day in the grubby clothes he wore at sea. Frequently he 'forgot' to wash or shave.

It was relatively easy to renovate the house. Improving the man in it was another story. She used to enjoy trudging through the mud of Spain's foothills with him. It was less fun seeing him bringing muddy boots into the kitchen of their home.

Martha was the only one of his wives who criticised his writing. Though she went into ecstasies about *For Whom the Bell Tolls* when he first showed her drafts of it, she found much of it trite. When she said as much to him, it proved to be yet another excuse for him to vent his rage. Literary critics, he thought, were bad enough in the media. Having one living under the same roof as him was too much.

He thought their relationship could have been saved by her having a child by him. Sadly, the idea held little interest for her. She lacked a maternal instinct. Books were her substitutes for children. Literary creation was better than procreation as far as she was concerned. Writers were spared the hassle of getting up in the middle of the night to feed a book. There were rumours that conception would have been difficult for her due to complications from an abortion she had years before. Martha said these were untrue, that she did actually become pregnant by Hemingway once but aborted the baby.

Like Brett Ashley in *The Sun Also Rises*, she disparaged the idea of being 'one of those bitches that ruin children'. She preferred ready-made families like Hemingway had. Children that were already raised required less effort than ones you conceived. This was one of the reasons she bonded with Patrick and Gregory so well. The fact that she was closer to them in age than they were with Hemingway's previous wives also helped.

Hemingway was older than Martha by as many years as Hadley had been older than him. That thought made him feel ancient. He told himself he could never match her enthusiasm for life. Feeling older than his years, he wanted to be cossetted by a woman. She would have been ideal for him in Paris in the '20s or even Key West in the '30s. Maybe that was his tragedy. He wanted someone with Martha's zest when he was married to Hadley. Now that he had that woman, he longed for the care Hadley could have provided.

They argued with one another like two cocks. She described him as a cobra, never knowing when his temper was going to erupt. He said she gave as good as she got. His hangers-on enjoyed his boorishness, or at least put up with it, but he got under Martha's skin when he became pompous. Her fuse was almost as short as his own. They were like two pieces of metal scraping against one another.

There were times when the marriage descended into farce. One day after she was away for a few months on assignments, he drew up a contract for her that suggested she devote herself to him body and soul like some kind of feudal chattel. 'I, the undersigned,' it went, 'hereby guarantee and promise never to brutalise my present and future husband in any way whatsoever, neither with weapons nor pointed instruments nor words, nor uncalculated sudden phrases nor looks. I recognise that a very fine and sensitive writer cannot be left alone two months and sixteen days.'[20]

Addressed to 'Mrs Martha or Mrs Fathouse Pig' and witnessed by two judges, 'R. R. Rabbit and P. O. Pig', it was like something he might have written for the magazine he contributed to in high school. Gellhorn just shook her head when she read it.

America entered the Second World War after Japan invaded Pearl Harbor in 1941. Hemingway, as always when war loomed, decided he wanted to be part of it. He thought it could be like 1918 for him all over again. He may have been forty-two years of age, but the lust for action was still alive in him. He went to the US Embassy for permission to turn the *Pilar* into a submarine chaser.

He armed it with machine guns, hand grenades, bazookas. The idea was that he would locate enemy submarines and try to lure them to the surface. Then he would either explode them by flinging grenades down the spouts or ram them with the boat. The embassy, amazingly, bought the idea.

He continued such intelligence activities through 1942 and 1943 with commendable enthusiasm despite failing to locate any enemy vessels. He was reported to have sighted one on a certain occasion but it was going too fast for him to close in on it.[21] All of these escapades were like an effort to recapture the glory of 1918. Patrick described them as 'surreal'.

Patrick had been a prisoner of war in 1942 after being wounded in the arm during a reconnaissance mission in France. That was actual combat. This, on the contrary, was make-believe.

Patrick and Gregory enjoyed being part of what Hemingway referred to as his 'Crook Factory'.[22] Patrick described it as 'the last really great time we all had together'.[23] They joined Hemingway's drinking friends in his mirage pursuits of the enemy during their summers in Havana without passing any judgment on him.

Martha was different. She accused him of gallivanting across the Gulf Stream with 'some over-the-hill jai-alai players who have more guts than brains' while preserving the illusion that he was doing something noble for the war effort. The fact of the matter, she told him, was that he was wasting scarce government-issued gasoline.[24]

He told her he would have the last laugh on her when he sank a U-boat. She asked him how he planned to do that. He said if he got close enough to one, he could hurl a grenade into the open hatch of its conning tower. She pointed out that the tower of a U-boat was higher than the bridge of the *Pilar*.

'What if you miss?' she asked. If that happened, the grenade would most likely end up blowing the *Pilar* to smithereens.

'Don't you think I know the realities of war?' he replied. He reminded her that he was hit by 237 pieces of shrapnel in 1918.

'If your bomb misses,' she pointed out, 'There'll be more than 237 pieces of shrapnel in you. There'll be 237 pieces of you floating around the ocean.'[25]

Such sarcasm cut him to the quick. He was used to being the authority on such matters. 'Kitten,' he harumphed, 'You need a vacation.'

He started contributing articles to *Collier's*. His motive was obvious. This was Martha's outlet rather than his. He was basically saying to the editor, 'Either her or me.' There was only going to be one winner in that scenario.

For Whom the Bell Tolls was made into a film in 1943. Hemingway received $100,000 for the deal. 'Rather a long cry from his poor rooms over the sawmill in Paris,' F. Scott Fitzgerald remarked when he heard the news. He saw Hemingway as having sold out to commercialism. 'Do you remember,' he wrote to Zelda, 'how superior he used to be about sales?' (He meant superior in the sense of not caring about them.)

Hemingway wrote to Charles Scribner in February 1940: 'I have to write to be happy whether I get paid for it or not. It's a hell of a disease to be born with. I like to do it, which is even worse. That makes it from a disease into a vice. Then I want to do it better than anybody has ever done it, which makes it into an obsession.'

Now, it appeared, he was compromising. The fee for the film was the most money he ever earned. Cynical about films of his books up to now, he hoped this one would reverse that trend.

Gary Cooper played Robert Jordan. Both Hemingway and Gellhorn were instrumental in getting Ingrid Bergman cast in the role of Maria. Gellhorn had met her on a ship going from Genoa to New York. When she mentioned her to Hemingway, he was all ears. He became entranced with her after meeting her, telling her, 'If you don't act in the picture, I won't work on it.'[26]

Another actress, a dancer called Vera Zorina, had been selected originally. She was on the set for three weeks before being dropped. 'She's a lovely dancer,' Hemingway allowed, 'but she has a face like a dachshund.'[27] Bergman thought she would be too 'Nordic' for Maria. Hemingway told her not to worry about that. He had encountered many blonde Spaniards in his time. The only concern he had was that she would have good ears. Maria's hair had to be short as it has been shorn by rapists in the book.

Bergman displayed her ears to Hemingway when she met him. To his relief, he saw that they were fine.[28]

Many people felt Bergman was too glamorous for the role. Hemingway had to agree. He fell out of contact with her after the film came out. His silence spoke volumes to her about his views on it. 'When he didn't call,' she sighed, 'I knew it wasn't a good sign. He never mentioned my performance.'[29]

Her idealised nature clashed with the rest of the guerillas. So did the romantic element of the film in general. Critics chortled over the earth moving under the sleeping bag in the novel. On celluloid they had even more fuel for their misgivings. Bergman's beauty, as predicted, became a target for the critics. 'Miss Bergman,' one reviewer wrote, 'weeps convincingly but after nine months in a mountain cave she looks as if she'd just been voted the prettiest polo player in Pennsylvania.'[30]

Hemingway also had problems with the dialogue in the film. The guerrillas were given words like 'assassin' and 'treachery', which, he pointed out, were hardly in a peasant's vocabulary. And they wore long moustaches. These were Hollywood affectations rather than depictions of Spanish styles. He even found their bandannas too gaudy. And one of the characters in the film (Rinaldo) spoke Italian rather than Spanish.

He flew to England without Martha the following year in advance of D-Day. She wanted to go with him. He said, 'The plane doesn't allow women.' This was a lie. Gertrude Lawrence and Beatrice Lillie were on his flight. She ended up having to go by freighter.

When she got to London, she learned that he was involved in a car accident. After a party in the home of his photographer friend Robert Capa, he took a lift back to his hotel room from a man who had been with him at the party. Both of them had been drinking heavily. It was three in the morning and the streets were black. The car crashed into a steel water tank. Hemingway was thrown against the windscreen and knocked out. Both of his knees were injured. He also had a gash across his scalp that needed fifty-seven stitches.

When he woke from his operation, there was a nurse standing by his bed. She was far from pretty, but he still found himself kissing her. 'I've always found being in hospital romantic,' he exclaimed, evoking echoes of his 1918 experience with Agnes von Kurowsky.

Leicester visited him. Hemingway always tried to say something kooky to his younger brother. 'Took my pulse this morning,' he announced, 'just by listening.'

Martha visited him too. She failed to take his injuries as seriously as she should have. A bandage the doctors had placed around his head made her laugh. 'It looks like a turban,' she observed.

Hemingway was shocked at her frivolousness. He was in a lot of pain. She thought he was exaggerating this. She felt he was partly to blame for what happened to him. 'You took a lift from a drunk man,' she snorted.

He was partying a lot at this time. Gellhorn spotted a number of whiskey bottles under his bed. He was ordered not to drink because of his concussion. Hemingway never heeded instructions like that.

After he was released from hospital, he went to Normandy, finding himself a place on a military vessel in advance of D-Day. When the day arrived, however, like all the other war correspondents, he was refused permission to go ashore.

Gellhorn found a way around this stipulation by hiding on board a Red Cross hospital ship. She locked herself in a latrine, staying hidden until the ship docked at the beachhead. She then stole a medical auxiliary's uniform. With this on her, it was relatively easy to pose as a stretcher-bearer.

When she got ashore, she helped the wounded. Hemingway was reduced to watching the action from a distance. He was furious that she upstaged him. It could have been his finest hour. Instead he was just a spectator.

Gellhorn was the only woman to land on the beach that day. The deception she employed was like something Hemingway himself might have pulled off as a young man. Maybe that was why he found it difficult to forgive her for it. She out-Hemingwayed him.

By way of consolation, he became an honorific captain of a unit of Resistance fighters in France. He mixed his drinks in this guise, becoming part soldier and part war correspondent. Carrying weapons as a correspondent was against the Geneva Convention. He was hauled up for a military interrogation by George Patton's inspector general. Some of the reporters attending it accused him of overstepping his status as a journalist. They had damning facts at their disposal. The most serious charge was that he took command of the French Resistance forces at Rambouillet—a bridge too far by any estimation.

He was undaunted by the charges. Maybe he was even flattered by them. Just as he warmed his hands at a military fire in 1918 by getting into the action under the wire in a civilian guise, so also did he repeat the trick here. He lived most of his life so far with a gun in one hand and a pen in the other. Why stop now?

In the course of the interrogation, the reporters told him they saw rifles and maps in his room. They even saw hand grenades, and they had heard him addressed as 'Colonel' on patrol.

If he was found guilty, he was informed, he would be expelled from France and lose his accreditation as a correspondent. He took this possibility seriously. The situation was ironic. In 1918, he was accused of pretending to be a soldier without being one; now he was pretending not to be one when he was.

He was solid in his defence of himself. The address of 'Colonel', he explained, was a gesture of affection rather than anything else. The arms were stored in his room for soldier friends of his rather than for himself. The maps were for non-military use.

Such arguments were all false. He was perjuring himself, going through the motions of a hearing that came about for no better reason than to pacify the 'complainers'. Nobody expected a guilty verdict, especially since he was so good at defending himself by bending the facts. Two officers on Patton's staff even advised him to perjure himself.

He was acquitted. The charm of the old rascal worked a treat. 'I beat the rap,' he beamed to Buck Lanham.

Soon afterwards he stood at Lanham's side as he won a landmark battle against the Germans in Hürtgen Forest. This was as close as he got to the heat of real battle. He conducted himself well here, showing both bravery and humour as the Nazis were routed despite having caused over 3,000 American casualties. Afterwards he travelled back to the Ritz Hotel in Paris. He had 'liberated' it sometime previously—by pointing people the way to the bar.

The war was nearing its end now. So was his marriage to Martha. When he met her in France that Christmas, their reunion was a disaster. He drank too much. She became furious with him as a result. One night he confronted her outside their hotel room with a chambermaid's bucket over his head. It was meant to be a helmet. He was pretending to be a soldier. The chambermaid's mop deputised as a lance. He proceeded to 'attack' Martha. She found herself yawning. 'Go away,' she droned, 'you drunk.'[31]

They traded insults like two second-rate comedians. He accused her of having had affairs with generals, of marrying him to advance her social and literary standing. She retaliated by saying he was one of the cruellest men she ever met. She said she had more of a social conscience than him, that she went on assignments to do something about injustice. He went on them just to write books.

She had a point. The young Hemingway was an assiduous reporter who flushed out buffoons like Mussolini. A few years after Martha met him, he became jaded. 'Ernest's commitment to the Spanish Civil War was the last time he cared about anything beyond himself,' she sighed.

On 22 November 1945, the day after their fifth wedding anniversary, she filed for divorce from him. 'I'm having my passport changed back to Gellhorn,' she threatened, 'I want to get out of the whole picture fast.'

He charged her with abandoning him. Under Cuban law, this meant he was entitled to everything they owned. He interpreted it to the letter, laying claim to everything from her typewriter to a pair of cashmere underpants he once bought her as a present.

The pair of them had sputtered on for five years before the inevitable meltdown. They spent less than half that time together. His reaction to their parting was typically eccentric: 'I hate to lose anyone who can look so lovely and who we [*sic*] taught to shoot and write as well.'

He was more emotional after his previous marriages broke up. Hadley's love had been pure. Pauline's ran hot and cold, but the split from her still cut deep with him. The one from Martha merely left him feeling blank.

'I made a very great mistake with her,' he wrote to Patrick, 'or else she changed very much. I think probably both—but mostly the latter. I am sick of her Prima Donna-ism.' For his next wife, he told his son, 'I'm going to get me somebody who wants to stick around with me and let me be the writer of the family.'

His previous wives had 'stuck around' through thick and thin. It was unthinkable that a woman would walk out on the great Ernest Hemingway. Unthinkable to the world and unthinkable to Hemingway. But the Squaw managed it. She dealt a severe blow to that gargantuan ego.

After he left Pauline, he said, 'Those that live by the sword must die by the sword.'[32] Now those words were coming back to haunt him. If Hadley was too old for him when he met Pauline, now he was too old for Martha. What goes around comes around.

As well as feeling betrayed that she left him, he was also 'damned lonely'. How could he be lonely for someone he hated? More likely he was angry. This seems obvious from the fact that he sued her for desertion, going into every nook and cranny of the aforementioned Cuban Law. By invoking it, Hemingway discovered that he could demand $500 from her bank account, her shotgun, her typewriter, her tennis racquet, and, bizarrely, her 'long underwear'.[33]

After the conditions were finalised, Martha and himself badmouthed one another both in print and verbally, each claiming the other got the thin end of the wedge. 'A man must be a very great genius,' Martha huffed, 'to make up for being such a loathsome human being.'[34] Hemingway had more to lose by the bad press generated by the divorce. He described marrying Martha as the biggest mistake of his life.[35]

As was the case with Pauline, the best times he had with her were before they married. It was the forbidden fruit that enticed. He had been happily sleeping with her for years before they tied the knot. Once they did that, carnage ensued.

They spent less than half their married life together. What time they shared was often contentious, a war of words on both sides.

Martha had no interest in hearing anything about Hemingway after they split up. She skimmed through newspaper articles about him with a vague curiosity. Most of them only confirmed what she knew—that he was declining both physically and artistically.

The more his writing disimproved, she noticed, the more extravagant his defences of it became. This was pitiable to her. She thanked her lucky stars she got out of the marriage when she was still young enough to explore life away from him.

Her time with him soured her feelings about marriage in general. She came to believe that bickering couples could improve things between them 'if they shot one another'.

She told Hemingway's biographer Jeffrey Meyers that after she left him she found it difficult to think of him without getting stomach pains.

14
Pocket Rubens

Hemingway met Mary Welsh, the woman who would become the fourth Mrs Hemingway, during his time in London. Shortly after meeting her, he told her he wanted to marry her. 'That's fine,' she said, 'but there's one slight problem. Both of us are already married.' Her husband was Noel Monks, an Australian reporter for the *Daily Mail*.

The serial monogamy he practised all his life continued with Mary. 'When I was young I never wanted to get married,' he revealed, 'but after I did I could never be without a wife again.' He slept with her while he was still married to Martha just as he slept with Pauline while still married to Hadley.

He once said the reason he never cheated on Hadley before Pauline was because of the lack of a need to. He may have slept with Duff Twysden if she was interested. His infidelities were hardly as plentiful as they were for other famous people who were handsome and who believed in indulging their instincts. Jane Mason was one of the few mistresses he had while he was married to Pauline. If Mason was more balanced, he might have married her too. 'He always marries the women he sleeps with,' William Faulkner noted. It was generally true. Martha filled a gap for him when Mason went out of his life. Mary now did so in the absence of Martha.

When Scott Fitzgerald observed that Hemingway needed a new woman for each book, he was only partly right. It would be truer to say he needed a new woman for each war. Agnes fulfilled that function for the First World War and Martha for the Spanish Civil War. Both Martha and Mary fulfilled it for the Second World War. Love and war inspired him in similar ways. Maybe it was all part of the one strain.

He kept a photograph of Martha on his desk at the Finca during his marriage to Mary. 'It's for the boys' sake,' he explained when she asked him about it. It sounded as if he was still carrying a torch for her.

'I cannot help wondering,' she accused, 'whether or not you kept pictures of Pauline around for the sake of the children when Marty was here.'[1] He had no answer for that.

Mary felt he carried a bigger torch for Pauline than for Martha. One night as he outlined all her good points, she said, 'You must still be attached to her. You're a bloody fool not to go back to her. You could start again where you left off. Your children would have their own mother instead of a phony. I'm easily disposable.' Her self-deprecation failed to sway him. 'We made too many cruelties to each other,' he explained, 'We couldn't erase them.'[2]

Mary ticked all his boxes at the beginning of their marriage. He said of her, 'She is an excellent fisherwoman, a fair wing shot, a strong swimmer, a really good cook, a good judge of wine, an excellent gardener, an amateur astronomer, a student of art, political economy, Swahili, French and Italian, and can run a boat or a household in Spanish.' He called her his 'pocket Rubens'.[3] She referred to herself as 'the short, happy wife of Mr McPapa'.

She was half Irish and half German. 'That,' said Hemingway, 'makes for a merciless cross and a lovely woman.' The 'lovely woman' was also subjugated to his wishes. In all his marriages, he was so determined not to become a henpecked husband like his father that he went to the other extreme. He told Mary what food to buy, what jobs to do around the house, what meals to prepare. If he disapproved of something she cooked, he threw it on the floor.

He lost his temper with her in public, prompting people to predict the marriage would be over within the year. He told a friend of his one day that he wanted to give her the clap. She responded by telling him Irwin Shaw had a bigger penis than him.[4] Mary had slept with Shaw in the past. She complained:

> Whatever else the critics say about Ernest, they're certainly right about him and women. He wants them like Indian girls, completely obedient and sexually loose. That I think I might learn to handle but the long intelligent speeches about the inadvisability or expense of something.... After about 5 samples in one day I get that smothered feeling. I wish the hell I were out of here and running my own household and my own life with no dictatorship. This is like being a high-priced whore.

Marlene Dietrich thought it was a marriage built on 'shifting sand'. That was an understatement. They fought like cats and dogs. Most mornings, Mary wrote in her autobiography, Hemingway woke up 'cheerful and with budding plans', but breakfasts of Scotch and champagne quickly turned Dr Jekyll into Mr Hyde. 'I feel more like his sparring partner than his bride,' she sniffed. Clearly, not too much had changed since the Martha days.

In April 1946, Mary faced a new kind of threat when 'Slim' Hawks entered his life. The attractive wife of the film director Howard Hawks, she later married Leland Hayward, the man who produced *The Old Man and the Sea.*

Mary hated her and the feeling was mutual. She described Mary as 'a fidgety hen of a woman, always scurrying around doing needless things that she thought made her indispensable'. Hemingway enjoyed flirting with her to annoy Mary.

He celebrated his forty-seventh birthday on the *Pilar* with a few friends, afterwards inviting them back to the Finca for drinks. A birthday letter from his mother informed him that she was vacationing at Walloon Lake with Marcelline and her family.

Windemere, she told him, was in a dilapidated condition now. Mice had gnawed holes everywhere and the roof and floor were rotted. People in the surrounding area called it 'The Haunted House'.

A week later he learned that Gertrude Stein had died of cancer. Another link to the past was gone. Stein had maligned him in her autobiography. He resolved to get her back one day. (He would do that in *A Moveable Feast.*)

He showed his best side the following month when Mary almost died. She was pregnant at the time. Both of them were hoping for a daughter. She woke on the morning of 19 August with a crippling pain in her stomach. It was so bad he called for an ambulance.

The surgeon on duty diagnosed her as haemorrhaging from a ruptured fallopian tube. It was what was called a tubular pregnancy. The egg was fertilised in the tube instead of the uterus.

Her regular obstetrician was away on a fishing trip at the time. She hovered on the brink of death. Her pulse faded and she lost consciousness. The substitute surgeon told Hemingway there was no hope. He advised him to take his final leave of her.

He was unwilling to do that. Knowing a little about medicine from having watched his father deliver babies as a boy, he advised the surgeon to probe for a vein.

Directing him from the door of the operating theatre, he told him to open the vein and inject blood into it.[5] Four bottles of plasma and two blood transfusions later, Mary's pulse returned to normal. He had saved her, as she put it, 'from Boot Hill'. But he still regretted the death of the baby. 'It would,' he said cruelly, 'have taken the taste of Gregory out of my mouth.' He had been angry with Gregory for some time now.

He was severely disappointed not to have the daughter he always craved. It was ironic that he saved his wife's life shortly after a possible one perished. (Nobody knew the gender of the baby.)

Mark Hellinger directed *The Killers* that year. Hemingway liked it even though Hellinger used less than five minutes of his dialogue in it.[6] He admired it so much he said he was thinking of rewriting it as a novel.[7] Hellinger gave Hemingway the print. He often showed it to guests at the Finca on his projector.

Gregory and Patrick were involved in a car crash in the spring of 1947. Gregory was driving but Patrick was more seriously injured. He hit his head off the dashboard and suffered a concussion as a result. If he went to bed after it, he may have been all right. Instead he played six sets of tennis. He was bedridden for sixty-four days, having to be fed rectally for forty-five of these.[8]

Pauline and Mary became unlikely friends at this time. Mary's father was undergoing surgery in Chicago and she had to be with him. Pauline was recruited to help nurse Patrick until she came back. She put her bitterness with Hemingway behind her to deal with the situation.

She spent the summer flying back and forth between Key West and Cuba as Patrick recuperated. When Mary returned from Chicago, she came down with flu. Hemingway was afraid of getting it from her. Pauline then came up with a suggestion. Why not have Mary go to Key West and leave Hemingway with Patrick?

Hemingway disapproved of the relationship that developed between the two women as a result. He imagined the two of them giving out about him to one another and he was right. Pauline vented about Hemingway to Mary in a way she was never able to before. Hemingway came to resent her presence in Havana. This was especially the case when it interfered with Mary accompanying him on fishing trips. He brought her to Italy the following September to get her away from Pauline, staying there for the next eight months.

Maxwell Perkins died of pneumonia later that year. It was another shot across the bows for Hemingway. 'We understood each other so well,' he pined, 'It was like having a part of myself die.'

Perkins had been his 'go to' person in publishing for so many years. He probably wrote more letters to him than anyone else he knew. Perkins had great patience with Hemingway's tantrums over publishing deals, none of which ever seemed to his satisfaction. Now he would have nobody to complain to about 'the writing racket'.

Charles Scribner put his son, also called Charles, into Perkins' position. Hemingway wrote to Charles Snr about Perkins' workaholic nature. 'Using up all his resistance,' he said, 'by not taking some lay-offs to build up is a good lesson to the rest of us.' He became closer to Scribner now. 'Don't you get to overworking,' he said to him, 'at least until young Charlie gets to know the business. I want to be able to see your alcohol-ravaged face when I come into the office for at least the next twenty years to help me feel someone in N.Y. has a worse hangover than I have.'

He was spending a lot of time in Ketchum now. He loved hunting there in the fall. That year he stayed there with Mary until Christmas. Gary Cooper and Ingrid Bergman joined them. It was the first time he saw Bergman since the filming of *For Whom the Bell Tolls.*

Hemingway always enjoyed seeing Bergman. His disappointment over that film was a distant memory now. 'The Swede', as he called her, lifted his spirits, both in person and in her films. Jack recalled an episode where he watched *Casablanca* with him one time when he was suffering from depression. The pair of them shot buzzards from the rooftop of the Finca with generous helpings of martini and then went in to look at the film. It reminded him of *To Have and Have Not* because of Humphrey Bogart being in it.

Hemingway was still calling Jack 'Bumby' at this time even though he was a grown man. Jack objected to this. 'I tried to give him the message by naming my dog Bumby,' he laughed, 'but he still persisted.'

Hemingway's anger with Mary grew worse. Everything she did seemed to ignite it. On one occasion, he called her 'a goddam smirking useless female correspondent'.[9] He became physically violent with her as well, slapping her one day for no reason. She was shocked to see him doing that. Maybe he was too. Violence towards women was unusual for him. She called him 'a poor fat feather-headed coward'. Afterwards the two of them laughed about the incident. Humour was always Mary's trump card in situations like that.

She had great resilience, rolling with the punches no matter how bad things became between them. Hemingway was left in little doubt that she was determined to go the distance with him. One day she said to him, 'Try as you might to goad me to leave you, you're not going to succeed.

No matter what you do—short of killing me, which would be messy—I'm going to stay and run your house until the day when you come here, sober, in the morning, and tell me truthfully and straight that you want me to leave.'[10]

She entered the marriage with an inferiority complex. Because of not being able to give him children she felt she had to try harder to please him in every other way she could think of.

She did her best to relax him when he was stressed. He became particularly so in 1949 when he received a demand from Pauline for $3,000 from a royalty statement of $7,271. 'Not a bad take,' he grunted, 'for a woman you slept with last in 1937.'[11] 'When I die,' he told a reporter sometime later, 'it will be from writing cheques.'[12]

Mary worried about other women taking Hemingway from her. She dyed her hair blonde to try and make herself more attractive to him. This was an effort to make it resemble Slim Hayward's.[13] The colour change was reminiscent of Pauline's after she became threatened by Martha.

She did everything she could think of to make the marriage better. She swam daily. She passed pleasing comments about Hemingway's writing. She manicured his hands and feet. She went to Spanish classes. She learned how to fire a 20-gauge shotgun.

Even so, he continued to behave boorishly. One night he boasted to Buck Lanham about his past sexual conquests in front of her. She showed no reaction. What would have been the point? She was married to a man who delighted in embarrassing her.

The older he got, the more he seemed to need to boast about his *machismo*. He reached the age of fifty in July 1949. On his birthday he wrote to Charles Scribner, 'I fucked three times today, shot ten pigeons, drank with five friends and searched the ocean for big fish all afternoon.'[14] The only part of that sentence that rings true is the one about drinking.

Mary visited her parents in Chicago that September. In her absence, Hemingway invited a seventeen-year-old prostitute called Xenophobia into the Finca to keep him company. It was hardly the first time he recruited the services of ladies of the night. 'Whores are more emotionally trustworthy than other women,' he insisted, 'especially about money.'

Xenophobia's 'madam' was a woman called Leopoldina. She had a good sense of humour, telling Hemingway one time that her favourite book of his was one called *Too Many Short Stories*. She entertained him over a number of visits when feelings of isolation got too much for him. He said to Peter Viertel, 'Had hoped to be a good boy but this is hard when one is a lonesome character.'

Roberto Herrera took photographs of the two of them to keep as mementoes. Mary saw them and blew a fuse. Xenophobia had different clothes in them. To her, this was evidence that she was in the habit of spending a lot of time with him. Another woman would have walked out. She stayed.

By now Hemingway was on the ropes artistically, having published nothing of note for nearly ten years. Depression was also starting to become a problem. He wrote a letter to Lillian Ross that year in which he confided that after taking a dive off the *Pilar* some time before, he was tempted to let the air out of his lungs when he was under the water. The title character in Jack London's *Martin Eden*, a book he admired, had done that. The only reason he came back up was because of his sons.

His mood lifted when he started working on a new book. It was a love story set in Venice. He wrote to Buck Lanham in September to tell him he left his heart there, 'and I haven't been able to find the son of a bitch ever since.'

The 'heart' ache was because of a woman called Adriana Ivancich. She was only nineteen years of age, the youngest daughter of an aristocratic Italian family.

He fell in love with her almost as soon as he met her. It was at a duck-shooting event in Latisana in Northern Italy. The weather was rainy. She was drying her hair at a fire. He was always attracted to women's hair—the auburn of Hadley, Pauline's bob, Martha's curls. In *A Farewell to Arms*, Frederic Henry says of Catherine, 'I loved to take her hair down. I would take out the pins and lay them on the sheet of the bed. It would be loose and it would all come down and she would drop her head and we would both be inside it.'

When Ivancich told him she had no comb, he broke his own one in half and handed it to her. The gesture led to a friendship that lasted over many years.

Sadly for Hemingway, it never went further than that. He was far too old for her. And he was married. She was also closely protected by her family.

Ivancich had a beauty that you had to look twice to see. There was a kind of inaccessibility about her that enthralled him, a Mona Lisa coyness. She was like a Renaissance painting, he enthused, a porcelain model come to life. For a man undergoing a kind of male menopause, she was like a fantasy. Each of his wives had been progressively younger than the last. Adriana was thirty-one years younger than him, putting her more into the daughter mould.

The fact that he never had a daughter of his own led him to gather around him a crew of adoptive ones over the years. Ava Gardner fulfilled that role for a time. So did Ingrid Bergman and Marlene Dietrich. Now Adriana was doing it. She was born in 1930, the same year as Gregory. Hemingway said to her one night, 'He could have been you.'

When he got to know her better, she filled him in on her history. Her family had suffered great losses in the war. Their estate had been burned and her father murdered. Her brother, Gianfranco, had also been wounded.

Hemingway wrote over sixty letters to her over the next few years. They were characterised by the kind of schmaltz he could never have abided in his books. In one of them, he wrote, 'When I am away from you I feel as though I were exiled from my country.'[15] He signed another one 'Hemingstein-Ivancich'.

He asked her to design the dust jacket for his new novel, one he was going to call *Across the River and Into the Trees*. It dealt with a character called Robert Cantwell. He was a colonel with a heart complaint—in all senses—who falls in love with a young girl called Renata. She was obviously based on Adriana just as Cantwell was on Hemingway. Once again Scott Fitzgerald's dictum held true about him needing a new woman for every book. And the corollary: a new war as well. This time it was the Second World War.

The title was a paraphrase of Stonewall Jackson's dying words.[16] Renata's name translates into English as 'reborn'. The symbolism was obvious. Cantwell's heart is about to give up. The novel chronicles his last three days. Once again, as in *For Whom the Bell Tolls*, time is compressed. He seeks a rebirth—or rather a stay of execution—through love.

Mary was worried about Hemingway making a fool of himself with Ivancich. She saw his fascination with her as an attempt to try and become Cantwell in real life. The inverse was closer to the truth. The relationship between Cantwell and Renata came about because of his fascination with Ivancich.

It was hopeless to imagine he had a chance of becoming intimate with her. He said to her on one occasion, 'I would ask you to marry me if I didn't know that you would say no.' The fact that their relationship was platonic enabled him to romanticise Renata more than he might otherwise have done. It was reminiscent of Agnes von Kurowsky's refusal to sleep with him after his Fossalta wounding.

In *Across the River and Into the Trees* we see evidence of a style of writing infatuated with its own excesses. The reticence of the early stories is replaced by bluster. This is one of the reasons he failed to finish so many books in the last ten years of his life. Some of the writing he did at this time reads like bad imitations of him done by others.

Mary found the book dire but refrained from telling Hemingway this. 'I kept my mouth shut,' she said, 'Nobody appointed me my husband's editor or the bombardier of his self-confidence.'[17] She kept her fingers crossed that someone at Scribner's would tell him it needed major surgery. Wallace Meyer, the editor who had been dealing with him since Maxwell Perkins died, saw the weaknesses in it but stopped short of pointing them out to him. How could he? Hemingway was the firm's most lucrative author.

Adriana was braver. She told him she found Renata boring, that she just sat around all day listening to the colonel's stories. This was true. The book is little more than a series of soliloquies from Cantwell, briefly interrupted by platitudes from her.

Renata was also an inconsistent character, Adriana pointed out. No Mass-going Venetian girl having recently left a convent would be as promiscuous as she, or drink like she does.[18]

Adriana, like Agnes, saw Hemingway as immature. Not much had changed between Milan and Venice, between the adolescent and the middle-aged man. Denied physical love, he consummated his passion on the pages of his books instead.

He tried to buy Adriana's love by offering to let her design his book. She had ambitions to be an artist but her talent was limited. Hemingway strong-armed Maxwell Perkins into accepting her design. It was so poor it had to be re-done by the in-house artists in Scribner's.

When Hemingway met Adriana's brother, Gianfranco, he became almost as fond of him as he was of her. He was walking along a street with her when he first saw him. Gianfranco had a limp. 'He walks like an Indian,' Hemingway observed, 'I like that.'

After he got to know him, he showered him with favours. He gave him a free run of his house in Cuba and offered him money to buy a house of his own as well. The fact that he was wounded as a soldier—he fought for Italy under Rommel in North Africa—endeared him to him.

Though Adriana was flattered by the way he fawned over her, she made it clear early on that things would go no further than that. Hemingway seemed content with this. He had the relationship on such an idealistic footing, maybe he felt a carnal element would spoil it.

Dora, Adriana's mother, complained about an ageing married man spending so much time with her daughter. She accepted him seeing her now and again, but when it became an everyday occurrence, she grew worried.

Hemingway behaved like a child with Adriana. He engaged in juvenile talk with her that she only half-understood. She kissed him one day, afterwards telling him it was a mistake. 'If that's the case,' he countered, 'It's one I wish you would make more often.'

When Adriana cut her finger on the dorsal fin of a fish on the *Pilar* one day, Hemingway knelt before her and sucked the blood out of it. Mary was there at the time. She became so disgusted she had to turn her face away and go to another part of the boat.[19] She knew there was 'no fool like an old fool' but hardly felt it was her business to tell him so. She doubted that any 'cautionary phrases' of hers could stop him drooling over her.[20] Adriana knew she had only to flick her fingers and Hemingway would leave Mary for her.

He went to the Bahamas in the summer of 1949. Mary went to Paris with Patrick and Gregory. They visited Hadley during the trip, finding her to be as ladylike as she always was, despite all that had happened between herself and Hemingway. From there she went to Venice to see Adriana, staying in Europe while the boys went back to college.

Hemingway, meanwhile, finished his novel, imagining it to be one of his best.

His radar was seriously on the blink. *Across the River and Into the Trees* is a banal book, as Mary noticed.[21] For a writer who once said prose should be like architecture, it was an embarrassment. One can only understand his lapse on the grounds that he was writing it as a valentine to Adriana. 'It nearly kills me every time I read it,' he told her, 'and I have read it now 200 times.'[22]

Most of what we get is a clapped-out character mainlining on reminiscences about ducks and sausages. It resembles a pulp version of Thomas Mann's *Death in Venice*, a meretricious example of Hemingway being 'lulled and dulled by the fable of himself', as one critic expressed it.[23] The sleeping bag of *For Whom the Bell Tolls* is replaced by a US Army blanket for the climatic love scene and is almost as farcical.

This is emotion recollected in pedantry. Cantwell is a broken record as he reminisces in his buffoonish manner over his past. How did Hemingway not see this? 'I have moved through arithmetic,' he pronounced, 'through plane geometry and algebra and now I am in calculus.'[24] He often told people he was looking for the 'fourth dimension' in writing.[25] This composition, sadly, was more like a child's abacus.

Everything is treated like a military operation: shooting duck, eating, even making love. Reaching for a bottle of champagne has to be done 'accurately and well' by the bumptious Cantwell. Digesting a good lobster becomes as important as storming a beach head. Is it possible to take a man like this seriously? He even keeps his flanks covered in the bar: his last battle zone. E. B. White wrote a satire of it called *Across the Street and Into the Grill.*

Love always clouded Hemingway's artistic judgement. We saw it with Catherine Barkley in *A Farewell to Arms* and Maria in *For Whom the Bell Tolls.* He got away with it in these books because they were so well crafted otherwise. This one lacked such craft, which means its weaknesses are thrown into high relief.

The most impressive character in it is neither Adriana nor Cantwell but the city of Venice. Hemingway describes it with the reverence he once showed for Paris. 'It's my city,' he rhapsodised, 'I fought for it when I was a boy.' The inhabitants knew that: 'Now that I am half a hundred years old they treat me very well.'

If *A Farewell to Arms* was Hemingway's *Hamlet*, *Across the River and Into the Trees* was a stab at *Lear* that goes from pathos to bathos. John Dos Passos, normally a man sympathetic to Hemingway, wrote, 'How can a man in his senses leave such bullshit on the page?'[26]

Tennessee Williams predicted that the book would be disliked by the critics but popular with readers and he was right. Despite its crucial lambasting, it sold well. It was surprising that readers who grew up on Hemingway's great novels could have accepted it. If Maxwell Perkins was alive he would never have allowed the sloppy prose on view here to pass his eagle eye unedited. His demise gave Hemingway the freedom to rant.

Cantwell is really talking to himself in the book rather than to Renata. Her interjections of 'Go on, please' and 'Tell it to me,' etc. are little more than jaded attempts by Hemingway to inject an illusion of dialogue into the proceedings. Dutiful promptings give his lapidary reminiscences a cosmetic justification. As is the case in *For Whom the Bell Tolls*, a woman acts as the pupil to Cantwell's teacher. In the earlier novel, Maria performed the function a lot less consciously because there was so much plot. We only get the bones of one here.

War was an important backdrop to *A Farewell to Arms* and *For Whom the Bell Tolls.* In *Across the River and Into the Trees*, the action is recounted rather than enacted. To quote Shakespeare, 'Aye, there's the rub.' The book is reflective of Hemingway's lack of involvement in the Second World War. Did we have the right to expect a great war book from him since his participation in it was so marginal? Hardly.

He defended the book resolutely against infinitely superior war novels like James Jones's *From Here to Eternity* and Irwin Shaw's *The Young*

Lions. Hemingway had problems with Shaw. The fact that he had a relationship with Mary before he met her was partly responsible for them. He liked him even less when he found a character based on him in his novel. Shaw had portrayed him as a short, fat, heavy drinking correspondent from *Collier's* in *The Young Lions*. There was also a character based on Mary in the book. She was described as having 'a deft, tricky way with men'.[27]

When Hemingway invited Mary to dinner, Shaw thought he was muscling in on his scene. Hemingway may well have been spoiling for a fight. If Martha committed a 'crime', as she put it, for having been at war when Hemingway was not, Shaw committed one by writing a book about a war Hemingway regarded as his personal property.

He started telling people he was going to punch Shaw on the nose the next time he saw him. A few weeks afterwards he was sitting in a hotel with Harold Ross, the editor of the *New Yorker*, when Shaw appeared in front of him. 'I heard you were going to punch me in the nose the next time you saw me,' Shaw taunted, 'Well here I am.' Hemingway was too drunk to fight at the time. Instead he started insulting Shaw, calling him 'The Brooklyn Tolstoy'.[28] He apologised to Mary for his outburst the following morning.

Why was he so critical of *From Here to Eternity*? He told Charles Scribner it was 'an enormously skilful fuck-up'. He was probably threatened by Jones. He witnessed the raid on Pearl Harbor, so was well qualified to write his book. He also saw active service in Guadalcanal, having been wounded by Japanese mortar fire there.

'Things will catch up with him,' Hemingway predicted, 'and he'll probably commit suicide. Hope he kills himself soon so it will not damage your sales. Make all the money you can out of him as quickly as you can and hold enough for a Christian burial.'[29]

He was even more vicious about him in a letter he wrote to Maxwell Perkins, saying, 'If you give him a literary tea you might ask him to drain a bucket of snot and then suck the puss out of a dead nigger's ear.' In an age before political correctness, he blithely used terms like this ('Wop' was another favourite) without fear of redress.

He was similarly dismissive of Norman Mailer's war novel *The Naked and The Dead*, describing it as 'Crap.'[30] Mailer sent an inscribed copy of a subsequent novel, *The Deer Park*, to him years later hoping he could give it a puff. The book was accompanied by a defensive note from him saying, 'If you think this is crap, fuck you'—a classic case of biting the hand you hope will feed you before you know what it might do.

Hemingway never got this delivery, but one day he bought a copy of *The Deer Park* in a shop. It did even less for him than *The Naked and the Dead*. All the more surprising, then, that Gregory said his father once gave this tribute to him:

> Mailer's probably the best post-war writer. He's a psycho, but the psycho part is the most interesting thing about him. Chances are he won't be able to throw another fit like *The Naked and the Dead*. If he does, I better watch out. There'll be another Dostoevsky to contend with and no one lasted more than three rounds with Mr Dostoevsky.[31]

This contrasts dramatically with his earlier description of the novel as 'poor cheese pretentiously wrapped' and 'verbal diarrhoea'. Did Gregory fabricate the kinder quote to please Mailer? Possibly. They became friends after his father died. Mailer even wrote the preface to a memoir of Gregory's, thereby 'fasten[ing] onto the son after he failed to meet the father'.[32]

Hemingway had been a role model for Mailer like so many others when he was growing up. After he went to Harvard, his worship of him amounted to something of an obsession. He fought like him, drank like him, tried to write like him, and became combative in the same way. Both of them also had many wives. They personified the idea of 'The Writer as Personality'. In both their cases, early success with war books spoiled them, making them create personas that eventually became like albatrosses round their necks.

In the introduction to *Advertisements for Myself*, a book Hemingway described as 'a ragtag assembly of ramblings, shot through with occasional brilliance', Mailer wrote: 'Every American writer who takes himself to be both major and macho must sooner or later give a faena which borrows from the self-love of a Hemingway style.' Such self-love was everywhere in *Across the River and Into the Trees*.

Hemingway insisted that its Italian translation be delayed. There were many rumours about his relationship with Adriana in the Italian press. He tried to avoid adding fuel to the flame by having it available to buy over there. Dora was relieved. She felt her daughter's reputation would be disgraced if it was.

The American press lionised the book. Martha Gellhorn felt sick after reading it. Part of that sickness was at Cantwell's self-righteousness. This, of course, was Hemingway's too. 'He will go on always feeling misunderstood,' she contended, 'always feeling everything is someone else's fault. I think he'll end up in the nut house.'[33] This was strong language. Maybe Martha had an extra motive in being so aggressive as Hemingway takes a sideswipe at her in the book at one point, saying of a character based on her, 'She had more ambition than Napoleon and about the talent of the average High School valedictorian.'[34]

Despite the rumours about his relationship with Adriana that were flying around the place when the book came out, he still invited herself and Dora to be his house guests in Cuba. Mary was livid when she heard about this. She accused him of drooling over her like 'a pimply adolescent'. He responded by throwing his typewriter on the floor and flinging wine in her face.

She got revenge on him by flirting with Gianfranco one day during the visit. This incensed him further. He reached for his rifle and shot a lamp on the veranda of the house. He then threatened to shoot Gianfranco. 'I know I'm a son of a bitch,' he told Harvey Breit, 'I can't help it.' Mary tried to stay out of his way as much as she could. At the end of the visit, she drove Dora and Adriana around Florida to show them the sights. They spent a few nights in the Ambos Mundos hotel and also visited New Orleans before making their way back to Venice.

Left on his own without Mary, Hemingway became lonely. It was often the way with him, bursts of temper being followed by remorse and self-recrimination. He threw himself into 'the Cuban fisherman book' to take his mind off himself. This was *The Old Man and the Sea*. 'Am in the very toughest part of the story,' he wrote to Mary, 'He has the fish now and is on the way in [but] the first shark has shown up.'

He showed an unsavoury side of himself again later that year when Xenophobia made a reappearance on the *Pilar*. Most men hide their infidelities, but Hemingway seemed to enjoy confronting his wives with his lovers. It was a practice that went all the way back to his honeymoon with Hadley when he brought her to Petoskey to meet the objects of his adolescent desires.

By now Mary had had enough. 'As soon as it is possible for me to move out,' she threatened, 'I will. In 1944 in bed at the Ritz Hotel in Paris I thought you were a straight and honourable and brave man and magnetically endearing to me. I believed in you.' That belief was now gone, she informed him: 'Both privately and in public you have insulted me and my dignity as a human being. You have debased my pride.' It sounded like the end, but Hemingway prevailed on her to stay.

Lillian Ross wrote a profile of him the following month in *The New Yorker*. It was subsequently published in book form. Hemingway had mixed feelings about it. It confirmed many peoples' views of him as an irascible old coot. In the course of it, he declaimed hyperbolically on life, love, and the whole damn thing. He drank, philosophised, said 'How do you like it now, gentlemen?' an inordinate number of times to people (without explaining to them what 'it' meant), and spoke at length about defending his 'title' against the young pretenders of the writing trade.

He told Ross that you had to act pompous to be taken seriously as a writer. He hated arrogance but he also hated being trivialised. Putting on a pose was the lesser of two evils.

Ross caught him off-guard in the profile. Her insights into him were all the more valuable for that. She also caught him at a time when he was taking a break from work. That meant he was more likely to sound off at length on non-literary matters. He left himself open in a way he rarely did before or after.

In some ways it was an unbalanced portrait. Hemingway was a severe disciplinarian at his typewriter. Off-duty, as we have seen so many times, he could be a pain in the neck. That was fine for those who knew him. His charm overrode it. But the profile was being read by people who had no acquaintance with him.

Ross admired him a lot. That was probably the reason she felt comfortable portraying him as a scoundrel. He makes an exhibition of himself at two main stages in the book—at New York Airport and afterwards in a cocktail lounge where he rants like a pub bore.

This is a domesticated Hemingway, far from faenas and Indian camps and the deep blue ocean. We see him buying a coat, turning down the offer of attending a boxing match, being proud of his slim waist, going a few metaphorical rounds with Chekhov and Co.

He liked the piece when he saw it in proof form, but after it appeared on the shelves people told him he was 'ruined' because of it. At this point, he suffered a sea-change in his attitude. 'I like Lillian,' he assured, 'We're good friends. But it's like being good friends with a circular saw.'[35]

The timing of the profile probably explained why his critics were so vicious over *Across the River and Into the Trees*. They identified Colonel Cantwell with the Hemingway who spoke to Ross like 'a half-breed Choctaw'. These were his own words.

She saw her piece as a Rorschach test.[36] Dwight MacDonald thought it glorified a 'grotesque philistine'.[37] Arnold Gingrich said Ross saw 'the emperor's bare behind while everyone else was oohing and aahing over the cut of his clothes'.

Hemingway stayed friends with Ross all his life. He also wrote her many letters. In one of them he said, her profile made him 'as many enemies as we have in North Korea. But who gives a shit.'[38]

15

The Explainers

Hemingway always hated what he called 'The Explainers'.[1] These were the people who tried to tell him what his books were about. Frequently they were the people least equipped to do so.

He had a particular problem with a Yale lecturer called Charles Fenton. At the time Ross did her profile of him, Fenton was digging up his past for a proposed tell-all biography.

Hemingway warned him off the project. He said nobody had a right to investigate his life in Oak Park because he never wrote about it himself. 'I had a wonderful novel about Oak Park,' he said in 1952, 'The reason I didn't write it was because I didn't want to hurt living people.'[2] He continued, 'I don't think a man should make money out of his father shooting himself or out of his mother who drove him to it.'

Anyone who has read his work closely, of course, would realise that he never stopped writing about Oak Park. He may not have mentioned it by name, but it was implicit in almost all the early stories. One of the reasons he refrained from direct autobiographical writing was because he knew it would leave him open to people like Fenton drawing false conclusions. 'If you tell these people the truth about anything,' he said, 'they reject it for anything more sensational.'

Biographers were starting to become more like detectives than scholars. He steered them away from investigating his youth. When there was a suggestion that his mother was being sought for an interview by a journalist from *McCalls* magazine, he threatened to withdraw her allowance if she broke silence.[3]

The situation was ironic. She spent most of her life asking her son not to delve into sensitive personal areas. Now he was muzzling her. Ever since he heard she sold some of his high school writings, he distrusted her. It was time for *omerta*, a Mafia-style silence.

He asked her to forward him some photograph albums she had. They had pictures of him in the effeminate pink dresses he loathed so much. The timing of his request was significant. It hinted at a fear of her blowing his macho image for keeps. Thankfully such an eventuality was avoided. The photos were burned.

He told Malcolm Cowley: 'I truly think that we suffer in our times from an exaggerated emphasis on personality. I would much rather have my work discussed than my life. Criticism is getting all mixed up with a combination of the Junior FBI men and a sort of columnist peephole and missing laundry list school.'

Hemingway became more worried about Fenton when he started quizzing Marcelline and Carol about his past. He even contacted Dorothy Connable, the daughter of the couple he stayed with in Toronto all those years ago. This was strictly off-limits. It marked the turning point in his relationship with him. From here on in, it was 'Cease and desist' time.[4] He advised Connable not to speak to Fenton under any circumstances. He told her he even copyrighted his Toronto articles so Fenton could be kept away from them.

He scolded Fenton saying, 'I would no more do a thing like that to you than I would cheat a man at cards or rifle his desk or wastebasket or read his personal letters.' He was fed up of authors trying to dig under his fingernails. It was enough 'to disgust a guy to the point of tickling his own throat and making him vomit'.

Fenton eventually got the message. He apologised for badgering him. When his book appeared on the shelves, however, it suffered from Hemingway having denied him so much potential material. All one got of him was an author gleaned from quotes and actions rather than anything more cerebral.

Fenton's life ended dramatically when he committed suicide some years later, jumping out a hotel window for reasons that were never explained. Hemingway mused, 'I wonder what he thought about on the way down.'

He made up a jingle about people of Fenton's ilk afterwards:

Sing a song of critics
Pockets full of lie
Four and twenty critics
Hope that you will die.[5]

He saw them as people who looked for meanings in books that were mostly made up by themselves. 'The way things are going,' he predicted, 'pretty soon there will be no writers. The critics will go to the coast to try and write the way the writers have done but they will not be able to do it. Then the motion pictures will die.'[6] When he heard someone was giving lectures on *A Farewell to Arms*, he said he thought it would be fun to walk into the university and ask a few questions about it incognito. Then he could reveal himself and say to the lecturer, 'Shit, sir, I do believe you are mistaken.'[7]

He baulked at the notion that there was symbolism in his work. If the 'explainers' wanted to look for things like that they were welcome to do so. They should remember, however, that a book was only as good or bad as the readers it found. He refused to run 'guided tours' through the more obscure territory of his work.[8]

'Symbols shouldn't be thought of before a book is written,' he believed, 'If they are they stick out like raisins in raisin bread. Raisin bread is all right but plain bread is better.'[9] When he learned that a course in Princeton had him as its subject, he said to Jack, 'If I could disguise myself as a student and attend that course incognito I'd bet anything I wouldn't pass it.'[10] If there had to be criticism, he thought, it should only be of the famous dead. That way, academics would be prevented from interfering with the creative process.

He said to Maxwell Perkins once, 'There are a lot of critics out there who really seem to hate me very much and would like to put me out of business. Don't think I mean it conceitedly when I say that a lot of it is jealousy. I do what they'd like to do and I do what they're afraid to do and they hate me for it.' He added wryly, 'Sometimes I find out what I'm supposed to mean when I read the books on my work.'

As well as Fenton, at this time he was being plagued by another biographer called Philip Young. Young's main thesis was that he never recovered from the trauma of Fossalta. He believed such a trauma was evident in almost everything he wrote afterwards. Hemingway hated this kind of thinking. 'Sure, plenty trauma in 1918,' he said, 'but symptoms absent by 1928. None in Spain in 1937 or 38. None in China in 40 or 41. None at sea, none in air. None in 155 days of combat. I suppose when Archie Moore loses his legs, P. Young will diagnose him as a victim of trauma.'[11]

It seemed to him that any kind of argument was accepted in the current climate of exegesis: 'All these guys have theories and try to fit you into them.' They were like sparrows chasing after carthorses for droppings.

Young also promulgated the theory that Hemingway was suffering from 'repetition compulsion.' He argued that he could only exorcise his war wound demons by acting them out again and again in what he called 'staged circumstances'. This argument gains credence from the fact that he spent most of his life entering situations of danger. Was he trying to expiate his pain by exposing himself to scenarios that would help him to re-experience it and thus transcend it? It was also possible that he put himself into these situations in order to steel himself against the fear of death.

A psychiatrist called Irvin Yalom came up with yet another theory: i.e. that Hemingway's virile pursuits resulted from an over-reaction to his parent's stuffiness. He was trying to create a heroic alter ego, Yalom contended, but could never live up to it.

Mary was as phlegmatic as her husband about these theories. 'Everybody,' she huffed, 'and his brother and cousin and uncle and aunt all think they're the definitive authorities on Ernest.'

Hemingway vowed to do everything he could to block the publication of Young's book. Despite this, he decided to press ahead anyway, with or without his blessing. The absence of such a blessing, as was the case with Fenton, meant he could quote him only in paraphrase. He told Hemingway this would be a disappointment to readers.

He was using psychology here. The comment appealed to Hemingway's vanity. He later heard Young had been wounded in war. No more than with Gianfranco Ivancich, such an event proved to be a game-changer for him. He did an about-turn, allowing Young to go ahead after all.[12] He even offered to lend him money.[13] Young had mentioned being in debt in another example of throwing himself at the author's mercy.

A Princeton professor called Carlos Baker was also in communication with Hemingway at this time. It was to do with a proposed biography of him. Baker, he knew, was different to Fenton. Neither was he a Philip Young. He felt he could trust him to give a balanced perspective of his life, so he agreed to the book.

He outlined the topics he wanted Baker to avoid: 'The suicide of my father, Pauline moving in on Hadley, *coitus interruptus*, Martha moving in on Pauline, and whores and nice girls until I run into Mary.' Baker got the message. He promised to focus on his writings as much as his life. This relaxed Hemingway hugely. He pleased him even more by enthusing about *Across the River and Into the Trees*. He was almost in a minority of one among critics in this respect.

This was a busy time for Hemingway. By now both *The Short Happy Life of Francis Macomber* and *The Snows of Kilimanjaro* had been made into films. Gregory Peck played Walden in *The Snows of Kilimanjaro*. Ava Gardner starred opposite him. Hemingway dubbed it '*The Snows of Zanuck*'.[14]

It was directed by Darryl F. Zanuck, a man who 'Hollywoodised' it too much according to Hemingway. 'He made one minor alteration to the story,' he denounced, 'in letting Walden live.' He was being sarcastic. By minor he meant major. As far as he was concerned, that was like Shakespeare letting Hamlet or Lear live—or Catherine Barkley in *A Farewell to Arms*.

He said to Leicester, 'Now all we need is for some Hollywood gag writer to take that poor bloody Colonel Cantwell out of the back of his Buick and let him hike to Venice down the middle of the Grand Canal and into Harry's bar dry-shod. They'll probably call it *Across the Selznick and Into the Zanuck*.'[15]

Hemingway had been instrumental in Gardner being in the film, having phoned Zanuck personally from Cuba to secure her.[16] When it turned out so badly he regretted this. He said to Gardner in pained tones after he watched it, 'The only good things about it were you and the hyena.' She refrained from telling him the latter was a dubbed human voice.

The ending was treacly. Planes rescue Walden. It was typical Tinseltown sanitisation. One was reminded of the proposed finale of *The Sun Also Rises* where the sun was supposed to light up the screen during the final scene between Jake and Brett.

The film made from *The Short Happy Life of Francis Macomber* was called *The Macomber Affair*. Starring Gregory Peck again, this time he had Joan Bennett as his co-star. The poster screamed, 'Gregory Peck Makes That Hemingway Kind of Love To Joan Bennett!' For those who could have been forgiven for asking what, exactly, was 'that Hemingway kind of love', we were informed that it was 'Love like the lash of a whip.'[17] He took all this in his stride, adopting a take-the-money-and-run attitude to the film as he did to most of the adaptations of his work. A print was sent to the Finca. He fell asleep watching it.[18]

Another problem was bothering him now. He was satirised by John Dos Passos in his *roman à clef*, *Chosen Country*. Dos Passos featured him as an overbearing character called George Elbert Warner. Hemingway saw it as revenge for his own caricaturing of Dos Passos as Richard Gordon in *To Have and Have Not* some years previously. The reasons for that are hazy. Jealousy was the most frequently ascribed motive. Dos Passos had started to outstrip Hemingway in his work by then and Hemingway was hurting. Dos Passos was even on the cover of *Time* magazine in 1936.

Hemingway believed he got the material for *Chosen Country* from things said to him in the past by his wife, Katy, whom Hemingway knew long before he did. 'He takes badly remembered anecdotes,' he snarled, 'and fouls them up.'

Katy had died four years previously, having almost been decapitated in a car accident. Hemingway blamed Dos Passos for her death, He was driving the car. His vision had been impaired by the sun shining in his eyes just before the accident. He crashed into a parked truck. Katy was thrown through the windscreen. He lost an eye himself. Thereafter Hemingway referred to him as 'that one-eyed Portuguese bastard'.[19] He had Portuguese blood and was born out of wedlock. 'He killed her off,' he fumed, 'and now he's stealing my material.'[20]

Hemingway's mother died later that year. Her life had been full. She even learned to drive at one stage, going on trips to places as far afield as Nantucket and California. She painted the scenes she saw around her on easels she placed in front of her on the steering wheel, the windows of the car closed to keep mosquitoes out. When she reached her sixties, she became a lecturer, giving talks all over the country on history and art. She used her paintings as the background to them. One of her landscapes fetched $1,000, a huge sum at the time. She gave her last exhibition at the age of seventy-seven.[21] A formidable figure even at that age, she was once listed in the *Who's Who of American Art.*

She developed dementia in her last years after an accident in a nursing home. It was due to the negligence of an attendant when she was in her wheelchair. She received a blow to the back of her head.[22] Afterwards she slipped in and out of lucidity. Sunny took care of her. Some days she said she was like a child, playing hide-and-seek with her. Other times she played difficult piano pieces from memory.

Hemingway never lost his hatred of her. He only allowed her to visit him once after he moved to Key West. That was in 1938. She stayed in a hotel rather than at his house. He was working on *For Whom the Bell Tolls* at the time. She said she hoped the book would be 'constructive, for a change'. Even at sixty-six, she was able to deliver one of her familiar barbs. Any chance she might have had of reconciling with him was killed off by the comment. When she was there, Hemingway wrote a passage into the book blaming her for the death of his father.

She stayed for six days. This was mainly to get to know her grandsons. The last time she saw Patrick, he was a toddler. Gregory she had never seen at all. At one point of her visit, she gave Patrick a penknife. She claimed it belonged to his grandfather. This was a lie. Patrick recognised it as a trinket from a local dime store. In that moment, any credibility she might have had for him disappeared. He joined his father in his disdain for her. This was sad. Hemingway had starved her of their company over the years. She entered the house like royalty, according to one of Hemingway's biographers.[23] Now she was reduced to the role of a lonely old woman telling a petty lie.[24]

Hemingway's feelings were mixed when he heard of her passing. 'I don't believe she had the grace of a happy death,' he surmised, not realising he was making a pun. He allowed himself a moment to remember how beautiful she was when she was young. He had 'the bells toll' in his local church to commemorate her. A few hours later, however, he was refusing to go to her funeral. 'The coffin might be booby-trapped,' he suggested.[25] Such a comment says more about his neurosis than anything Grace had ever done to him in the years of their *mesalliance.*

No matter how far he travelled around the world, her presence continued to haunt him. His father died when he was a relatively young man. Grace outlived him by over twenty years. Why was it not the other way round? He harboured suspicions about women right through his life as a result of her influence on him. Such suspicions were partly assuaged by Hadley but reinforced by his subsequent wives. He called her 'the All-American bitch' to people behind her back, but his letters to her right up to the day she died are polite. He never fully expressed his anger towards her after those early altercations in Oak Park and at Lake Walloon, letting it fester inside him like a character in one of his stories. That made it worse.

Pauline also died in 1951. It was from an aneurysm. For years she had high blood pressure. It was caused by an undiagnosed adrenal tumour. Her death was accelerated by an incident that occurred shortly beforehand involving Gregory. He had been arrested for entering the toilet of a cinema in Los Angeles in women's clothing. Cross-dressing had been a penchant of his for years. He was recently married and due to become a father in a few months.

Pauline visited him in the jail. Gregory thought she looked terrible. This was due to a pain in her stomach. She employed a lawyer who said he would do everything he could to keep the incident out of the papers.

She told Gregory she was going to tell Hemingway about it. He begged her not to, but she thought it was the best thing to do. Hemingway had berated her in the past for keeping things from him. She was staying in Jinny's house at the time. Jinny was living with a violinist called Laura Archera. She had been lesbian for some years now. As long ago as 1937, she tried to seduce Jane Mason in Mexico.[26]

Pauline phoned Hemingway as soon as she got back to the house. The call became heated. He grew enraged after she told him what happened. His roars thundered down the phone. 'You're to blame for the way Gregory turned out,' he fumed. Pauline started roaring back at him. Then she broke down. She went to bed after putting down the phone.

Later in the night she woke up. The pain in her stomach that she first experienced at the jail was now excruciating. She went into Jinny's bedroom to tell her about it. Both Jinny and Archera realised the gravity of the situation. They decided to drive her to the local hospital to find out what was causing it.

After she was seen by a medical team they realised how ill she was. She was operated on by the emergency staff. One of her blood vessels ruptured during the operation, causing a violent reaction in her system. She died from shock.

Everyone was incredulous. Pauline was still a relatively young woman. There was nothing in her medical history to indicate anything was wrong with her. Had the argument with Hemingway been responsible for her going into shock? Nobody could say for sure.

She was denied a funeral Mass in her local church because of her divorce from Hemingway. The church also forbade her body to be put in a Catholic cemetery. Jinny decided to bury her in Hollywood Memorial Park Cemetery instead. It was beside Paramount Studios. She was laid to rest beside famous people like Tyrone Power and Cecil B. DeMille. No headstone was placed on her grave. Her grandson saw this as the result of her children not being bothered to erect one.[27] It was a sad end for someone who was once the toast of Paris. In her Key West years, she was more noted for being married to Hemingway. The following day's newspaper had the headline, 'Hemingway's Second Wife Dies in Hospital'.[28] Even in death she had to play second fiddle to him.

Hemingway was unusually quiet when he heard about her death. He refused to accept responsibility for it but deep down he must have known that his argument with her was a contributory factor. Mary expressed her grief more volubly, her recent closeness to Pauline making her feel emotional about what had happened. When a cable arrived from Jinny to say she died, Mary ran down to her rose garden 'to try to find some sort of stability to contain this unexpected blow'. Pauline, she remarked, was 'an accidental friend to me, both generous and loving. I would miss her for a long time.'[29]

She was nonplussed by Hemingway's under-reaction to the tragedy. 'How can you be so cold?' she snapped at him. In retaliation he spat in her face.

His real feelings were expressed in a letter he sent to Charles Scribner sometime afterwards. 'The wave of remembering has finally risen,' he wrote, 'so that it has broken over the jetty that I built to protect the open roadstead of my heart. I have the full sorrow of her death with all the harbour scum of what caused it. I loved her very much for many years and the hell with her faults.'

The 'harbour scum' was a reference to Gregory's arrest. He continued to badger him about this in subsequent phone calls. Gregory held to his belief that Hemingway was responsible for Pauline's death.[30] His attitude led to an irrevocable split between them.

A few months after the funeral, Gregory showed up at the Finca with his wife, Jane, and new baby, Lorian. He married Jane in a hurry after she became pregnant by him. Towards the end of the visit he said of his arrest, 'It wasn't too bad.' The opportunity was there for Hemingway to mend fences, but he refused to. Instead he replied, 'No? Well it killed Mother.'[31]

Hemingway had been against Gregory marrying Jane. He even threatened to disinherit him if he went ahead with it. He thought he was too young to marry.

'You're only doing it,' he said to him on a phone call sometime before, 'because Jane is pregnant.' Gregory exploded with rage at Hemingway's accusation. He tore strips off his father. It was like a precursor of the call between Hemingway and Pauline on the night Pauline died. Hemingway told Gregory he was crazy at the end of it. Gregory retaliated by saying he was ashamed to carry the Hemingway name.

Hemingway refused to attend his wedding in protest. Neither had he attended those of Jack or Patrick. Pauline was furious with him. 'How can you behave so badly about the women your sons marry?' she remonstrated at the time, 'They've had to take four wives of yours. I think they've been damned cooperative about it.'

Gregory wrote a scurrilous letter to his father in 1952 outlining all his grievances with him. He called him 'a gin-soaked monster' in one part of it. When his life story was told, he predicted, biographers would say he wrote a few good books but that he destroyed five people's lives. He was referring to Hadley, Pauline, Martha, Patrick, and himself.

'God damn you,' he rasped at him for the things he did to Pauline. Pauline once told Gregory that when he came home from the Spanish Civil War in the '30s she met him at the boat. She tried to put her arms around her, but he brushed her aside, making for his luggage instead.

'You accused me of killing her,' he wrote. Afterwards he gave him some medical advice: 'For your information, a heart attack is incurred over a period of time.' Of Mary, he wrote, 'She's taken more shit from you than they dump in Havana harbour.'[32] 'If I ever meet you again,' he said at the end of the letter, 'I'll beat your head into the ground and mix it with cement to make outhouses.'[33] One day soon afterwards he ran into a Borders bookstore and pulled all Hemingway's books off the shelves. He wrote his own name on the title pages over his father's one.[34]

The latter action points to some jealousy on Gregory's part, a resentment of his father coming out as anger. It recalls an incident of years before when he was a schoolboy. On that occasion he passed off a story by Turgenev as his own. He changed the words slightly to fool his teachers.[35] Hemingway was fooled too. It was years later when he learned of the deception. He always hated plagiarists. Now he had one in his own family.

Gregory spent the rest of the '50s in a fog of booze and unemployment. He squandered his inheritance from Pauline on safaris. Hemingway funded some of them but then became tired of his extravagance, writing him business-like letters similar to the ones he wrote to his mother when he thought she was shelling out too much money on her cottage on Lake Walloon.

Gregory once boasted of having killed eighteen elephants in a month.[36] No matter how much cross-dressing he did, he still had some of the Hemingway bravado in him. He later admitted this was a lie.[37]

Of Hemingway's literary aspirations for the future, he fumed:

> You'll never write another great novel because you're a sick man—sick in the head and too fucking proud and scared to admit it. There's nothing I'd rather see than you acting intelligently but until you do I'm going to give you just what you deserve, and in extra large handfuls to make up for all the trouble you've caused me.

Gregory subsequently went back to university to study medicine. He thought it would please Hemingway because of his own father having been a doctor but nothing he could do at this stage, it appeared, would please him.

'I doubt you'll have much success in your chosen profession,' he wrote when Gregory told him he was applying to medical school, 'I see you've mis-spelled the word "medicine" in your application.' This was rich coming from such a terrible speller as himself. A later letter was more amusing. 'The deterioration in your spelling,' he wrote to his son, 'is a very alarming symtom [*sic*] of your condition.'

He continued to blame Gregory for Pauline's death. Hemingway always had to scapegoat people for events. His mother was the cause of his father's suicide. Pauline stole him from Hadley. Martha stole him from Pauline. And so on. Much of this was the result of an over-active imagination. Writers are sometimes described by people as 'licensed liars'. Fiction was often a euphemism for mendacity in Hemingway's case.

When Gregory was in medical school he sent for the autopsy report on his mother's death. It said the tumour she had in her adrenal gland caused her blood pressure to soar on the night she died as a result of her emotional upset. Then it dropped to nothing, causing the shock that killed her. This linked the argument with Hemingway to her death. Gregory sent the report to him. Hemingway was enraged when he got it. Then he went quiet.[38] That was usually how he reacted when he felt guilty about something.

Pauline left nothing to Hemingway in her will. Everything went to her sons. He did, however, succeed in cajoling from them the original manuscript of *A Farewell to Arms*. The fact that they were now independent of him changed their relationship to him. There was no need to be deferential to him anymore.

Jinny adopted children in the '50s. It was unusual for a single woman to do this at the time. She said she needed to fill the gap in her life left by the death of Pauline. Her parents were also dead by now and so was Gus. Both she and Laura Archera later became friendly with the writer Aldous Huxley and his wife, Maria.

When Maria died of cancer in 1954, Archera married Aldous. They moved into a house near Jinny and continued their friendship with her. There was a fire in Jinny's house in 1961 which destroyed, among other things, all of Hemingway's letters to her. Huxley died on 22 November 1963, the same day as John F. Kennedy's assassination. Archera remained friends with Jinny afterwards.

Jinny never married, her suspicion about Hemingway's mercenary motive in marrying Pauline souring her attitude to men in general. Hemingway always defended himself on this charge, insisting that the original manuscripts of his 'big' novels, which he gave to Gus as gifts, aptly compensated for his various generosities. Jinny died of cancer in 1973, having been fighting the disease for many years and surviving much longer than anyone expected.

Hemingway met Tennessee Williams at a party a few years after Pauline died. Williams asked him how it happened. He paused for a moment before saying, 'She died like everybody else and after that she was dead.'[39] It was like a sentence from one of his stories.

Charles Scribner died the following year. Maxwell Perkins had also died by now. So had Scott Fitzgerald, James Joyce, Katy Dos Passos, Gertrude Stein, Sherwood Anderson, and Archibald MacLeish. 'Writers are dying like flies,' was the way Hemingway put it.[40]

It was a lot of candles to light.

16

Back to Basics

'He was an old man who fished alone in a skiff in the Gulf Stream and he had gone eighty-four days now without taking a fish.' So Hemingway wrote on the opening page of *The Old Man and the Sea.* He was an old man himself now too.

He had written many books but they had not received the attention they deserved, especially the last one about a Colonel and a young woman. It was a true book, and one that was deeply felt, but the critics made fun of it. They made fun of it because they knew nothing about writing. He was hurt by their words, so much so that he was tempted to give it all up. But then he told himself it was not his way to give in. He decided that he would make one last attempt at a book. Maybe he could still summon the ability up to write 'the one true sentence.'

He started writing the story of a fisherman, a fisherman like one he had known once in another country many years ago. The memory had stayed with him. He knew that if he wrote it truly and well it would find its readers. He might be lucky again with the people who knew he had it in him to write a good book about the things that meant something to him even though he had many health problems now, and other problems too, with wives and his family and even his friends, or those who called themselves his friends.

He had gone 84 months without success. What chance was there for him with an old man who wanted to fight the moon and the stars? He was also fighting a fish that could pull him out farther than where he wanted to go, out to where the sharks were, sharks who could pick his bones clean, leaving him with nothing at the end of it except his dreams.

*****

Despite the vicious critical reception unleashed upon *Across the River and Into the Trees*, Hemingway galvanised himself for another literary surge. He wrote a book that, as he put it, 'would not go bad afterwards'. The simplicity of the title gave it all away: *The Old Man and the Sea.*

He wrote a synopsised version of the story in a 1936 work called *On the Blue Water*. Now, twenty years later, he took it to another level. Maybe the stories you carried round in your head, he thought, were better than the ones you actually wrote.

His hero, Santiago, is a bruised and battered soul. He fishes for marlin on a small boat as his assistant Manolin watches from the sidelines. He hooks the fish, but sharks eat it at the end, leaving him with nothing.

This idea could have been inspired by an incident in 1933 when Hemingway was fishing with his friend Mike Strater. Strater hooked a 12-foot marlin, but sharks were hovering nearby. Hemingway shot them with his Thompson submachine gun. This was ostensibly to 'save' the marlin, but their dead bodies attracted even more sharks, so his action was counterproductive. By the time Strater reeled in the fish, there was little of it left.[1] Maybe Hemingway shot the sharks because he was envious of Strater's catch and sought a way to destroy it.[2] Strater said he caught a big fish once in Bimini and Hemingway stood in front of him every time it was photographed as if to make out it was he who caught it.[3]

Hemingway was proud of his book. He looked forward to seeing how it would be perceived by the public. This time, he told Perkins, there was no need for disclaimers in the frontispiece. Sharks were unlikely to sue. He was tired of being threatened with legal suits from people who thought they recognised themselves in his books. The prototype for Santiago, he claimed, was Carlos Gutierrez. Gregorio Fuentes was another possible model for him.

Simplicity is the keynote of the book. We have a fisherman, a boat, a boy, a marlin, the sky, the sea, the sun, the moon, and the sharks. Hemingway always maintained that the test of a good story was what you left out rather than what you put in. Much is left out here.

It was twenty-seven years since Nick Adams fished the big two-hearted river. He was hardly recognisable in the Bible-spouting Santiago, but the same dynamic was at work, the same Emersonian struggle of man against the elements.

Hemingway's fans always felt he had one last great book in him no matter how many times he faltered, but who would have believed it was going to be such a small one? Every novel he ever wrote started out as a short story. This one stayed that way. Was it a long short story or a short novel? Who cared? It was a masterpiece.

He received over a hundred letters a day in fan mail. People warmed to the simplicity of the style. The dethroned heavyweight was having yet another shot at 'the title'.

The Old Man and the Sea had nothing startlingly new either in style or content, but it crystallised all his themes. Academics went overboard looking for symbols. They said Santiago was Hemingway. The marlin was his savaged books. The sharks were the critics.

He begged to disagree. As he wrote to Bernard Berenson: 'The sea is the sea. The old man is the old man. The boy is a boy and the fish is a fish. The sharks are all sharks. No better and no worse.'[4] No good book, he insisted, had symbols arrived at beforehand and stuck in. Only if they emerged in the process of the composition were they allowable.

He was returning to his minimalist roots at the age of fifty-three. Why had it taken him this long to leave out so much? It must have been a source of amusement to him, as it was to all his readers, that he had spent so many years looking for success through major projects and found it in a fragment.

The book could have been over a thousand pages long, he claimed, with a plethora of characters in it, including details of how they were born, educated, and bore children. That kind of thing had already been done excellently by other writers. He preferred to work by a process of exclusion.[5]

It was originally meant to be a part of a bigger opus, a trilogy that comprised manuscripts called *The Sea When Young*, *The Sea When Absent*, and *The Sea in Being*. Such titles went no further than the work-in-progress stage.

John Dos Passos had by now forgiven Hemingway for wrongs perpetrated against him in the past. He was generous in his praise of it. Its style was so clever, he said, 'I could hardly judge the story. It was like a magician's stunt. When he makes a girl float through the hoop you don't notice whether she's pretty or not.'

Gregory was vicious about the book. Still holding bitterness against his father, he said it was 'as sickly a bucket of sentimental slop as was ever scrubbed off the bar-room floor'.[6]

It ends sadly. The world breaks Santiago like it breaks all people, but he keeps himself 'strong at the broken places'. He lives to fight another day.

The Old Man and the Sea, once again, epitomised Hemingway's idea of life as a struggle nobody can win. The only pride to be gained is in giving in gallantly. It may be cold comfort but nothing else is available to us. To that extent, we should make a virtue out of necessity. Oak Park's self-confessed 'lousiest Catholic' is really outlining a 'vale of tears' *zeitgeist* here. One became purified by suffering.

Santiago's botched mission comes to us with messianic overtones. He resonates as a thinly disguised Christ figure crucified by the sharks. The only surprise is that he survives at the end. Mary was responsible for this. Hemingway originally intended to kill him off. She thought that would be too predictable a finale. The closing page, where he lies dreaming about the lions, is stronger as a result.

The book gave Hemingway his best notices for over a decade. Bernard Berenson said it was 'as unByronic and unMelvillian as Homer'. It netted him the Pulitzer Prize in 1952.

Its essential conundrum was encapsulated by Hemingway's biographer Kenneth Lynn. How was it, he wondered, that a book that 'lapses repeatedly into lachrymose sentimentality, and is relentlessly pseudo-Biblical, that mixes cute talk about baseball with crucifixion symbolism of the most appalling crudity, have evoked such a storm of applause from highbrows and middlebrows alike?'

One theory he propounded was that Hemingway's fans were rooting for him to write a decent book after the disaster of *Across the River and into the Trees*. Their generosity of spirit, he contended, was born as much from relief as adulation. He bathed in the glory of their renewed faith in him.

Shortly afterwards, however, disaster struck when he suffered back-to-back plane crashes. It had been the pattern so often in his life, euphoria followed by mishap.

He was on safari with Mary at the time. The first crash happened when they were on the way to see Victoria Falls. The pilot ran into a flight of ibis near the Belgian Congo. They forced him to dive. As he did so, he struck an abandoned telephone wire. In order to miss the birds, he knew, he had to either land on a sandspit where six crocodiles lay basking in the sun or on an elephant track through thick scrub. He opted for the latter.

Misfortune struck again two days later when another plane Hemingway was in caught fire on take-off. This time everyone was trapped inside, including himself and Mary.

She was small enough to fit out the front window. His own height came against him in this respect. The door beside him was also jammed shut. His right arm and shoulder were dislocated so were unusable to try and open it. He headbutted it instead, suffering a bad concussion as a result. It was the fifth major concussion of his life. He called it his 'coup de tete,' a pun on *coup d'état.*

When he woke up the next morning there was cerebral fluid leaking out of his head. It trickled down his face behind his ear and onto the pillowcase, mixing with caked blood. Outside the window there were hyenas howling as they smelt it. He was given primitive first aid in a local bar by a physician who poured gin into his skull fracture to prevent infection.[7]

Many other problems were caused by the crash. His sphincter was paralysed. He had double vision. He could only hear from one ear. He had multiple burns. Crushed vertebrae made his lower back feel as if he was being prodded by a hot poker. There was also damage to his kidneys and spleen. A doctor in Nairobi he told him it was a miracle he was still alive.

He appeared at a press conference a few days later, his head swathed in bandages. He was clutching a bottle of gin and a bunch of bananas. Gin was the last thing he should have had in his hand. Alcohol made his concussion worse.[8] He told reporters in his beloved quasi-Choctaw dialect, 'My luck, she is running good.'[9] The incident became the subject of Ogden Nash's poem, 'A Bunch of Grapes'. Afterwards it was made into a song sung by Jose Ferrar and Rosemary Clooney.

He played down the severity of his injuries. Between the two crashes, he told people, all he worried about was the fact that Mary's snoring was drawing an unusual amount of attention from a group of elephants that were hovering nearby.[10] He said they were as large as mountains. There were wild dogs around too. By making wild howls he was able to gauge their whereabouts.

Mary, he chuckled, had never seen a plane burn up: 'That's an impressive sight—especially when you're in the plane.'[11] Before she left it, he noticed, she took care to bring her vanity case with her. 'Never been in a crisis yet,' he informed Aaron Hotchner, 'that a woman forgot her jewels.'[12]

He should have rested afterwards. Instead he went fishing at a beach camp in Kenya with Mary and his safari guide, Philip Percival. When a bush fire broke out near their camp, he tried to fight it, but he was too weak. Mary was away from him at the time. In his clumsiness he tripped and fell into the flames, suffering severe burns on his legs, stomach, chest, arms, and legs. When she came back, she found him nursing patches of raw flesh. His hands, she said, looked like hamburgers.

He was presumed to be dead by anyone who heard about the crashes. A search plane had spotted the wreckage of the first plane and reported no sign of life.

Stories started to circulate. The most ridiculous one came from a German newspaper. It reported that Hemingway had crashed into Mount Kilimanjaro while searching for the frozen carcass of the leopard he immortalised in his story.[13]

He spent the next few weeks reading obituaries of himself in newspapers from around the world. Rumours of his death, he said *à la* Mark Twain, were exaggerated. Forest Lawn would have to wait a while yet.

Reading the obituaries, he confessed, became a 'a new and attractive vice' for him.[14] 'In most of them,' he noted, 'it was emphasised that I sought death all my life. Can one imagine that if a man did that, he could not have found her before the age of 54?'[15]

Other articles regurgitated the old chestnut about him wearing false hair on his chest or whistling in the dark to try to prove to himself that he was fearless. Some writers speculated that he was a lifetime coward who sought out all those death-defying situations to test himself.

Such theories he saw as simplistic. One could only be courageous, as he often pointed out, when fear was present. Cowardice should not be confused with panic.

The need to keep proving himself may have hinted at some inner insecurity but to call it a death wish was too strong. He never acted self-destructively in his daily life. If anything, he was over-careful about his health. His bathroom in Cuba was never painted, for instance, because he liked writing details of his blood pressure and weight changes on the walls. He also stored his urine and checked it periodically for purity. This was hardly suicidal behaviour.

The crashes meant he had to curtail his alcohol intake. Doctors kept booze away from him when he was in hospital and forbade him to indulge in it when they released him. The deprivation made him realise how much he needed it. Jack once said he drank a quart of whiskey almost every day for the last twenty years of his life. Most people failed to realise how much he was ingesting because of his high threshold of tolerance. Maybe Scott Fitzgerald was luckier when he passed out after a few glasses of wine.

He travelled to Europe two months after the second crash. In Venice, he again met Adriana. It was over three years since he saw her. That was, as he put it, 'twenty years too long'.

She wrote to him when he was in hospital. 'I didn't know I loved you,' she said, 'until I knew [*sic*] you were dead. I started crying and my heart was heavy like a stone. The only thing I could do was lie in my bed. I was too weak to get up. I looked at my face in the mirror and it wasn't any more my face.'

She sought his help in trying to get a book of her poems published. He told her they were very good but one wonders. His love goggles were probably on again.

That was the last time he saw her. It was an emotional farewell for him. 'Look, daughter,' he said as he pointed to his tears, 'You can now tell everybody that you have seen Ernest Hemingway cry.'[16]

Their relationship continued from a distance. He put money into a savings account for her and sent her regular transfers from it. When she asked him if he could afford this, he said, 'I have two rich sons, and I have just re-financed Bumby. You are my true and only daughter.'[17] He felt the inheritances Patrick and Gregory received from Pauline's estate freed him from any further responsibilities towards them.

Towards the end of the year, he was awarded the Nobel Prize. He cast scorn on the news, referring to it as the 'Ignoble Prize'. He said he always thought of it as 'Something you got when your beard was long and white and you needed to put your grandchildren through Devil's Island.'[18] Nobody who ever won it, he maintained, 'ever wrote anything worth reading afterwards'.[19]

When he said this, he was thinking of William Faulkner, the man he referred to as 'Corn-drinking Mellifluous'.[20] He claimed to always know when Faulkner had 'had one'.[21]

Faulkner won it in 1950. Hemingway sent him a cable of congratulations, but Faulkner failed to acknowledge it.[22] Hemingway's editor later asked him to review *The Old Man and the Sea*. Faulkner ignored the request, causing Hemingway to become outraged. He eventually did review it, saying in the course of the review that it was Hemingway's best book. This makes his initial reluctance to write about it baffling.

Hemingway believed he was a better writer than Faulkner. 'When I get tired sometimes,' he bragged, 'I imitate him a bit just to show him how it should be done. It's like loosening up with five finger exercises. Anyone who's not a musician could mistake them for music.'

Faulkner had recently published *A Fable*. Hemingway thought it was overwritten. 'One shouldn't win the Nobel Prize,' he pronounced, 'and then rewrite the Bible.' He said of Faulkner in general, 'Writing would sure be easy if you went up tin a barn with a quart of whiskey and wrote 5,000 words a day without syntax.'[23]

Faulkner had been bothering him since 1947. He gave an interview to a journalist that year in which he accused Hemingway of cowardice. The term was used in a literary way. He believed Hemingway took fewer risks than other writers, being content to stay in his own groove stylistically.

Hemingway misunderstood him. Outraged at the slight, he had Buck Lanham write to him to tell him how brave he was during the war. Faulkner afterwards apologised for the misunderstanding but Hemingway was slow to forgive him. The award of the prize, however, pacified him. He was now in the same league as Faulkner as far as global recognition was concerned.

The win also had its downside. He told Robert Harling:

> They called me from New York to tell me I was going to get it. I didn't think that was right. I don't think anyone should know about that kind of thing in advance. Then the journalists came. I don't know how many. A crowd. I'm not used to that kind of thing. I'm more used to attacking than accepting. Prizes aren't good for writers.[24]

Despite his denunciations, he was more than proud. This was the award he always wanted. It was up there with hooking the biggest marlin the world had ever seen or going fifteen rounds with Tunney. The quintessentially unliterary man had scooped the ultimate literary accolade.

He told Harvey Breit he thought it should have gone to other people before him, like Isak Dinesen.[25] Some people thought it was given to him for sentimental reasons. It had come so soon after his supposed death in Africa. That may have been a factor, but nobody could deny the effect *The Old Man and the Sea* exerted. A film version of it was even being talked about. Gary Cooper was being suggested for the title role.

Cooper had returned from the brink of oblivion a few years previously with *High Noon*. It won him an Oscar. Like *The Old Man and the Sea*, it was a simple story that worked the miracle. Cooper, like Hemingway, had done nothing different to what he did all his life. But somehow the formula worked. *High Noon* was a critical and commercial bombshell.

Hemingway was expected to go to Stockholm for the presentation ceremony. The idea fazed him. He told Buck Lanham, 'I'm thinking of telling them to shove it.'[26] Lanham said that would be silly, that apart from everything else it came with a $35,000 price tag. He took the point but still dug in his heels about going to Stockholm. He hated rituals. The thought of having himself measured up for a monkey suit horrified him. 'Wearing underwear is about as formal as I get,' he sniffed.

It would have stuck in his craw to appear in front of a congregation of stuffed shirts and mutter bromides about 'The Craft'. Lanham told him he could tape a speech and have it read out. He thought that sounded like a good idea. 'I'll start on one,' he promised.

It turned out to be very profound. Writing, he said, was a lonely life. Though organisations for writers palliated such loneliness, they hardly improved anyone's writing. As a writer grew in public stature, he shed the loneliness, but the writing often suffered as a result.

A good writer, he continued, must face 'eternity, or the lack of it', each day. For a true writer, each book should be a new beginning where he tries again for something that is beyond attainment. He should always try for something that has never been done or that others have tried and failed. Sometimes, with great luck, he would succeed. How simple the writing of literature would be if it were only necessary to write in a different way what was already well written. It was because the world had such great writers in the past that a writer was driven far out past where he wanted to go, out to where nobody could help him.[27]

There was a buzz of activity around his house at this time. 'I feel like an elephant in a zoo,' he grumbled.[28] To escape reporters he took Mary to the coast in the *Pilar* for a few days. When he got back to the Finca, he found the 'Swedish gong' was still sounding.

All sorts of people arrived at his door to interview him. Others called to pay their respects. Some of his visitors stayed with him for days, even weeks. One day he was cutting up some turtles to put into his freezer when a delegation of Portuguese and Chinese reporters appeared. 'I took what pleasure there was,' he jibed, 'in shaking them by the hand with a turtle-smeared hand and wishing them God speed.'[29]

Mary's father died now. She told Hemingway she intended to go to her mother to take care of her. He drank to excess in her absence. In the autumn of 1955, he took to his bed for two months suffering from hepatitis. His blood pressure was dangerously high.

When he recovered, he went on another trip to Europe with Mary. Peter Viertel met them at the Ritz Hotel. Hemingway started flirting with a woman he met there. She called herself La Comtesse. By now Mary had become more bored than angry by his dalliances.

A few days later, he joined Viertel for a meal with some Hollywood people who wanted to meet him: Rita Hayworth, Audrey Hepburn, and Mel Ferrer. Things were going well until an autograph-seeker approached their table. Everyone signed except Hemingway. When the autograph-seeker got to him, he looked him up and down and snapped, 'Sir, you look to me to be a cocksucker.' Ferrer laughed nervously. Hepburn was shocked. Hayworth looked into the distance. He apologised to them, saying he was becoming cantankerous with age, but it led to a very tense atmosphere.[30]

Adriana wrote to him in February 1956 to say she was getting married. It was to a Greek man, Spiros Manos. He owned coffee and hemp plantations in Tanganyika. Hemingway was glad for her, at least until she told him Manos was jealous of him and demanded she burn all his letters. 'I wouldn't want you to do that,' he pleaded. She acceded to his wishes.

Filming of *The Old Man and the Sea* began the following month. A crew from Hollywood arrived in Cuba. Nobody expected Hemingway to be enthusiastic about it. His books usually received a mauling when they were put on celluloid.

He seemed unusually interested in this one despite the fact of Cooper not having been cast in it. He even started making suggestions about how it should be directed, making some very uncharacteristic noises about wanting to adopt the 'New Realism' style of European cinema in bringing it to the screen. 'We need Vittoria de Sica,' he demanded. It was surprising he wanted this man as he had directed the remake of *A Farewell to Arms*, a film that underwhelmed him, as we saw. Instead they went for a more 'old school' director, Fred Zinnemann.

Hemingway asked that cameras be placed on the flying bridge of the *Pilar* to give the camerawork an authentic look. He also wanted the marlins to be shot in close-up. 'Let's make audiences feel they're in the film,' he enthused.

He had a mixed reaction to the news that Spencer Tracy was going to be playing Santiago. Tracy had been so moved by the book that he cried while he was reading it.[31]

Hemingway, however, thought he was unsuitable for the part. In the absence of Cooper, he wanted Humphrey Bogart to play it. Bogart would have been nervous working with Hemingway despite his reverence for his writings. Hemingway thought Tracy was too fat to play a fisherman, especially a Cuban one.[32] He liked his voice, which was important as there were going to be a lot of 'voiceovers' in the scenes, but thought his hands were too soft.[33] 'He's probably going to look as if he just walked out of a five-star hotel rather than an adobe hut,' he derided. Neither was he impressed with the actor chosen to play Manolin, Santiago's friend. He thought he looked like 'a cross between a tadpole and Anita Loos'.

Viertel was doing the screenplay. Hemingway knew he was friends with Tracy—and that Tracy had a drink problem. 'Will he be able to stay sober for the duration of the shoot?' he asked him. Viertel told him he fell off the wagon on his last film. This was the last thing Hemingway wanted to hear.

Katharine Hepburn was with Hemingway when he first met Tracy. She assured him he would stay off the sauce. When Hemingway told her what Viertel said about his last film, she was furious. The revelation almost ended her friendship with him.

The idea of Hemingway disapproving of somebody because he liked to drink was ironic considering his own intake. He travelled to Peru during the shoot, drinking so much at one of the bars there that the owner claimed his bill 'kept us operating for a year'.[34]

Back in Cuba he appeared on the set many days, sometimes spending hours reeling in marlin. Unfortunately, none of them were big enough to be used in the final cut.

There were also problems with Zinnemann. He argued with both Hemingway and Viertel about the way scenes should be shot. In the end he walked off the set. John Sturges replaced him. Sturges had some impressive work behind him but described *The Old Man and the Sea* as 'the sloppiest picture I ever made'.[35]

As was the case with every other Hemingway book that had the life sucked out of it by Hollywood's compromises, this morphed from an elemental story into, as the billboards put it, 'Rugged, ripping and real drama as man meets tiger sharks head-on in the most exciting adventure ever filmed!'

Other slogans went: 'Man Against Killer Monsters of the Raging Seas!' and 'The Most Dramatic Man-Against-Monster Battle Ever Shown!'

To help Viertel with the screenplay, Hemingway put him into a dilapidated hut like Santiago's. He thought the environment might summon his muse. He also brought him fishing for marlin. One day he got seasick on the *Pilar*. This disgusted Hemingway. How could a man who suffered from seasickness, he wondered, get into the heart of his hero?

Viertel felt the material was too thin for a film. He wanted to flesh it out by adding a scene where Santiago travels to Havana to find work. He also wanted a scene with Manolin's parents forbidding him to go into the boat with him. Hemingway strenuously objected to both of these proposals.

The film relied too much on the script. Film is primarily a visual medium. It would have been difficult for any director to maintain audience interest in Santiago over ninety minutes no matter how evocative the voiceover was.

The Old Man and the Sea 'cured' Hemingway of Hollywood. Gary Cooper tried to interest him in another project on which they could collaborate, but he said no. 'The picture business isn't for me, Coops,' he informed him, 'no matter how much dough we could make. How would we spend it if we were dead from dealing with the characters we would have to deal with?'

He hated everything about Sturges's film, including the fish. It was made of rubber. 'No movie with a rubber fish,' he admonished, 'ever made a dime.'

If he lived long enough he would have seen *Jaws*.

17

Black Ass

Hemingway aged almost visibly before people's eyes in the mid-'50s, becoming old and frail so suddenly it was almost as if he lost the picture in the attic.

He started to think about death a lot. Not a dramatic one in a plane crash or being gored by a bull but death that was banal, domesticated, absurd. Coming so close to dying as a young man in Fossalta gave him a fatalistic attitude to it. When Tennessee Williams asked him how Pauline died, as mentioned, he replied baldly, 'She died like everybody else and now she is dead.'[1] After Katy Dos Passos died in the car accident of 1948, he wrote to Marion Smith: 'She is dead and so will we all be and there is nothing to do about it.'

To avoid dwelling on these matters he drank and worked—or vice versa. Such activities were at best only temporary alleviations of what he called his 'black ass' moods.

When he was nineteen, he wrote, 'How much better to die in all the happy period of undisillusioned youth, to go out in a blaze of light, than to have your body worn out and old and illusions shattered.'[2] Ivan Kashkeen, who translated two of his short stories into Russian in 1934, summed him up with the phrase: '*Mens morbida in corpore sano*.'[3]

'I'm not a depressed rat naturally,' he told Pauline in 1926, but the condition was always burrowing down inside him waiting to be unleashed. When life became troubled for him, as it did in the late '50s, he was on a collision course with disaster in some shape or form. William Walton insisted he was a manic depressive all his life but managed to conceal it by drinking.

His friends now noticed the change in him. They wondered if his concussions might have caused brain damage. He seemed to shrink physically as the '50s went on. Even his gait changed. He used to walk on the balls of his feet. Now he just loped in a flat-footed manner.

His kidneys were damaged. The plane crash injuries continued to trouble him. His hair was thinning too. He combed it to the front to hide his bald patch in a rare example of vanity.

He also did his best to hide his agitation. After the derring-do of past years, it was difficult to accept the fact that he was falling prey to nerves like his father. Nerves were for weak people in the Hemingway canon. To acknowledge he had them was tantamount to resigning his status as role model for a generation of adventurers.

Silence meant the wound festered. Bewilderment mixed with rage inside him. He started to give vent to feelings he suppressed during the years of plenty.

It was as if he was going through a protracted adolescence, but without a tutor to guide him. He could find his way through deepest Africa without a compass but left to negotiate his own inner traumas, he was lost. His philosophy of *Il faut d'abord durer*—'One must endure above all'—was no more.[4] He was approaching a personal Gethsemane. But unlike the Jesus of his story 'Today is Friday,' he was anything but sure he was going to be 'good in there'.

The problems of hunting or running with the bulls were easier for him to negotiate than what he saw as a 'disease of the intellect'. He had no matador's cape to help him with it, no long-range rifle lens. Depression was a beast that sneaked up on you when you least expected it, demanding submission without a struggle.

At this point of his life he was profoundly alone. As alone as Santiago stripped of his booty, as alone as Frederic Henry having lost a wife in childbirth, as alone as Robert Jordan lying on the pine needle floor of a forest.

His eyes were bothering him as well. It was as a result both of a congenital weakness and many years reading in poor light. His vision was so bad, one of the only books he could comfortably enjoy was a large-print edition of *Tom Sawyer.* He was terrified of going blind.

Doctors ordered him to cut down on his alcohol consumption. He did so for a while, resulting in him producing some good work. 'This non-drinking thing is a bastard,' he said to Mary, 'but it pays off terrifically in the writing thing.'

Drink had been a big part of his life from his teens. Henry Villard, who shared a bed in the hospital he was in when he was wounded in the First World War, claimed he was lowering huge quantities of cognac and vermouth as far back as 1917. He once described alcohol as 'Central heating.'[5] 'I'm shy,' he claimed, 'I drink to make other people bearable.'[6]

The habit began to affect his body more after the plane crashes. The damage done to his liver in the second one made it a worry. George Plimpton said it stuck out from his body 'like a long fat leech'.[7] Hemingway was aware of the danger it posed. 'You can live on one kidney,' he pointed out, 'but if your liver goes, you're through.'

His body had been bruised long before the crashes. The many accidents he had in his life saw to that. The first one, as already mentioned, was when he pulled a skylight down on himself in a toilet in Paris in 1923, mistaking the cord for a flush chain. It required nine stitches and left a permanent scar that had to be airbrushed out of most of the photographs that were taken of him afterwards. The car accident he had in London in 1944 necessitated fifty-seven stitches to his head. A 1952 bust-up on board the *Pilar* required stitches there too. On another occasion he shot himself in the leg while trying to kill a shark. Then there was the time he cut a finger to the bone when he over-exerted himself with a punchbag—and a riding accident in Wyoming after his horse bolted.

Another time his friend Slim Hawks, the wife of Howard, almost blew his head off with one of his guns. It happened one day when he was bending down to unlace his boots after a hunting expedition. She was unaware there was a bullet in the gun when she pulled the trigger. It zinged past him, grazing his head and singeing the hairs on the back of his neck.

She was distraught. Everyone went quiet. She threw the gun on the ground. Hemingway was shocked for a moment. Then Hawks started to cry. He went over to her. 'It's all right,' he consoled. 'It's not!' she shrieked. Hemingway said, 'We're going home now. We'll have a drink and then it won't look so bad. Besides, think of how famous you would have been. The woman who killed Hemingway.'[8]

He downplayed incidents like these because his code demanded it. His strength helped him bear the pain better than other mortals. But when he got to sixty, such strength began to desert him.

'My luck, she is running good,' were his famous words after he survived the second plane crash. But was it? In retrospect, he might have been better off to have died that day. If he had, neither he nor the world would have been privy to the Stygian darkness of his last years.

'The real reason for not committing suicide,' he said in 1926, 'is because you always know how swell life gets again after the hell is over.'

The hell came back once too often, however, at this time of his life. Neither were there enough 'swell' times between the black periods.

He went to Spain in 1953 to see if he could recapture the excitement he portrayed in *The Sun Also Rises* but failed to do so. It was a different country now. Later that year he went back to Africa, the scene of all his safaris, and again found it to be irrevocably changed. In the '40s, he had visited Fossalta with Mary and buried a 1,000 lire note there as a kind of memorial to his war wound. In every decade he tried to recapture something that was gone, like Fitzgerald's Gatsby, only to find it out of reach. 'Never go back,' he advised finally, 'It's like going into the empty gloom of a theatre when the charwomen are scrubbing it.'[9]

'Where the hell does a man go now?' he asked rhetorically in 1951. For the next ten years, some good moments apart, he never really got an answer to that question.

It was never in him to bask in the afterglow of fame. Aaron Hotchner told him he should retire. 'Retirement is the filthiest word in the language,' he shot back. Like Santiago, he had to go on proving himself every day. You were only as good as your last book. It was acceptable for a boxer or a bullfighter to hang up their boots but not a writer.

The Sun Also Rises was made into a film in 1957. Errol Flynn was one of the stars. Hemingway commented drolly, 'Any film with Flynn as its best actor is its own worst enemy.'[10] This was harsh. Flynn turned in one of his best performances here, probably because he was playing a character close to himself—a lush. Tyrone Power was also effective, his reserve suitable for the emasculated Jake, and Ava Gardner was born to play Lady Brett. It was her third appearance in a Hemingway film after *The Killers* and *The Snows of Kilimanjaro*. Robert Evans was artificial as Romero but because this was an idealised character he got away with it.

The central theme was problematic. Impotence was hardly a commercial subject. As Darryl F. Zanuck put it, 'How the hell can you make a story about a guy who can't get it up?'

The fact that Barnes's doctor actually uses the word 'impotent' in one scene was a milestone for the cinema. The Hays Code had bowdlerised such dialogue up to now. Hollis Alpert wrote in his review of the film, 'One has the sense of an historical occasion.'[11]

The original draft stipulated that the sun comes out from behind the clouds as Brett speaks the last line in the film. Such a line went, 'There must be an answer for us somewhere.' Thankfully, such a finale was dispensed with. Everything is left hanging in mid-air instead.

A remake of *A Farewell to Arms* also came out that year, starring Rock Hudson and Jennifer Jones. The original director was John Huston. David O. Selznick was the producer. He told Huston he wanted Hemingway to like it but knew how fussy he could be. 'If a character goes from Café A to Café B instead of Café B to Café A,' he opined, 'or if a boat heads north instead of south, he's upset.'[12] He advised Huston not to see the book as Holy Writ. In other words, there should be no 'Papa-worshipping grovelling' in the film.[13] Huston was eventually replaced by Charles Vidor. For Hemingway this was a bad move. Huston was more his kind of man. He hated Vidor's film and walked out of it after half an hour.[14]

If he made some money from it his mood might have been better. He cursed himself for signing a contract with Darryl F. Zanuck that denied him any percentage on remakes of his works. 'I'll castrate that bastard if I ever see him again,' he said one day as he strode around Pamplona with a penknife.[15]

Selznick tried to pacify him by offering him $50,000 from the profits. 'What profits?' he asked. He doubted it would even make that *in toto*. If by some miracle it did, he advised Selznick to have the money given to him in nickels, which he should then shove up his ass until they came out his ears.

He now travelled to Spain to cover a *mano a mano* between Antonio Ordonez and his brother-in-law Miguel Dominguin. *Life* magazine had commissioned him to write a piece on it. He decided to call it 'The Dangerous Summer'. The term was applicable in more senses than one.

Mary went with him. So did Hotchner, Gianfranco Ivancich, and his new secretary, a nineteen-year-old Irish girl called Valerie Danby-Smith.

He was cantankerous on the trip. When they got to Madrid, he seemed confused. Crowds queued up to welcome him back to a place he immortalised in his work. A party was thrown in his honour, but he drank too much at it. His kidney started to bother him. His physician George Saviers happened to be in Madrid on holiday so he treated him.

He tried to write about the bullfight, but his concentration was dim. The words failed to come. His creativity was ebbing, but he refused to admit this to himself. If anyone else suggested it, he flew into a rage.

The atmosphere was wrong, he contended. The city was overrun with tourists. Non-aficionados had taken over.

The Madrid that Hemingway visited in his youth had no more than a few dozen tourists at a time. By the late '50s, that figure had leaped up to 100,000. He felt like an anachronism.

The new breed of bullfighters were hardly what they used to be either. They were superstars now, celebrities rather than romantics going into the valley of death. The duel between them and the bull was in danger of turning from ballet to pop art.

Autograph hunters besieged him. So did the hangers-on and the expats. There was still the beauty of the corrida, but he was drinking too much to appreciate it properly.

He was abusive to Mary. When it became too much for her, she went home.

Hotchner helped him edit the 'Dangerous Summer' article. 'Hotch is my eyes now,' he accepted. But he became crabby anytime he criticised what he wrote. He wanted to be told he still had 'the juice', that he could still get the 'gen' on his beloved toreros without being shepherded along by a mentor.

Hotch felt he was over-writing. The more turgid the article became, the more his defensiveness increased. Nobody edited him when he was writing *Death in the Afternoon*, he reminded Hotchner. Neither would they now.

Life had originally commissioned just 5,000 words. Hemingway's final tally reached a whopping 120,000. Even after he cut it down to half that length it had to be run over three separate editions of the magazine. Some readers were turned off by it. 'All those mean men,' one sniffed, 'trying to kill the poor bulls.' Hemingway raised his eyes to heaven. '*Life* is not life,' he sputtered.

'The Dangerous Summer' was subsequently published in book form. It was well written in parts but overall was a much lesser work than *Death in the Afternoon*. The beauty of the feria is there, and the sweep and swirl of the language, but there was something missing.

If *Death in the Afternoon* was a lecture, this was more of a diary. It would have benefited from more cuts from Hotchner if Hemingway allowed them but he didn't.

His sixtieth birthday approached. He was hardly in a celebratory mood. Mary broke her toe shortly before it. Hemingway acted as if it meant nothing to him. 'Something was changing in him,' she wrote in a memoir, 'or in both of us.' He was drinking more than ever and averaging just three or four hours' sleep a night. He drank in a place called the Plaza del Castillo. It was far from salubrious. 'I was increasingly repelled by the dirty tables,' Mary wrote, 'the sour smell of spilled wine, the stupid chit-chat with strangers who moved in for autographs and free drinks, and Ernest's endlessly repeated aphorisms.'[16]

When he learned that his birthday coincided with Ordonez's thirtieth, he thought it would be an idea to combine the two occasions. Ordonez agreed.

It proved to be a gala occasion. Dominguin also attended. Other guests arrived from overseas. There were forty altogether.

The festivities began at 10 a.m. There were seventy-two bottles of wine and forty-eight of champagne, as well as liberal supplies of whiskey and gin. Much hell was raised. There were flamenco dancers and guitar players and Japanese lanterns in the gardens. At midnight, Hemingway was presented with a three-layered cake. Fireworks were set off. At one stage, a firecracker became stuck in the top of a palm tree outside the house and set it ablaze. The ladders the partygoers had were too short to reach the flames and the hoses too feeble to put them out. Finally, the fire brigade was called. Hemingway posed for photographs with the firefighters wearing one of their hats.

Mary had put great care into preparing for the night. She even set up a shooting booth that she hired from a travelling carnival. Maybe she was trying to get Hemingway to forget the fact that he had just hit the three-score mark.

He hit a different kind of score as the party went on, shooting ash from cigarettes in Ordonez's mouth with pellets from an air gun. This understandably made the bullfighter nervous. Hemingway was still a good shot, but in view of his declining eyesight he could hardly be depended on to hit the target every time.

'Even though they're not real bullets,' Ordonez pointed out, 'They could still damage my face.' Hemingway just laughed. He continued firing until Ordonez said, 'Ernesto, we've gone as far as we can go. The last shot just brushed my lips.'

Hemingway was tempted to continue performing the same trick with Saviers. He refrained because, as he pointed out, he was 'the only doctor in the house' if he misfired. Even so, the riotousness continued throughout the night. When Mary went to bed at 6:30 a.m., there were still people sitting around the pool. They were even there when she woke up three hours later, eating eggs and drinking coffee. Hemingway toasted the last of them, Toby Bruce and his wife, with champagne as they made their way towards the aeroplane that would take them home. Maybe it was the last truly happy night of his life.

Ecstasy, once again, was followed by agony. Shortly afterwards he received a tax bill for $30,000. It was due to inefficiency on the part of his accountant, Alfred Rice. He misrepresented Hemingway's income on the sales of his books. It was an honest mistake, but Hemingway was furious. Rice paid the interest on the bill, but this was only a drop in the ocean

Hemingway had been having problems with tax for years. He turned down $50,000 for his story 'Fifty Grand' once because of the taxes that were going to be levied on it. 'For two bits I would quit writeing [*sic*],' he wrote to Rice, 'Nobody would get any money; neither the govt, nor agents nor anybody and I could fish and not have to knock my brains out and be a hell of a lot better off.'[17]

Money concerns continued to occupy him in subsequent weeks. He started blaming Mary for the expenses incurred at the party. This was unfair as it was her own money she used, a stipend from an article she wrote for *Sports Illustrated*.

Hemingway now travelled to France, bringing Valerie with him. Mary was threatened by Valerie, seeing the same excitement in Hemingway when he was with her as she had with Adriana Ivancich a decade before. Adriana was more beautiful but because of Hemingway's fascination with younger women and the increasing friction with Mary, she became a worry to her for a time.

When they returned to Cuba, his decline into mental illness became more apparent. Valerie became more of a friend to him than a secretary as she tried to stabilise his moods.

He spent a lot of time talking to her, asking her questions about her life as well as relating anecdotes about his. He told her of the Irish writers he admired, especially James Joyce. He always admired Joyce for freeing writers up in their use of language.[18] He also liked Brendan Behan, especially his book *Borstal Boy*.[19] As Mary watched them chatting in a non-romantic way, she relaxed, not seeing Valerie as a threat anymore. She went shopping with her in Havana and started to bond with her.

Valerie swam nude in the Finca with Hemingway. This became almost a demand from a man who always liked to feel natural, right back to his skinny-dipping days on Lake Walloon.[20] He did twenty laps every morning before going to his study to write.

He wrote every morning no matter how hungover he was. It had been the pattern all his life. He sweated out his hangovers in boxing and in games of tennis, pelota, and jai alai. The writing may not always have been as good as he might have wished but he kept at it as he had in the old days, agonising about the right paragraphs, the right sentences, the right words. He 'bit on the nail', as he put it, until he got 'pooped'.

After his morning's work was finished he dictated letters to Valerie. Then it was time for cocktails. He entertained visitors nearly every night. Nobody got in his gate without being expected. He drank a lot. Sometimes his 'Papa Dobles'—a personal cocktail made with Bacardi, lime, grapefruit, and six drops of maraschino—made him engage in extravagant displays of affection with his guests—unless they went down the wrong way, which brought out the 'other' Hemingway.

Valerie saw his relationship to her as paternal. He did his best to disabuse her of this view. One night he told her his marriage with Mary was over, that she no longer cared for him and was talking about divorce.[21] He said he wanted Valerie to be his wife so he could have the daughter he always longed for. It could even be a Catholic marriage, he urged. He was only married once in the church, he pointed out, and the wife from that marriage was dead.

Valerie laughed off his offer as 'charming and harmless'. She knew it was part of the fantasist Hemingway was. Mary was similarly amused. She joked about Hemingway 'kidnapping' Valerie.

His fascination with her youth was part of a pattern with him. In his former years, he fell for four women who were older than him: Agnes, Hadley, Duff Twysden, and Pauline. When he was in his thirties and forties, he fell for younger ones: Jane Mason, Martha, and Mary. In his fifties, he was attracted to two women young enough to be his daughters: Adriana and Valerie.

In all the women he referred to as 'Daughter' (Ava Gardner, Marlene Dietrich, Ingrid Bergman) and all the younger ones he wanted to marry (Adriana, Valerie) it was really his youth he was chasing rather than the women themselves. Prematurely old from hard living, he thought their presence in his life might take his mind off time's winged chariot.

Valerie and Adriana could have been gold-diggers who took him up on his proposals of marriage and then left him. If they succumbed to his charms, or pretended to, he would most likely have spent his last years alone.

18

From Cuba to Ketchum

Hemingway's life was about to change significantly now. Cuba had become a virtual war zone. There was a revolution brewing there. Fidel Castro's rebels had mounted a campaign against the dictator Fulgencio Batista.

A bomb went off outside the Finca one night. On another occasion, Batista's soldiers were looking for an escaped rebel. They thought he might be hiding in Hemingway's house. His watchdog, Blackdog, was guarding it at the time. When he barked at one of the soldiers, he struck him in the skull with the butt of his rifle. The dog died instantly.

Hemingway was heartbroken. He had a special relationship with him. Blackdog used to croon in mourning anytime he was away.[1] He even went off his food. When he came back he followed him everywhere.

They had many fun times together. Blackdog came to understand the relationship between typing and food. When Hemingway stopped typing, it was time to eat. That was nearly always in the morning. 'I fooled him sometimes,' Hemingway chuckled, 'by typing in the afternoon.'

He lodged a protest against the killing in Havana but no action was taken.[2] It was courageous of him to do that under the circumstances. He was lucky to avoid prison for having the audacity to stand up to the government in this way.

Blackdog's death was just one in a series of incidents troubling Hemingway in Cuba. Some thieves had broken into his house some time before. He shot at one of them but he got away. There was a time he never had to lock a door. Now he did it every night.

He wondered if Batista's soldiers might invade the Finca at some stage. There were a lot of guns in it. Maybe it was also time to dispose of any ammunition Batista's army might seize from his boat. He went out on the *Pilar* with Gregorio Fuentes one day to expedite this, collecting all the weapons he had from the days when he was hunting for Nazi U-boats. With a heavy heart, he threw everything overboard. 'Better in the sea than in Batista's hands,' he told Fuentes. Later that evening he swore Mary to silence about the dumping. She was unaware of what he was doing up to this.

He left Cuba in 1960. Before he went, he presented Castro with a prize for fishing. He was personally friendly with him despite disavowing his politics. 'I'm afraid to go there,' he told his friend Forrest MacMullen, 'because I'd never get out of it.' He withdrew his support for Castro when he became, as he saw it, a puppet of Nikita Khruschev.[3] Russian influences were everywhere in Cuba now. He even found difficulty paying his bills with American dollars because Castro froze them, having to use Canadian ones instead.

He wondered where he was going to live from now on. Mary remembered how much he loved hunting in Idaho. She wrote to his friend Lloyd Arnold to ask him if they could visit him in Sun Valley. There was a neighbouring town called Ketchum. Could this be a permanent home for him? A major stumbling block was that it was landlocked. 'Summers without the boat?' Hemingway queried.

He eventually agreed to go there. Mary found a house with a commanding view of the mountains. 'It might inspire your writing,' she suggested. Unfortunately, it was heavily fortified. Gregory said all it lacked was 'an electrified fence to be as secure as Trotsky's redoubt in Mexico'.[4]

Peter Viertel's wife, Jigee, died that year, having set herself on fire when she was lighting a cigarette in the bathroom of her home. She was drinking at the time. Hemingway felt guilty as he had gotten her in on drink. It was years before. They were crossing the Atlantic on an ocean liner. She had flu. 'Dr' Hemingway prescribed a course of whiskey sours for her. It was the beginning of a habit that proved to be her undoing. She was teetotal before that. Her marriage to Viertel broke down shortly before she died. That caused her to hit the bottle harder than usual.

It was Hotchner who gave Hemingway the news. 'I suppose you heard about Gigi's death,' he wrote in a letter to him. Hemingway thought he meant Gregory. Hotchner had spelt Jigee wrongly. 'He meant Jigee, not Gigi,' Mary corrected. Hemingway felt a mixture of grief and relief.

'I'm the son of a bitch who gave her her first drink,' he told Hotchner when he met him later in Idaho.

'If it wasn't you,' Hotchner consoled, 'It would have been someone else.'

'Maybe,' Hemingway allowed, 'but I was the one. I could kick my brains out for that.'

Jigee's death was something he could have dealt with better any year but this. Events he would normally have been able to handle now became momentous.

His moods became unpredictable. One day he developed a paranoia about being stalked by the FBI.[5] Valerie was another worry. He was terrified of being hauled over the coals by the immigration authorities after she mislaid her passport. He also worried about how he was going to pay her for her services. She was without a work visa.

The thought of hunting with his friend Bud Purdy even gave him pause. He became nervous going into a field with him one day to shoot pheasant. 'It's trespassing,' he quivered, 'We could be arrested.' Purdy explained to him that he had permission from the owner, but he still vacillated. It took him half an hour to coax him out of the car.

He always had a terror of being arrested ever since breaking the law in the woods one day as a boy in Michigan. He shot a heron and a game warden had given out to him. He turned up at his house to arrest the young Ernest later in the day. This was one of the few times Grace took his side, telling Sunny to get a shotgun if the warden refused to leave the house.[6] Apprehension about the law was a very unusual characteristic of someone who was allegedly 'afraid a nothin.' These days, it seemed, he was afraid of everything. 'Try always to stay out of any court of law,' Hemingway advised Leicester one day, 'They can twist you around so you end up mucking yourself.'[7]

Hemingway had many delusions at this time. The weirdest one was a fear that his friend Bill Davis was planning to murder him by boobytrapping his car.[8] Mary hoped the move to Ketchum would calm his nerves. The best way of him doing that, she thought, was by him getting back to his writing.

He thought so too. Every morning he got up at dawn to see if he still had 'the gen'. He stood in front of a chest-high bookcase in his bedroom beneath the horns of a water buffalo in front of a window. 'I like to write standing up to reduce the old belly,' he told Aaron Hotchner, 'It also gives you more vitality. Who ever went ten rounds sitting on his ass?'[9]

Mary told him he could get haemorrhoids if he stood too long. 'Old Ernie Haemorrhoid,' he sniggered.[10] He was still capable of the occasional joke. But then the black moods would come again. Nobody knew what Hemingway to expect on a given day.

He was working on the book that would become *A Moveable Feast* now. It was a series of sketches of literary figures he knew from the '20s in Paris. He wrote them at that time. They went missing for years. He retrieved them from a hotel basement in Paris in 1956. He now decided to rework them.

Maxwell Perkins loved what he saw of the book. Hemingway thought it was cruel, that he was too hard on Hadley, on Pauline, even on the tragic Scott Fitzgerald. He feared libel suits from those who were still living. But the writing of it galvanised him, helping him to stave off the depression engendered by his new home, as Mary predicted.

He found Ketchum glum. When he went walking with her by the Big Wood River, he castigated her for bringing him to this godforsaken place. The fortress in which he lived overlooked a barren landscape, acting as a kind of objective correlative of his state of mind.

Overriding his dark moods was an almost omnipresent worry about money. One night he noticed the lights of the local bank on after hours. For reasons best known to himself, he deduced that the staff were combing his accounts for irregularities. It was probably just the cleaning lady he saw but there was no point in telling him that. He also suspected the bank's vice-president was trying to fiddle his account.

Another worry he had at this time was the fact that he might face charges as a result of an accident he had on the road one day. His car scraped against another one. A more serious concern was the fear that Mary would have him committed to a psychiatric institution if his demons got worse. His preoccupations, she remarked, 'seemed to enclose him as the tentacles of an octopus envelop a mollusc'.

They continued to argue. She talked of leaving him, of moving into a New York apartment to resume her career as a journalist. When he abused her, she abused him back, telling him his writing was useless, that he was 'past it'.

By now he was starting to lose weight. His clothes hung off him. Mary pretended not to notice this for fear of worrying him even more. His posture became sunken and his voice lower. He was like one of those timid recluses Sherwood Anderson captured so vividly in *Winesburg, Ohio*. He feared his weight loss was due to cancer.

Was this the man who fought so bravely with the Loyalists against Franco? Who was given a medal for valour in Fossalta? Who spent his life giving two fingers to figures of authority?

It was as if the emotions he suppressed in the characters of his stories over the years were now tumbling out to exact revenge for such subjugation.

He reverted back to the small child he was in the summer dress, to Dutch Dollie rather than Pawnee Bill. He was his mother's compliant son again, the one she wanted to be a daughter.

It was 1902. The oak tree had become a weeping willow, the handsome hulk a piece of broken porcelain. 'If I'm going to be a vegetable,' he told Bud Purdy, 'I don't want to live.'

The author Leslie Fiedler visited him one day to ask him about an essay he was writing on him. He got a shock when he saw him.

'He looked much older than his 61 years,' he said, 'He was broken beyond repair.' He tried to engage him in conversation but without success. 'It's hard enough for me to write,' Hemingway told Fiedler, 'much less talk.' Fiedler recalled his comment to Gertrude Stein all those years ago when Hadley became pregnant with Bumby: 'I'm too young to be a father.' He wrote an extensive account of the visit, saying at one point, 'I could hear him in my inner ear crying out that he was too young to be an old man.'[11]

Mary witnessed his deterioration with a mixture of sadness and stoicism. If you were Hemingway, she knew, youth was always going to be a tough act to follow. The pain of a battlefield had a certain legitimacy attached to it. That of old age was simply ignominious. Hemingway was never going to be a candidate for dying in his bed at eighty-five.

He betrayed one of the classic symptoms of depression by telling people his literary career had been a fiasco, that he never wrote anything that was 'worth a damn'. This remark was made not long after he was awarded literature's especial honour. Other things being equal, he was on the verge of a renaissance with many unfinished novels waiting to be worked on.

But other things were not equal. He contemplated the '60s not so much with hope as dread.

Every decade seemed to begin slowly for him and end well. The end of the '20s produced *A Farewell to Arms*, the end of the '30s *For Whom the Bell Tolls*. The '40s both began and ended badly for him. The '50s inverted the usual pattern, starting promisingly and fizzling out with half-baked projects that were postponed indefinitely or abandoned. Maybe if he gave the '60s a chance, something would have come of that decade too. He thought this was unlikely.

The way he saw it, his spring was dry. Rewriting the Paris sketches became drudgery for him. The man who could once crank out 5,000 words a day had writer's block. He chopped paragraphs up in an attempt to breathe life into them, but they refused to bend to his wishes. They mocked him with their emptiness, laying inert and lifeless before him, refusing to yield the old riches. The white spaces between the lines were just white spaces now, not implications. It was as if the ringmaster at the circus had lost control of his animals. They were rebelling against him.

A Moveable Feast revived him for a time, but every good day seemed to be followed by a string of bad ones. At the end of 1960, he rang Hadley to ask her something about the Paris years. They were long gone out of her memory now, so the call went nowhere. As she left down the phone, she found herself in tears. A woman who knew him better than any other, she sensed his depression more from his demeanour than his words. She was well trained by 'The Master' to read between the lines of his speech. This time it was for real rather than in the pages of a book.

The early months of 1961 exacerbated his decline. John F. Kennedy invited him to his inauguration in January. He was a great admirer of Hemingway's writing. A few months earlier, he had written to him asking him if he could use his phrase 'Grace under pressure' in the opening sentence of his book *Profiles in Courage*.

Hemingway was unable to attend the inauguration. This was the pass his life had come to. He was asked to write a tribute to Kennedy the following month. This he agreed to. It took him the best part of a week to do it.

He refused to sign himself into a psychiatric clinic for fear the public would say he was losing his mind. Vanity had always been one of his greatest vices. Admitting he had 'nerves' was still impossible for him. It was the affliction of weak people like his father. To be classified as a psychiatric case would have been even worse. It would be the ultimate ignominy. He was always cynical about the people he called 'shrinks'. Asked once to name his psychoanalyst he replied, 'Corona, Smith Corona.'

After much persuasion from Mary, he finally agreed to be placed under medical supervision. It took place in the Mayo Clinic in Minnesota. He registered under George Saviers' name.[12] By now he was in such a state of tension he feared this slight subterfuge might be deemed a felony by the FBI.

He entered on the pretext of having tests for a blood pressure problem. The hospital was chosen because it treated both physical and psychological maladies. As such, it would avoid the attention of the media.

He underwent multiple electroconvulsive therapy sessions in the following months. The staff were chuffed to have such a famous writer in their wards. After befriending them, he arranged for Scribner's to send them copies of his books. His spirits picked up a little at this. He played the role of 'The Writer' to his new fans.

Things appeared to be going well at first. A doctor called Howard Rome began treating him. He felt he was getting somewhere. What he failed to realise was that he was dealing with a master psychologist.

Hemingway washed down pills with vodka to kill the pain of a lifetime of hellraising. Or maybe to anaesthetise himself to his depression. Rome oversaw repeated doses of the electroconvulsive shocks. Hemingway had eleven bursts of them in all. They destroyed his memory. 'And what,' he asked, 'is a writer without his memory?' In the middle of his gloom, he was able to quip, 'What I need is a shrink who's done a creative writing course.'[13]

His paranoias continued. He suspected one of the hospital interns was a 'fed' in disguise. Exactly why the FBI should be after him was never properly explained. His tax affairs were in order.

His dignity was stripped from him in the hospital. Items with which he might do damage to himself were removed from him. Doctors had the freedom to enter his room whenever they liked, even when Mary and himself were making love.[14]

Nobody knows why he had so many shock treatments when it became obvious that they were having no effect. Rome swore by this form of treatment. According to Hemingway's biographer, Jeffrey Meyers, 'If somebody came in to him with cancer or a hanging nail, he'd probably get it.'[15]

Instead of solving his problems, the clinic intensified them. Matters became bizarre when he succeeded in persuading the doctors to release him from their care. That happened at the end of January. The Old Artificer convinced them all that he was cured. Mary knew what was happening but was powerless to do anything about it.

Hemingway watched Hollywood's Oscar ceremonies in April. Gary Cooper was given a Lifetime Achievement award. Cynics dubbed this 'The Deathbed Oscar'. Cooper had prostate cancer. It was inoperable.

Mary rang him to congratulate him. Hemingway was reluctantly dragged to the phone to add a few words. Cooper died the following month. His wife, Rocky, persuaded him to convert to Catholicism on his deathbed. 'Now,' Hemingway scoffed, 'he can have all that money *and* God.' It was like the pot calling the kettle black. He had converted to Catholicism himself to avail of Pauline Pfeiffer's millions all those years ago.

Hemingway and Cooper had a long-standing bet whereby each promised the other he would win 'the race to the barn'—i.e. die first.[16] Though 'Coop' got to it before him, Hemingway felt his own 'high noon' was fast approaching.

The photographs taken of him around this time show a man who seems dazed by life. He looks through the camera rather than at it. He was lost inside himself as he searched his memory-banks for the treasures that refused to come. Sometimes he put a laboured smile on his face. He was like Nick Adams in the early stories, telling himself everything was 'quite fine'.

The post-ECT Hemingway, patched up to return to his bleak mountain home, looked tortured. There was no way he could numb himself with sex or drink or a new blockbuster anymore. All he had was the chaotic intensity of his thoughts.

Thoughts of suicide hinted. They had always been lurking, both in his work and his life. How else could someone capture the dark night of the soul so adeptly? Was 'A Clean Well-Lighted Place' his promissory suicide note in this regard? Would he, like the waiter in that story, have said, 'Our nada, who art in nada, nadą be thy name' when his luck was bad? Would he have said it when the writing failed to come, or things went 'to hell' with 'Miss Mary', as he called her, or Miss von Kurowsky or Miss Mason or Miss Ivancich? Was he like the hyena in *The Snows of Kilimanjaro*, waiting for Dr Hemingstein to slip up so it could get out?

In *For Whom the Bell Tolls*, he wrote, 'Dying is only bad when it takes a long time and hurts so much that it humiliates you.' In an unpublished fragment from the '30s, he wrote, 'My old man was a coward. He never had any fun and was married to a bitch and he shot himself. I am not a coward. I've had a damned good time, plenty of fun, been married to two good women and I think I will shoot myself.' Elsewhere he said chillingly, 'I would have stayed in the plane that burned in Butiaba once Mary was out if I could have seen the rest of 1954.'

By now, as Dwight MacDonald put it in the kind of asyndetic prose Hemingway would have appreciated, 'The position is outflanked the lion can't be stopped the sword won't go into the bull's neck the great fish is breaking the line and it is the fifteenth round and the champion looks bad.'[17]

In *To Have and Have Not*, he had a character speculate on ways he might kill himself: 'Some made the long drop from the apartment or the office window. Some used the native tradition of the Colt or Smith and Wesson.' In *Death in the Afternoon*, he wrote, 'When a man is in rebellion against death he has pleasure in taking to himself one of the godlike attributes: that of giving it.'

He was like an animal with his foot caught in a trap, a tethered lion without the ability to scream. An almost surreal vacuum loomed.

It had its roots as far back as the Nick Adams of 'Indian Camp'. His future seemed to be mapped out for him even from that early story. In his youth he watched his father dealing with brutal scenarios. Now he was immersed in his own one.

The poor reception given to *The Dangerous Summer* put him off going to Pamplona in 1961. It seemed to prove to him that he could no longer write eloquently about his favourite subject. If that was beyond him, what point was there in attending the event? Instead he stayed in Ketchum.

He continued to give Mary grief. The only time of the day that he talked to her, she wrote in her memoir of life with him, was when she turned off her light to go to sleep at night:

> Then he would stand beside the open door of my room and at length upbraid me. [He'd say] I didn't appreciate the dangers of living in Idaho where we would be taxed if we remained more than one hundred days. I was not helping him find someplace safe from taxes. I was spending too much money on groceries. I had neglected him throughout his stay at St. Mary's [hospital]. How could I have enjoyed a TV program when we were in such great danger? I was betraying our well-being.[18]

On 21 April of that year, she came down from her bedroom to find him in the sitting-room with a shotgun in his hand. Two shells from it were standing upright on the windowsill in front of him. Instead of getting hysterical, which most women would have done in the circumstances, she expressed a wish to go on a fishing trip to Mexico. The comment confused him. She was using a stalling tactic. Saviers was due to call. She thought he might pacify him.

'Honey,' she reproved, 'You wouldn't do anything harmful to yourself, would you?'

He put down the gun. Then Saviers arrived. Hemingway made a half-baked attempt to pick it up when he saw him but he was dispossessed.

Saviers told him he was going to have him readmitted to the hospital. Hemingway flew to it. When the plane stopped *en route* for refuelling, he went for a walk. In the course of this, he searched the glove compartments of parked cars looking for firearms. He then tried to walk into the whirling propellers of an aeroplane, stopping only when the plane cut its engine.[19]

After being readmitted to the hospital, he received more electroconvulsive therapy. It was as ineffective as previous doses, but he pretended they were working. Rome bought it. He proved himself to be an adept actor once again, fooling him into signing him out. The situation was farcical. He left the clinic on 26 June. Mary protested but nobody listened. As Gregory put it, 'What was one woman's intuition compared with all that medical expertise?'[20]

July was only a few days away. It had always been a special month for him. Michael Reynolds wrote:

> Born in July, blown up in July, Pamplona in July. On the first of July each summer of his youth the family boarded the steamer that carried them up to Lake Michigan for their two months at Windemere. July was the cottage, the lake, the woods. It was trout fishing and camaraderie with the summer people, baseball games in the village, campfires in the night. July was the big wound when he died for the first time only to come back out of the explosion to find his kneecap somewhere in his boot and his head ringing like a bell.[21]

On the night of 1 July, Hemingway went out for a meal with Mary and Saviers. A pair of travelling salesmen sat at a table opposite them in the restaurant. He panicked when he saw them. 'They're FBI agents,' he shrieked. He got up from his table and made Mary drive him home.

He slept in an adjoining bedroom to hers that night. They sang Italian songs to one another through the walls. His last words to her were 'Goodnight, kitten.'

At 6:30 a.m. the following morning, he went down to the kitchen as she lay asleep upstairs. It was a Sunday, a day he always hated. It reminded him of his mother's piety, of cello practice in Oak Park. He woke early as he did most days, his thin eyelids making him susceptible to the light streaming in through his window.[22] He once said he never missed a sunrise in his life no matter how many glasses of tequila he had the night before.

He made his way down to the kitchen in his bathrobe and slippers. The keys of his rifle cabinet lay on the windowsill. He brought them down to the basement where the cabinet was. From a box of 12-gauge shells, he removed two. He then took out his favourite Boss shotgun.

'I was certain,' his biographer Jose Luis Castillo-Puche wrote, 'that he picked up the rifle as he might have picked up his pen—quite willing to sign his autograph for the very last time, with a bold flourish.' 'He couldn't have killed himself in Spain,' Puche said, 'because he had too many memories of it.' The only place he could do it was Ketchum, 'a cold, neutral zone where he had no guardian angel'.

Better to burn out than to rust away, to extinguish the flame quickly than rage against the dying of the light. Drink, women, sex, safaris, corridas, and clean, well-lighted places could only stave off bleak thoughts for so long.

He slipped the shells into the rifle. Hemingway was an ace marksman like his father. He had to be now. No more than firing at a lion, you only had one chance when you fired at yourself so it was important to make it count. To only partly do the job, to have to live with a gunshot wound, that would have been even more nightmarish than death.

He had already died once when his soul left his body in Italy. This time there would be no medals for valour afterwards. Neither would Agnes sit by his bedside, or Ursula climb into bed with him, or lie beside him all night to stop him having bad dreams.

He put the rifle to his forehead and pulled the trigger. The power of the two barrels practically blew his head off. He had found his island in the stream, his sea in being. Life was complete for him. He had finally fucked 'the oldest whore in Havana'.[23]

But once again, the winner took nothing. Like the Pablo of *For Whom the Bell Tolls,* he had taken death as an aspirin. The silver cord was broken.

It was just two and a half weeks before his sixty-second birthday. He died like his father had, perhaps like everyone in every country in every era did, like all of those the world broke, the very good and the very gentle and the very brave, the beautiful and the damned.

The shot woke Mary. She compared the sound of the rifle to that of a bureau drawer being slammed shut.[24] Leicester had heard a similar noise in 1928 when he sat in his bedroom listening to his father shooting himself.

She rose from her bed and called out his name. When he failed to answer, she threw back the coverlet and ran down the hall to his room. The sheets on his bed were disturbed, but he was nowhere to be seen.

She ran down the steps to the basement. There she saw him lying on the floor surrounded by blood, the shotgun beside his body. It was over finally, his long goodbye to life executed cleanly and without fuss. She was shocked but not surprised.

She blamed herself for leaving the key to the basement in the kitchen. It made nonsense of hiding the rifles downstairs, of keeping the cabinet locked.

Her man was gone. Maybe he had been for years. She did everything in her power to keep him in the clinic. Even though he talked of suicide, she thought this very fact was a buffer against him carrying it out. Any attempt he made to kill himself so far was a public one. She saw some reassurance in that. It was as if grabbing rifles when others were present, or trying to throw himself off planes, was just Papa being his exhibitionistic self.

He was not being exhibitionistic on 2 July. He was being forensic.

She tried to compose herself to take in what happened. She had lost her husband. Papa's children had lost their father. So had the greater world outside. The instantly recognisable face that zoomed its way across the globe for so many decades on all those magazine covers would now be captured only in repose.

The man who preached endurance all his life had not himself been able to endure this final hurdle of his life. The people who looked to him for guidance, who expected him to lead them to the promised land of self-realisation, were without their leader.

Peter Viertel heard of his death on a news flash in Biarritz. He found it difficult to believe. When it was confirmed to him, he changed his attitude, seeing it as having a frightening inevitability to it. 'He's gone,' Antonio Ordonez consoled, 'It's better for him even if it's bad for us.'

As was the case after the death of John F. Kennedy, people remembered what they were doing when they heard the news. Hemingway had graced so many newspaper covers over the years, he was part of the national psyche. Even in hibernation he was still the king.

He was commemorated in Russia, France, Sweden, and Spain. People wept on the streets in Key West when they heard the news. Likewise in Cuba. No longer would they be able to shout out 'Papa!' to him in Sloppy Joe's or La Floridita. The *Louisville Courier Journal* wrote, 'It's almost as though the twentieth century itself has come to an end.' There were letters of condolence from the White House, the Kremlin, and the Vatican.

The funeral was delayed until 5 July to allow Patrick fly home from Africa. That was where he was living since his twenties. Jack flew in from Oregon and Gregory from Miami. A Catholic burial was planned even though Hemingway had been excommunicated by the church after his divorce from Pauline. A Mass was prohibited because of the rumour of suicide surrounding his passing.

At this time it was just that—a rumour. Mary insisted his death was accidental, that he was cleaning his rifle when it went off.[25] Most people were dubious about such a story. Hemingway would have been more scandalised by the suggestion of the clumsiness it suggested than he would have been by Mary telling people he intentionally ended his life.

Though telegrams came from all over the world, only a handful of people turned up at the funeral. Such a handful, according to Gregory, 'had enjoyed the periphery of greatness because they knew that was the closest they would ever come to it'. As they lowered his father into the ground, he felt a sense of relief: 'I couldn't disappoint him, couldn't hurt him anymore.'[26]

He met Valerie for the first time at the funeral. They felt a bond with one another that he thought came from being excluded from the main mourners. Mary had been alienated from Gregory for years. She was cool with Valerie because she suspected she was covering the funeral for *Newsweek* magazine. This was untrue. Though Valerie was a researcher for that publication, she was at the funeral only in a personal capacity.

The slim turn-out was a result of Mary's wishes. Policemen had been recruited to remove what she called 'the curiosity seekers'. Marlene Dietrich was even excluded from the guest list, despite being one of Hemingway's dearest friends. Mary was nervous of his great chemistry with the woman he called his 'Kraut'. Jack was delegated with the embarrassing task of telling her to stay away.[27]

The rifle Hemingway shot himself with was cut into pieces and buried. Nobody wanted it to be appropriated by a collector as a grisly souvenir. Mary placed a monument to him in Sun Valley. In Petoskey, Madelaine gave him the unlikely honour of a stained-glass window depicting the Nativity in her local church. No doubt Oinbones (her pet name for him) would have been amused.

In the months and years afterwards, literary gurus the world over queued up to give their views on the reason for his suicide. Every nickel-and-dime psychologist, it seemed, knew this. Most of the theories were either melodramatic or over-intellectualised. Anthony Burgess speculated that he had 'a self-disgust in his inability to live up to his Joycean ideal of total artistic dedication. Corrupted by the wrong kind of fame, he found it too late to retreat.'

It was more likely that writer's block was the catalyst for his suicide, amidst a welter of psychological maladies. He always saw writing as an adventure, an investigation into the safari of the heart. In 1954, he told Hotchner, 'It's the only thing that makes me feel I'm not wasting my time sticking around.'[28] When his inspiration went, he wanted to go too.

One of the more ridiculous theories about why he killed himself was that he did so to humiliate Mary, a woman he humiliated in every other way in the preceding decade or so. This was a sad example of how low Hemingway 'experts' were willing to stoop for a sensationalistic tidbit.

The other main reason for his desperate final act was probably genealogical. Its spectre hung above him all his life like the sword of Damocles. Clarence had set a dangerous precedent. He became a kind of inverted role model for Hemingway right through his life, making suicide an option for him anytime it got too tough.

At the end of the day, nobody had the full picture. All they knew was that, as he said of Pauline, 'He died and he was dead.' He had spent his life killing things on land, sea, and air. On 1 July 1961, in the words of Clive James, 'He bagged his last trophy.'[29]

19

Aftermath

In the fall the war was always there. So were the bulls and the fish and the lions and the frozen daiquiris. But he did not go to them any more. He was sleeping with that old whore Death, leaving Mary to clean up the debris. Posterity would perform a different kind of operation regarding his work. He often said he was vain enough to know his 'stuff' would last.

Gertrude Stein once declared, 'Hemingway looks like a modernist but he smells of the museums.' He never made a secret of the fact that he wanted to write literature that would be read long after he was dead. James Plath wrote, 'He's as culturally significant as Marilyn Monroe, Elvis or James Dean. That means the interest will probably never wane.'

Morley Callaghan liked telling people he was remembered more for the fact that he boxed with Hemingway than for all his books. Buck Lanham remarked wryly that his glowing military career only served as a footnote to his friendship with him in most people's minds. Harold Loeb never escaped from Hemingway's identification of him with Robert Cohn in *The Sun Also Rises* no matter what he did afterwards.[1]

He lived at least five lifetimes in one. Such a life was analysed to the nth degree by revisionists. He was hardly cold in his grave when biographies of him started appearing. Some of them were from friends or so-called friends. Others came from family members, casual acquaintances, literary scholars. He would have been equally unimpressed with all of them, particularly those that were in the works when he was alive.

Aaron Hotchner wrote one of the more intimate accounts of his life. Leicester believed he would have cut Hotchner out of it if he knew he was taking notes of all their encounters. Hotchner secretly taped many of their conversations. He was well known for his 'devil box'—i.e. his tape recorder. Hemingway refused to let anyone but Hotchner near him with such a device when he was speaking off the record.

Leicester himself also wrote a memoir of Hemingway. This was after he died. During his life he wrote different kinds of books. Hemingway was disapproving of these, not thinking he had talent. When Leicester told him he was in the process of writing a memoir about his youth, Hemingway stopped him. 'I forbid absolutely any such publication,' he wrote to him in a letter, 'If you're short of dough let me know by return mail. Sorry to be so stuffy and formal about something in the family but privacy is more limited each day and I want to keep what I have. It's damned little as it is.'

When Leicester sent Hemingway a novel he wrote once, Hemingway put it in a barrel without reading it and set it alight. Leicester never knew what happened to it. At his funeral, he tapped Valerie Danby-Smith on the shoulder and said, 'Excuse me, Miss, do you know where my manuscript is?' She politely refrained from telling him its fate.[2]

Leicester's memoir, when it was eventually published, was called *My Brother, Ernest Hemingway*. Its main thesis is that Hemingway needed a 'spiritual kid brother' all his life. This was a function Leicester failed to fulfil as well as people like Hotchner and Gianfranco Ivancich. As was the case with most members of his family, Hemingway stayed out of contact with Leicester in the last years of his life. The book is sketchy about this time as a result. We also learn little about Hemingway's early years. Leicester was dependent on other people's accounts of these years because of the large age gap between himself and his brother.

Gregory also wrote a memoir, *Papa*. Leicester helped him with it. He was expecting some acknowledgement but it failed to materialise. Gregory even denied him a percentage of the royalties from the book. Leicester took him to court for this. The pair never spoke again.

Papa was a kind of chronicle of death foretold. It was uncompromising in depicting the abrasive relationship Gregory had with Hemingway. Sentiment was at a premium in it but you felt you could trust it more for that reason. It was born out of Gregory's pain, his coming to terms with the uneven hand life dealt him. Like Martha, he stood up to Hemingway at times when other people would have been afraid to. Hemingway's tempers were fierce when he was confronted.

Gregory had many problems with his sexuality during his life. We saw evidence of his transvestism from the events of 1951 that resulted in Pauline's death. The fetish was ironic. Anytime Hemingway was annoyed with him, he used to say, 'When you were born I wanted a daughter rather than a son.'

The problems continued after Hemingway married Mary. When he was twelve, Hemingway found him trying on a pair of Mary's nylons one day.[3] He kept quiet about it but a few weeks later he said to him, 'Gigi, you and I come from a strange tribe.' (This phrase became the title of a future book by another family member in time.) Two years later, he started wearing some more of Mary's undergarments. He was in Cuba at the time, on a break from boarding school. Their maid was originally suspected by Hemingway and Mary. She pleaded innocence, but they held on to their suspicions about her, even when she broke down in tears. She was dismissed from the house as a result. The garments were discovered when Gregory went back to school. They were hidden under the mattress of his bed in the guesthouse where he slept that summer.[4]

Nothing was mentioned to Gregory afterwards. It was too much for Hemingway to deal with, another crisis he could do without. He always regarded Gregory as the biggest liability of his children. In *Islands in the Stream*, he wrote, 'He has the biggest dark side in the family except for me.'[5] Gregory was confused about why he wanted to try on Mary's clothes. Maybe, he thought, it was the result of a lack of love from Mary as a child. He always believed she cared for Patrick more than him. 'I think I was trying to get her attention,' he confessed years later.

He would have preferred if his parents confronted the cross-dressing problem when it first exhibited itself. That way he could have got some help for it instead of it getting worse in subsequent years. He thought it began with Ada Stern threatening to leave him as a toddler.[6]

The cross-dressing was indicative of larger confusions in his life, confusions that led to mood swings almost as great as his father's. His first wife, Jane, divorced him after he had an affair with the daughter of a plantation owner on a 1955 safari.[7] Afterwards he studied medicine in university for two years before dropping out. A chameleon like his father, he became a paratrooper in the army in 1956. Afterwards he succumbed to depression. Multiple bursts of electroshock treatment followed. He was finally diagnosed as schizophrenic.

He married Valerie in 1966. By the time of their marriage, she had a son by, of all people, Brendan Behan. She got to know Behan when she returned to Ireland after her time with Hemingway ended. He was fascinated to hear she worked for Hemingway, being a great admirer of his work.

The child was a boy. She called him Brendan. Behan offered to adopt him. He had no child of his own at the time. His wife, Beatrice, was against the idea. She later gave birth to a daughter, Blanaid. Behan died shortly after Blanaid was born.

Valerie brought Brendan up with Gregory. How amazing it is to think that two of the world's best-known writers were related through this woman. Valerie had three other children by Gregory afterwards. He had eight children altogether from four wives

He was abusive to Valerie both physically and psychologically during their marriage. His cross-dressing fetish continued during it as well. Sometimes he tried on women's clothing in department stores. He told Valerie he was in the process of having a sex change at one point. He was naive about the repercussions this could have on their relationship. 'If I had it,' he asked her, 'could we continue living together as girlfriends, going out shopping and to the beauty parlour?'[8] He attended many psychiatrists, but they failed to solve his problem.

Valerie divorced him in 1987. He continued to abuse her even after the divorce. There were many incidents where he was physically abusive to others as well, including police officers. It was incredible that he never served a lengthy prison sentence. He always found the money to get himself out on bail. People tended to feel pity for him rather than scorn. Most police officers agreed that he was 'a very nice guy'.

Valerie demanded barring orders against him in the following years. The 'sexual inversion' motif that excited his father carried a dark undertow for Gregory. He began the process of sexual reassignment to 'become' a woman. In 1988, he had a breast implant. Later on he fell under the spell of the Scientology guru Ron Hubbard. Hubbard advised him to take drugs to 'audit' his brain.

He died in the third-floor cell of a women's detention centre in Miami on October 1, 2001, fifty years to the day after his mother died. It was after being arrested for exposing his (female) genitals on a street in Biscayne Bay. He was carrying a woman's dress and a pair of high-heeled shoes at the time. His toenails were painted pink. He died of a heart attack in his cell. He was trying to get his legs into a pair of women's panties when he keeled over. He was just six weeks short of his seventieth birthday.

Other members of Hemingway's family wrote memoirs too. Marcelline's one was called *At the Hemingways*. She started it on the plane to his funeral. Gregory was sitting beside her. There was no conversation between them because, as he later wrote, she was 'too busy taking notes on the other people in the plane, notes that might prove useful for her forthcoming book'.[9] Hemingway described Marcelline to Carol as 'a bitch with handles'.[10] The slur got back to her. Her book at times read like revenge, a settling of scores under the cover of fondness.

Neither does it go into the important things in her life, like a nervous breakdown she had in 1921 to Hadley. She was the sister Hemingway liked least of all. Maybe he never got over being twinned with her. Or was it that she reminded him more of his mother than any of his other siblings? Grace comes across almost as a martyr in her book.

Sunny wrote a memoir called *Ernie*. It was more affectionate than Marcelline's one. She regaled the reader with a series of childish japes she and Hemingway engaged in during the years of killing skunks, hunting squirrels, and calling each other nicknames to emphasise their camaraderie. The tone was so happy it was almost unfathomable to think Hemingway could develop such dark sides to him in his later years.

Jack also wrote a memoir, *Misadventures of a Fly Fisherman*. It was an interesting book from an anecdotal point of view but was more about himself than his father. It lost a lot of interest because of that.

Hotchner's *Papa* came out in 1966. It became a best-seller because of its generous trove of anecdotes, many of them featuring a Hemingway few knew. Mary was bothered by its revelations and took him to court, pleading disingenuously that the conversations the pair of them had were private. Not surprisingly, the case was thrown out.

Many critics accused Hotchner of lifting anecdotes from other sources and making out they were his own. Be that as it may, there was still enough material here to give us a vivid picture of Hemingway at his highs and lows, a figure of huge mirth and equally large gloom. Mary's problem with it was the fact that it went into areas she felt were intrusive. She saw these as muscling in on her terrain.

Hotchner captures Hemingway both in fire and ice. His laughter booms but equally resonant are the cold silences and vast mood swings, particularly towards the end of his life when the writing of *The Dangerous Summer* became an ordeal. During his temper tantrums, pages fly about the room as Hotchner and Mary watch on helplessly.

Mary became even more protective of Hemingway's reputation in the following years. When unwanted visitors drove up to her door, she shot at their cars with a rifle, puncturing their tyres. She asked Valerie, who was Valerie Hemingway at this point because of her marriage to Gregory, to collate his papers for presentation to the John F. Kennedy Library in Boston.

Mary's relationship with Hemingway's sons was strained. This was partly due to the fact that they were denied the money they were expecting from his will. The disappointment hit Gregory especially hard. Mary got almost everything.

She published her autobiography, *How it Was*, in 1975. Many of the problems she had with him were airbrushed out of it. Neither did she mention a serious problem with alcohol that had been troubling her by this time, nor the fact that she found it difficult to cope with Hemingway's demons. Many people believed they were on the verge of divorce when he died, that his suicide saved her having to go to court to get away from him.[11]

The fact that he died in America rather than Cuba was another source of relief to her. After they left Havana the Finca Vigia was appropriated by Castro. It was subsequently turned into a museum. When that eventuality transpired, she was allowed bring its contents back to the US with her.

Hemingway was an incorrigible collector. Mary took as many of his possessions as she could from Cuba. There was everything from bullfight programmes to train tickets to manuscripts of early stories. She also found many interesting collectibles in the back room of Sloppy Joe's. Much of it was damaged by rats but much was also well preserved. She was nervous something would happen to all the items on her way back to Idaho, but thankfully they arrived in good condition.

Adriana Ivancich was displeased with the portrayal of her in Mary's book. Mary suggested that she tried to wreck her marriage to Hemingway. Such a suggestion amplified feelings of depression she was going through at this point of her life. Her husband tried his best to help her but without success. Neither could the two children she had by him do anything.

She wrote her own memoir in 1980. It failed to generate the interest she expected and promptly disappeared from the bookshelves. Whether as a result of this or a general feeling of depression, she hanged herself three years later from an olive tree on her farm outside Rome, thereby becoming another member of the extended Hemingway circle who could never quite recover from him.[12]

The number of books written about Hemingway written by people not related to him are too many to discuss here but some are worth mentioning. A man called Peter Buckley wrote a beautiful book about him entitled simply *Ernest.* It was distinguished not only by a set of evocative photographs but also a purity in the writing that put one in mind of Hemingway's own diction. It errs on the side of hagiography but is still a deeply evocative work.

Buckley leaves certain biographical gaps, like a treatment of the women in Hemingway's life, but the rhythms of his prose are so hypnotic one finds this easy to overlook. You put the book down feeling sure Hemingway would also have liked it. Buckley writes like a poet, setting much store by

Hemingway's perennial search for truth. *Ernest* is like an extended elegy to him, a paean both to him and the world of nature he loved so passionately.

Extensively researched biographies were also written about Hemingway by Jeffrey Meyers, Kenneth Lynn and James Mellow. Peter Griffin has written a series of books about him and so has Michael Reynolds. Reynolds tries to unlock his soul as a safecracker would a gold vault in his incredibly detailed works. This man has justifiably been called the definitive Hemingway biographer. Dennis Brian tried a different approach in *The Faces of Hemingway*, recording telephone interviews and playing them off against one another in a kind of ersatz open forum. Charles Fenton, like Philip Young—and indeed Griffin and Reynolds—emphasised his early years.

All of these books are explicatory in their way, but they all stop short of omniscience. Hemingway's tactics of concealment were as canny off the page as on it. He left clues about how he was thinking that often seemed to mock potential researchers rather than enlighten them.

Hadley wrote a memoir of him with Alice Sokoloff in 1973. She was eighty-two at the time and not welcoming of the attention it brought her. She soon grew tired of answering the same questions interviewers put to her over and over, especially the inevitably boring one: 'Wasn't it an awful letdown living with Paul Mowrer after Hemingway?'[13]

Posthumous publications by Hemingway himself are more intriguing than books about him. In the last years of his life, he found it impossible to finish anything—*The Garden of Eden*, *Islands in the Stream*, *A Moveable Feast*, *The Dangerous Summer.* After he died, however, work that was either cast aside or mislaid made its way onto bookshelves.

It was his friend Charles Ritz who found the manuscript of *A Moveable Feast* in a trunk in the basement of the Ritz Hotel in Paris. Hemingway had left it there some twenty years before and forgotten about it. This is incredible considering it features some of his most beautifully written sketches. The trunk also contained the original copies of some early stories which he was able to sell to collectors for large sums.

A Moveable Feast, as mentioned, contains closely observed character portraits of people he knew in Paris in the 1920s. In the absence of an Oak Park memoir, this is the closest he came to an autobiography. He often suggested he intended to write an autobiography. This became increasingly unlikely as the years went on. The 'Paris book', as he called it, will have to do in the absence of one. Just as *The Old Man and the Sea* was part of a bigger work that was abandoned, brevity worked in its favour. An intriguing mixture of vitriol and nostalgia, it puts everyone from Scott Fitzgerald to Gertrude Stein to the sword.

Writing it, for Hemingway, was an example of the salmon returning to the stream in which it was spawned. The present had stopped mattering to him by this time. Only memories of the glory years could spur him on. The fact that he brought attitudes of later times to bear upon his memories gives the book an extra dimension. Gianfranco Ivancich said a page from it was in his typewriter on the day he died. That in itself tells us how much it meant to him.

Islands in the Stream came out in 1970. It tells the story of an artist, Thomas Hudson, and his relationship with his children. He struggles against family ties and the failure of his art. The book avoids the more serious excesses of Hemingway's later work but leaves one with a curiously empty feeling. Apart from a few glimpses of his genius, it becomes increasingly weighed down by swathes of dour philosophising about bereavement and the like. One doubts he would have published it in this form in his lifetime. It goes on so long it becomes difficult to care what happens to Hudson in the end.

Perhaps Hemingway's most curious posthumous publication was his unfinished gender-bending book, *The Garden of Eden.* Telling the story of David Bourne, a First World War veteran honeymooning through France and Spain with his sexually adventurous wife Catherine—she likes to swap identities with him during lovemaking—the plot takes off when they meet a woman called Marita, who fancies both of them. This is new territory for Hemingway. It extrapolates themes that are dormant in his more famous novels. The problem is lack of direction.

Catherine's jealousy of her husband's writing puts one in mind of Zelda Fitzgerald with Scott, though David is no way as likeable as Scott. Hemingway might have got away with him in a short story. Over the course of the novel, he flounders.

As was the case with *Across the River and Into the Trees*, a lot of ink is spilled on issues like ordering the 'right' food and drinking the 'right' drinks. This is done in the kind of self-satisfied style that makes one wonder what happened to the Angry Young Man who wrote all those pulsating stories about characters who lived on the edge.

From another point of view, the book can be seen as an exemplification of his *ménage à trois* scenario with Hadley and Pauline. After Hemingway took up with Pauline, John Dos Passos said to him, 'Aren't we all expatriates from the Garden of Eden?' The comment may have given him his title.

Catherine seems like a composite of Hadley and Zelda. Marita is the Pauline character zoning in on the marriage. Bisexual by orientation, she sleeps with Catherine. (There was a rumour Pauline once slept with Hadley, and that she went on to have lesbian affairs after Hemingway divorced her.)

As well as dealing with a *ménage*, the book investigates the playful undercurrents made possible by the inversion of traditional sexual roles, thereby giving Freudians who suspected Hemingway of being a latent homosexual a field day.

Aaron Latham, the author of a biography of Scott Fitzgerald, believed Hemingway was 'a man who dreamed about going out and shooting lions all day and then coming home and making androgynous love'. He was indeed fascinated by the theme of sexual inversion, as is evidenced by the fact that he dealt with it not only in *The Garden of Eden* and some of his other novels but also in stories like 'A Simple Inquiry' and 'A Sea Change'.

The Garden of Eden almost matches *Across the River and Into the Trees* for self-indulgent conversations that appealed to few outside a very select readership. (You can only do so much with your hair.) It might be interesting to gourmands and amateur hunters but hardly to the general reading public. John Updike wrote of it, 'Hemingway reached back from his workroom in Cuba through all the battles and bottles and injuries and interviews to make mythic material out of his discovery that sex can be complicated.'

There have been more studies of this book by 'explainers' than any of Hemingway's other posthumously published ones. Most of them have been done not because of the book's literary riches, of which there are few, but because it goes into some kinky areas of its author's psyche. Its fetishisation of sex throws retrospective light on some of his earlier fiction.

The most recent posthumous publication was *True at First Light*, a painfully droll account of his 1953 safari experience. Patrick revealed that it was originally intended to be a book of short stories.[14] In its published form, it becomes little more than a melange of frothy ruminations. The lions are almost cuddly. We get the token fantasy woman. No matter how much Hemingway liked to embellish his legend, one feels he would have drawn the line here.

Patrick whittled it down from a staggering 200,000 words to roughly half that. No doubt Hemingway would have edited it differently. He disliked the book and abandoned it in mid-sentence on page 850. By that stage he had enough of it. Most other readers reached their exhaustion point much sooner.

It was published in 1999 to coincide with the centenary of his birth. This suggested it was a marketing opportunity as much as anything else. By now Hemingway had become a brand. Holidays to places like Pamplona and Kilimanjaro were tied in with the books. Rifles and fishing rods were also sold in his name around this time. As one writer put it, 'He'd become a version of Burberry or Dior for those with cultural aspirations and a gun licence.'

For literary merit one would be better employed surveying his letters. Carlos Baker collected these in 1981. They run to 921 pages and portray him in every possible mood. A more recent set edited by Sandra Spanier is almost that size in each of its many iterations.

The letters in these volumes are more disordered than in the Baker collection. He makes up words or misspells them intentionally. He goes into stream-of-consciousness diatribes. He mixes spacing styles. He draws sketches. He rants on interminably, at one stage giving us a fourteen page 'education' about wine.

Hemingway's word tally for the letters he wrote during his lifetime ran to over three million. There are over 10,000 of them in all. He could never resist replying to one he received. As he put it in that folksy idiom he enjoyed so much, 'Screedage occurs after instant wordage.'

The letters are free of the famous 'discipline' he swore by so much in his fiction. One enjoys seeing the 'real' Hemingway in their spontaneity, their wordplay, their childishness and—something notably absent from so many of his novels—their wit.

The overall impression that comes through them is his richness of spirit. If the stories and novels only show one-seventh of their author as per his iceberg theory, here we get the other six-sevenths. Fiery, melancholy, jocose, idealistic, defensive, depressed, jejune, self-parodic, self-congratulatory—the entire man is here.

Hemingway's almost Herzog-like obsession with writing letters seems to attest to an inability to spend any time alone without putting pen to paper. He could hunt and fish alone, but within the confines of whatever abode he inhabited, he found it difficult to tolerate his own company for very long. If he was between books, letters to all and sundry filled the gap for him. He sometimes begrudged the time spent on them, feeling they wasted his creative juice, but they were therapy nonetheless. They also gave him a connection with friends and colleagues—and even enemies. If he was born a century later, he might well have become addicted to emails.

He said to Scott Fitzgerald in 1925, 'It's such a swell way to keep from working and yet feel you've done something.' According to Gregory, letter-writing helped him unwind from what he called 'the awful responsibility of writing'. For such an exhaustive craftsman, this was sweet relief.

Bernard Berenson's biographer Meryle Secrest waxed lyrical about the letters, crediting them with being 'so spontaneous they banish forever the image of Hemingway as an anguished writer painfully producing a sentence every third day'. She also said they were 'indomitable and life-enhancing, full of whimsical reminiscence and unguarded insights into himself, written in a laboured hand, like a child learning to write'. They betrayed a tender and loving man, she praised, someone whose character was 'transparently insecure, and diametrically opposite to the almost ludicrous image offered to the world'. One would have to have a crystal ball to foresee the mind of a suicide at work in them, even down to the one he penned two and a half weeks before shooting himself. That was to an acquaintance of his called Frederick Saviers. It ends with the postscript: 'Am feeling fine and very cheerful about things in general and hope to see you all soon.'[15]

The curse of suicide plagued the Hemingway family. Gregory's son, John, spoke of it as being like a Faustian pact with the devil. Jack referred to it as 'the family exit'.[16] Both of Hemingway's grandfathers shot themselves. Ursula took a fatal overdose in 1966 when she was informed she had inoperable cancer.[17] Some of the Hemingway family even believed Marcelline's death—two years after her book appeared—was suspicious.[18] Leicester committed suicide in 1982 after being informed he would have to have his legs amputated because of diabetes. It was like a replay of his father's last days.

'With this much loss,' Paula McLain wrote, 'you begin to think it's in the blood, as if there's a dark magnet pulling the body in that direction.' Jack reflected in his old age, 'I'd like to hang around a while to see just how long a Hemingway can survive by natural means.' He got his answer in January 2001 when he died of complications from heart surgery.

One of Hemingway's first sketches features a wounded soldier who has lost both his legs in the war. He commits suicide with the words, 'I had a rendezvous with Death but Death broke the date and now it's all over. God double-crossed me.' Leicester may well have been thinking of these words when he shot himself.

A self-destructive urge even extended into the next generation of Hemingways. Jack jokingly observed that he spent the first half of his life as a famous son and the last as a famous father.[19] He gave birth to two daughters who became Hollywood actresses. Margaux, the elder one, died by her own hand at the age of forty-one in 1996 after a blighted career as an actress. It was overshadowed by that of her younger sister, Mariel. Margaux died on a significant date, 1 July. Hemingway had shot himself on the 2nd.

Margaux had well-publicised problems throughout her life, including bulimia, dyslexia, epilepsy, and alcoholism. She was divorced twice and also spent time in the Betty Ford Clinic. In 1990, she modelled nude for *Playboy*—a sign, perhaps, that her career had derailed.

Hemingway's reputation continues to grow today. The biographies keep coming. Some of them seem excessively critical of him, like the ones written by Paul Hendrickson and Richard Bradford, though both of these have been exhaustively researched. In more recent years there have been two biographies of him written by women, Ruth Hawkins and Mary Dearborn. Will Hemingway finally become a 'woman's writer'? Stranger things have happened.

Christopher Ondaatje explored his safaris. Michael Palin and Michael Katakis wrote coffee table books. Leslie Blume and Andrea di Robilant explored the embryology of two of his books, *The Sun Also Rises* and *Across the River and Into the Trees*.

Woody Allen put Hemingway into a film, *Midnight in Paris*. *The Sun Also Rises* was made into a play. There were two novelisations based on his life with Hadley, Paula McLain's *The Paris Wife* and Naomi Wood's *Mrs Hemingway*. Ken Burns and Lynn Novick directed a brilliant six-part documentary on him in 2021.

Hemingway's literary life began with a tragedy just as his actual one ended that way. In between the strained subtleties of 'Indian Camp' and the nervous panic of July 1961, he wove stylised tapestries that dwarfed his contemporaries.

He once told Malcolm Cowley, apropos his refusal to make excuses for his lapses:

> There are no bad bounces. Alibis don't count. Go out and do your stuff. You can't do it? Then don't take refuge in the fact that you're a rummy, or pant and crawl back into somebody's womb, or have the con. You only have to do it once to get remembered by some people. But if you can do it year after year after year, quite a lot of people remember and they tell their children and their grandchildren. And if it's good enough it lasts forever.[20]

With Hemingway it was. And it will.

20

The Man Behind the Myth

Like most geniuses, Hemingway was a mass of contradictions. He lived like a recluse a lot of the time and yet he was one of the most recognisable faces in America. He may have been a larger than life figure around the world as well but to the people in his inner circle, like his former chauffeur Toby Bruce and the people he hunted and fished with like Joe Russell, Bra Saunders, Roberto Herrera, Charles Thompson, Forrest MacMullen, Lloyd Arnold, and Bud Purdy, he was simply 'Ernie'.

He made an art form out of debunking 'litrachure', but he was a voracious reader, having almost 5,000 books in his library.[1] He could also speak various languages. He said he hated talking about writing but none of his contemporaries talked more about it than he did.

He was jovial, big-hearted, generous, outgoing, and charismatic. He was also vengeful, violent, insecure, jealous, unfaithful, self-obsessed, and manipulative. In the words of Norman Mailer, 'His dirty fighting and his love of craft came out of the same blood.'[2]

One of the main questions that intrigued people about him was how someone who appeared to be so charming could go out of his way to alienate his friends time and again. Hadley said there were so many sides to him, 'You could hardly make a sketch of him in a geometry book.'[3] She admitted he had a cruel streak but added that his kindness 'went just about as far in the other direction'.

He made friends quickly. His fiery temperament made him lose them nearly as fast. His ever-expanding circle of acolytes changed with the seasons. People soon learned exactly what it was they had to do to remain within that charmed circle. Those who broke the rules were more often than not denied a second chance. When he turned against someone, his anger paralleled the original adulation.

He fell out with most of his friends throughout his life. There was no chance of doing that with some of them. James Joyce died. Ezra Pound was locked up in an asylum. Maxwell Perkins and Sylvia Beach he rarely saw. Bernard Berenson he never met. Almost everyone else fell foul of him at some point, either due to offences real or imagined.

His relationships with members of his family were equally mercurial. He never forgave his parents for criticising his books. Nor did he forgive Marcelline for berating him after he left Hadley. Nor Carol for marrying a man he disapproved of. On the other end of the scale, he was strongly affectionate with people like Arnold Gingrich, Buck Lanham, Harvey Breit, Archibald MacLeish. He loved as he hated, with undiluted passion.

His saving grace was his sense of humour. No matter how 'black-assed' he became, he could retrieve any potentially disastrous scenario with a quip. In *A Moveable Feast*, he wrote: 'They say the seeds of what we will do are in all of us but it always seemed to me that in those who make jokes in life the seeds are covered with better soil and with a higher grade of manure.'[4]

His charm was so great he could sell ice to Eskimos. Like Arthur Miller's Willy Loman, he spent most of his life selling himself. Dorothy Parker compared the experience of meeting him with how a tourist might feel upon seeing the Grand Canyon for the first time.[5]

Humanity, he claimed, could be divided into two classes: the bastards and the sons of bitches. 'I try to be kind and Christian and gentle,' he told Robert Cantwell in 1950, 'and a lot of the time I make it. When I don't, it gets in the papers.'

The French novelist Pierre Drieu La Rochelle said of him, 'He is a man who is at once a camera and a phonograph. He has the shoulders of a porter and the soul of a hunting-dog, desperately aware of every living scent, pursuing every quarry with a tender and implacable desire.' Archibald MacLeish found it difficult to get along with or without him.[6]

He was pathologically sensitive. When Thomas Shelvin passed some mild criticism of *To Have and Have Not,* he threw the manuscript out a window into the snow outside and refused to retrieve it for three days. It was the first and last time he ever showed Shelvin work-in-progress. The experience made him stop doing that to others as well.

The issue of his bravery, or lack of it, is a continuous bone of contention among scholars. Was he pre-eminently courageous or a coward who took elaborate pains to camouflage that fact? Sometimes his bravado sounded adolescent, as when he claimed he killed 112 people in the war. He also said once that he shot a German through the head which resulted in his brains coming out through his nostrils.[7]

This was nothing more than locker-room banter. People took it with a grain of salt. One finds it difficult to imagine him killing even a single man, never mind 112. Some people believe the only shots he ever fired in the Second World War were at a photograph of Mary's previous husband, Noel Monks, which he placed on the commode of a toilet bowl in 1944 after being presented with a gift of a German pistol from Buck Lanham and wanting to try it out. He was tipsy at the time and annoyed by Monks being 'faintly difficult' about the divorce from Mary. Needless to say, he totally destroyed the commode and flooded the floor with water.[8] This seems more likely than the phenomenon of a gun-toting Hemingway taking on all comers in the trenches.

He was happier killing soulless creatures like lions and marlin. Even then there was some reluctance. He never killed an elephant, for instance, feeling such an act would be an abomination. When asked why he condoned cockfights in Cuba, he replied, 'What else does a fighting cock like to do?' He had a point.

His violence was never gratuitous. It was either a case of pitting himself against nature or against his fellow man in official or unofficial boxing matches. The official ones took place with people like Ezra Pound, Harold Loeb, and Morley Callaghan, the unofficial ones with Robert McAlmon and Max Eastman.

Hemingway's humour is something that has largely been ignored by biographers. It erupted at unusual times. During the Second World War, a soldier asked him why he had never been promoted beyond the status of captain despite his many scars gained in battle. He replied, 'The reason, young man, is a simple and painful one. I never learned to read and write.'[9]

When a member of a shooting club he belonged to came up to him in 1945 and said, 'Ernesto—you were never actually under fire, were you?' he replied gamely, 'Shit no. Do you think I'm crazy?' This is reminiscent of the mood he was in when he asked for the macho publicity puff advertising *A Farewell to Arms* to be watered down.

His practice of growing away from people he was close to was a continuing pattern in his life. It was most apparent in his relationships with members of his family. In time he broke with all of them except Ursula. She was like a second mother to him from the time he got his war wound.

He never liked Marcelline, as mentioned. Madelaine he saw as being selfish like his mother. He became bitter with Carol after she said she wanted to marry a Princeton student called John Gardner. Hemingway always had a chip on his shoulder about not having gone to university.

The anti-intellectual pose he adopted in his stories could be viewed as inverted snobbery.

Gardner struck him as being cocky. When he warned him away from Carol, he just laughed. Hemingway told her if she went against his wishes he would stop sending her money. Even so, she went ahead with the marriage. Hemingway blew a fuse, all but disowning her afterwards. Of Gardner he said, 'Only thing to have done would have been to shoot him.'[10] When people asked him about Carol in later years, he said things like, 'She's dead.' He also spread a rumour that she was raped as a teenager. Carol vehemently denied this.

Nobody has ever been able to explain why he took such a dislike to Gardner. He had an affable personality and proved to be an ideal husband to Carol. They had a happy marriage together. It lasted longer than any of Hemingway's ones. Some critics have speculated that Hemingway had unconscious sexual feelings for Carol. That meant he would have disapproved of her marrying *any* man. This is a theory with absolutely no basis.[11]

The fact that he had only one brother might lead one to expect him to have had a close relationship with him, but Hemingway had problems with Leicester's virility. Another problem with him was that he wrote badly. A third was that he physically resembled his mother. Every time Hemingway looked into his eyes, he saw Grace. This distressed him greatly. The only way he could get his mind off it was to keep his eyes shut as he talked to him.[12]

Hemingway's relationship to his children was also fraught, as I've been at pains to point out in the preceding pages. It alternated between extravagant displays of affection and glowering rages and was also unpredictable in regard to money.

In March 1955, he made two promises to Jack. The first was that he would never kill himself as his father had done, the second that he intended to leave him a large inheritance in his will.[13] He kept neither one of them. In fact, he left neither Jack nor any of his other children anything in his will. His siblings were also left out of it. Sunny was even denied the Michigan cottage he promised her. She had to buy it from Mary.

Outside the family he was equally unpredictable in his relationships. Gertrude Stein was a case in point, going from angel to demon in his eyes. His relationship to her is interesting as a kind of prism through which we can view the ever-changing filter of his reactions to other former friends. She appealed enormously to him after he arrived in Paris. Things deteriorated so much in the '30s that they stopped speaking to one another.

He spoke disparagingly of her to Arnold Gingrich: 'She was a fine woman until she went goofily lesbian with the menopause.'

A possible reason for her turning against him was because of the 'evil' influence of Alice B. Toklas. Toklas never liked Hemingway. 'Give up your friendship of Hemingstein,' she demanded of her one day, 'or you give up me.'[14]

One day when he arrived at her door she greeted him with the words, 'Hemingway, why do you always come here drunk?' 'I don't know, Miss Stein,' he replied, 'Unless it's to see you.' On his next visit, he was shocked to see a padlock on her door. There was a sign beside it that read, 'Keep out. This means you.'

Stein, he said in 1948, 'had a necessity to break off friendships. She only gave real loyalty to people who were inferior to her. She had to attack me because she learned to write dialogue from me.'

Some critics argue that he turned against her because he was homophobic. Stein was a nice woman, he wrote to Harvey Breit in 1956, 'until she had a change of life and opted for fags and fags only'. In 1933, he wrote to Janet Flanner, who was also lesbian:

> I never cared a damn about what she did in or out of bed and I liked her very damned much and she liked me. But when the menopause hit her she got awfully damned patriotic about sex. The first stage was that nobody was any good that wasn't that way. The second was that anybody that was that way was good. The third was that anybody that was any good *must* be that way.

Stein demonised Hemingway in her book *The Autobiography of Alice B. Toklas*, portraying him as an accident-prone coward who wrote as stupidly as he boxed. The immediate cause of their split was a discussion about sex that he accidentally overheard between herself and Toklas.[15] The surprisingly prudish Hemingway was shocked by their language.

He once said that he would like to have had sex with her, a distinctly unlikely possibility in view of that lesbianism. In an interesting aside, she told him she was repulsed by male homosexuality. She sometimes thought him to be gay himself, and in need of being 'outed'.

Hemingway wrote a number of stories featuring gay men. They fare badly in them. This fact has fed into the homophobia charges that are often levelled against him. But he had gay friends like Robert McAlmon and the bullfighter Sidney Franklin—though Franklin insisted he had such a bias against homosexual men that he once crossed a street in Spain for the sole purpose of knocking one to the ground.[16] He also fell out with

Jinny Pfeiffer, though this was hardly due to her lesbianism. It more likely resulted from her turning against him when he broke with Pauline.

Whatever about homophobia, he certainly seems to have suffered from sexism. Women in his books are largely killjoys. This is a strain apparent all the way back to the early Nick Adams stories like 'The Three Day Blow'. In that story, a character tells Adams, 'Once a man's married he's absolutely bitched. He hasn't got anything more. Not a damn thing. He's done for. You've seen the guys that get married. You can tell them. They get this sort of fat married look. They're done for.'[17]

Hemingway expected his women to be housewives rather than working mothers. He may have been thrown by the fact that his own mother was an independent spirit at a time before it was kosher for women to be like this. In his more outrageous moments—or was he merely being frivolous?—he was prone to make statements like:

> There's only one thing to do if a man is married to a woman with whom he has nothing in common, with whom there is no question of justice but only a gross fact of utter selfishness and hysterical emotionalism, and that is to get rid of her. He might try to whip her first but it would probably be no good.[18]

Any man who allowed himself to suffer from women, he alleged, had a disease as incurable as cancer.[19] This comment was made when he was getting a hard time from Pauline after their divorce. He may also have been thinking about his father's spirit being sucked out of him by his mother when he wrote this, or Scott Fitzgerald's by Zelda. Sometimes it might be necessary even to shoot a woman, he suggested, even if it got you hanged. A less drastic solution was to numb yourself so nobody could hurt you. But by that stage you were probably dead anyway.

Another example of his misogyny can be found in a letter he wrote to Bernard Berenson in 1953. 'God deliver us all from women's brains,' he wrote, 'They have a lack of imagination. When anything hits them they think they're the first person it ever happened to.'

Bernice Kert believed he was confused about the role women played in his life. She wrote in her book *The Hemingway Women*, 'The conflict between his yearning to be looked after and his craving for excitement and freedom was never resolved.' He needed the security of marriage but despised its claustrophobia. The Oak Park side of him wanted to legitimise his romances whereas the bohemian in him needed frequent breaks away from the crippling routines of domesticity.

His life would have been less complicated if he had less marriages and more affairs. Mary thought he was a victim of his time:

> [When he was young,] people were more or less committed to marry the woman they wanted to shack up with. That was the custom. It would seem to me that someone of Ernest's wide interests and exuberance, a normally healthy fellow, would be interested in more than one woman. He'd naturally have two or three girls. The fact that he faithfully got rid of one and married another is a circumstance of the recent past.

His grandson remarked, 'He was the kind of person who, if he went to bed with a woman on a semi-permanent basis, married her.'[20]

When he was courting Hadley, he slept with Kate Smith and an Armenian prostitute he met in Turkey while researching an article for the *Toronto Star.* He felt Hadley would like to have slept with the bullfighter Cayetano Ordonez, whom they met in Pamplona. He discouraged her from this. His own infidelity was 'merely' physical, he reasoned. Hers would be a betrayal of the heart. Such a doublethink was carried over into his relationship with Pauline. When he divorced her, a part of him felt it was no less than she deserved because she stole him from Hadley.[21]

He told Malcolm Cowley once that he bedded every woman he ever wanted to. He liked telling people not only that he caught frequent doses of venereal disease but that a prostitute once waived her fee thanks to his 'performance'. Boasts about boudoir exploits with Montmartre prostitutes rolled as trippingly off his tongue as tall tales about killing 'krauts' or catching bigger fish than he did.

Scott Fitzgerald's heaven, he theorised, would be comprised of wealthy monogamists heartily drinking themselves into the grave. His would be holding two *barrera* seats at a bull ring with a trout stream outside and two houses nearby. One would be for his wife and children, the other for his nine nubile mistresses.[22]

Hemingway wasn't the kind of man to have one life in the bar and another one at home with his little lady. He preferred his women to accompany him wherever he went. 'Any girl who marries Papa,' he told Lillian Ross, 'has to know how to carry a gun.'[23]

As the years went on, he needed to be away from his wives more and more. Martha went her own way from the beginning so that marriage was doomed almost before it started. The one to Mary lasted because, like Hadley, she soaked up everything he threw at her.

He often seemed to be closer to his female friends than his wives. One of the greatest friendships he formed with a woman outside marriage was with Marlene Dietrich. It never developed into an affair and was probably stronger for that.

She kept all his letters, refusing to allow them be published after his death. If he wrote something that pleased her, her approval meant more to him than that of any critic. She said he was 'my anchor, my sage, my best advisor, the pope of my personal church'. His body, she went on, 'seemed to emit sparks whose light fell on us and was reflected in our eyes'. Letters she wrote to him contain effusive comments like, 'I want to put my arms round you, and my heart. I want to kiss you forever for the beauty that is in you.' In 1953, she wrote to him, 'You are always in my thoughts. I look at your picture every morning and say Hello to you.'[24]

Would they have made a good husband and wife? She thought they would. One thing that appealed particularly to him about her was her androgynous look. Pauline had that too. So did Duff Twysden, Jane Mason, and Mary Welsh.

Dietrich and Mary were rivals for his affections. In 1944, he escorted both women to official receptions simultaneously in Paris, afterwards entertaining them in the Ritz. He termed this 'The command post for all veterans of the 22nd Infantry Regiment.'[25] Dietrich sang while Mary seethed. She was anxious to know if his recent marriage proposal to her was based on sound principles or merely uttered on the spur of the moment.

Hemingway called Dietrich 'a good General'. She used to sit on the edge of his bathtub as he was shaving, crooning songs like 'Lili Marlene' and 'Falling in Love Again' to entertain him. Mary made fun of her voice in an affectionate way. Dietrich was secure enough in her talent not to mind. 'If she had nothing more than her voice,' Hemingway wrote in a *Life* essay on her, 'she could break your heart with it.' He used to sing to her too, having a fondness for the song 'I Don't Know Why I Love You But I Do'. Hemingway was no Caruso. He enjoyed singing even when he was off key. Dietrich said of him, 'I honestly think if more people had friends like Ernest, there would be fewer analysts.' She saw him as the most positive life force she ever encountered.

Dietrich's daughter, Maria Riva, claimed her mother never really knew Hemingway the man, only the image. According to Riva he was for Dietrich 'the dashing war correspondent in the turned-up-collar raincoat; the hunter, shotgun cocked, standing strong in the path of charging rhino; the lonely philosopher of the bleeding hands, clutching the fishing line'.

Dietrich became an adoptive daughter to him in time like Ava Gardner and Ingrid Bergman. Gardner won brownie points with him by accompanying him to bullfights and visiting him under pseudonyms to throw reporters off the track.[26] He was physically attracted to her. When she swam naked in his swimming pool one day, he refused to have the water changed afterwards. He never became romantically involved with Gardner any more than he did with Dietrich or Bergman. Marriage to them was also out of the question for him. 'Would never marry an actress,' he propounded, 'on account they have careers and work bad hours.'[27]

He once called Bergman 'the best actress in the world'. When she was undergoing image problems in Hollywood as a result of being pregnant outside wedlock with Roberto Rossellini's child, he gave her much support. 'What's the problem?' he asked. 'They were both in love. Where's the sin?' He told her he wanted her to have twins. He would be the godfather, he promised, and carry them into St. Peter's Church with him, one on each arm.

When she expressed a desire to leave films and concentrate on being a housewife as a result of feeling unwanted by the top Hollywood brass, he dispensed some fatherly advice to her. 'Listen, daughter,' he expounded:

> I have looked into Dr Hemingstein's crystal ball and a housewife is one thing you ain't gonna be. When they are starved enough for you they will come to get you. In the meantime, anything I can do with my cheque-book or my 16-gauge Winchester or maybe just to cream a couple of characters that need creaming, you only have to say the word.

In these relationships, we see Hemingway in his natural state. He became as jovial as he was before success turned him in on himself. Marriage seemed to take away his spontaneity. Mary thought he was better at loving women from a distance than when they were with him twenty-four hours a day.

Adriana Ivancich was an example of this. He never lived with her, so the allure remained. She became famous for her association with him. In this she was like Agnes, another woman who rejected him and became known for that rather than anything else she did in life. In her later years, Agnes became a librarian in Key West. Tour guides pointed her out as the inspiration behind *A Farewell to Arms*. This caused her more distress than comfort. Her relationship to him may have only been a 'boy-girl thing' for her but it stayed with her forever even if Hemingway himself got over it.

His relationship to Ivancich also had lifelong reverberations for her, giving her ideas about herself she could never fulfil. When she married Spiros Manos, it was a disaster. The possessiveness with which he courted her was followed by indifference after he brought her up the aisle. He soon abandoned her. She went on to marry a count in 1964. He was eight years older than her. The Italian edition of *Across the River and Into the Trees* came out the following year. Whatever chance she had of forgetting Hemingway was destroyed by all the media attention around this. It engulfed her. In 1966, she put his letters to her up for sale at Christies, the ones she hid from Manos after he ordered her to burn them and she refused. The move was either one of opportunism or an attempt to exorcise the last vestiges of Hemingway's memory from her life. This was always going to be impossible. People kept asking her about him, right up to her tragic demise.

At the end of the day, one is left with the question: was Hemingway hero or villain, sinner or saint? In his alter ego Nick Adams, we see echoes both of the devil and the Garden of Eden. Both elements are implied in his name. It was possibly chosen to indicate this. Hemingway loved straddling extremes.

People find it easy to criticise him. Easy because everything in his life is so transparent. The mistreatment of his mother. The backstabbing of friends who put him on the road to success. The carousing. The sexual perversions, real or imagined. The alcoholic excesses. The sadistic putdowns. The trite pugilism. The desertion of wives. The wallowing in false glory. The refusal to work at relationships. The exploitation of pain. The tantrums. The slushy, sermonising style. The final descent into madness.

We need to place these things in the perspective of his overall character. He was well aware he was no angel, but his virtues were as big as his vices. They came from the same tortured heart. If he was unforgiving, it was because he set such rigorous standards. He loved and hated with more passion than the average soul and was finally overcome by it.

He was a braggart, but braggarts are often innocent. They need approval from others. If you scratch one you might find a soul too sensitive to admit its vulnerability. For such a successful writer, he displayed an incredible insecurity. It made him feed off adulation like oxygen. The flipside of this coin was that it made him react against so badly against criticism.

He had a huge impact on the lives of people who came after him, some of whom took his character into their own, even trying to mould it into it. I met one of them, a man called James Mitchell Lear. He was an actor who toured the world with his one-man show *Hemingway Reminisces*. In the late 1970s, Hemingway's granddaughter, Margaux, asked Lear to act as 'The Spirit of Hemingway' for a collection of photographs she was appearing in for *Town and Country* magazine. She was struck by his resemblance to Hemingway.

After posing for the shots, he became obsessed with the man he resembled. Over the next few years, he visited Hemingway's haunts in such far-flung locales as Pamplona, Key West, Paris, and Austria in an attempt to get inside his skin.

'There's been so much written about him,' he said to me when I interviewed him backstage during the Dublin run of his play, 'it gets difficult to separate fact from fantasy. What I try to capture in my show is his *joie de vivre*. We hear a lot about his dark side these days. That only came at the end of his life after electroshock treatment robbed him of his creativity.'

Lear had little truck with those who interpreted Hemingway's life backwards from the way it ended rather than forwards from the way it began.

I asked him if he thought he had a death wish. 'Why do you say that?' he asked, 'Because he went hunting? If that's the case then you have to say that anyone who ever went hunting had a death wish. Is that logical?'

His own belief was that his fascination with outdoor pursuits was a reaction to his upbringing. 'He came from Calvinist stock. Use the proper knives and forks, sit erect, do what you're told. The fact that he had a tyrannical mother made this worse for him.'

According to Lear, he was an average all-American boy who formed a dream of being a writer because of failing to measure up in other areas. 'He couldn't get on the first team in swimming or football. He was unspectacular academically and he had clumsy feet. He also a bum eye so he couldn't get into the army as a young man.'

It was his ability to embrace his demons that made the last twenty years of his life so resonant for Lear: 'He fulfilled a part of every person. We could all dream we were inside him.' His overall view of him was of a man with immense courage, immense fear, and immense capacity for pain. 'Did you know,' he said, 'that he once walked a mile in Madrid with a broken leg? He always acted on instinct. I think it grew from that need to be famous. He couldn't help himself—like all of us.'

Was he the brawler of legend? 'The jury is still out on that one. Toby Bruce once told me he never saw him starting a fight but he could finish one all right. If people rubbed up against him the wrong way he decked them. He hit a man so hard once, he somersaulted over a car. He had unbridled energy. It probably came from all that pain.'

He saw the same energy in Sunny when he met her. 'She was 83 at the time. She had emphysema and an oxygen tank but she was still able to bring me boating out on Lake Walloon.'

When they got to the cottage in Windemere she had a bottle of beer waiting for him. After drinking it, he looked out across the lake to the Indian camp of Hemingway's first short story. Beside an outhouse he saw a sign that said, 'Hemingway Sat Here.' It was written by the man himself. 'He was already,' said Lear, 'developing his myth.'

'Seeing things like that,' he said to me, 'is research. It's preferable to sitting for months in a library poring over books. I saw what he saw the way he saw it—the cottage, the lake, the way the sun set over Petoskey Bay. How can you match that?'

Epilogue

If this was enough of a book, it would have had everything in it.

It would have had the war, the last gentleman's war, and all the good thoughts he had about his life during it. It would have had the early ferias and deep-sea fishing and nights outside the cafes in Paris when no one asked him what he wanted to do with his life and he did not ask himself either because he was just going through the day and it was pretty and beautiful and the buildings were fine and there were many good friends and it was good to have them there by his side swapping talk about the *metier* and bullfighters and men and women who knew life was not easy but took the right chances at the right time.

The early years on Horton Bay where he lost his heart to women who might not have even known it, and the wind coming up sharp and cool in the long mornings afterwards to remind him of that. And walking with his grandfather on the beach at Petoskey and climbing the hill behind the cottage to see the sunsets.

Waking up to the sun in Key West feeling as if it was the first day of his life. The way the sea looked when it was cold and hard and inviting him into it with a sly elegance. And all those Cuban trips and the stories afterwards—even if half of them were false—and the good feeling he had about the writing and how it was such a hell of a thing not to feel guilty that he did not have a proper job. But he always knew this was his real job even if his mother did not think that way, or his father either.

Going hunting with him in Michigan and being shown how to trap wild animals. Watching the sun go down on the bay afterwards and carrying all his dreams with it and all his fears. Coming home late at night when the lights were on the river and the leaves falling from the trees. Telling stories that were true even if the person that told them was not him write. It was a long time ago and in another country so that might not have been important.

If this was enough of a book, it would have had him cycling up and down Kenilworth Avenue delivering *Oak Leaves* to the residents, or his Uncle Tyler proposing marriage to his maid, or Gertrude Stein throwing her head back and laughing raucously at yet another clever riposte from him, and then hitting him for his insolence. It would have him taking Hadley to Fossalta in 1922 and seeing no remnants of the war there at all, only the memories.

It is a pity the book does not have him fishing for trout in Michigan or for salmon in the Loire or relaxing with a book afterwards as he lay down with Hadley under the stars, marvelling at how lucky he was to have found a woman so pure and giving, and a life that allowed him to go anywhere he wanted without anyone breathing down his neck for deadlines or telling him how to write.

It should have had Marie Cocotte nursing Bumby through his whooping cough in the apartment at the Rue Notre Dame des Champs, or him wandering through the boulevards in search of inspiration, or going with Hadley to the six-day bicycle races in between skiing trips, or Scott and Zelda arguing fiercely, and the happy look that came into Zelda's face when she knew Scott would not be able to write anymore.

Why did it not have him going over his stories until he got them right, the hard work nobody knew about because they always thought Papa Hemingway was too busy chasing lions to care about his craft when the truth of it was that he cared almost too much to talk about it.

It should have had him shooting himself in the knees that day when he was trying to kill sharks, and the *mano a mano* bullfights, and talking about why he broke the comb for Adriana in Latisana in 1949, and meeting Marlene Dietrich when she refused to sit at a table of thirteen people because, like him, she was superstitious. It should have had him dancing in the square with senoritas at parties that went on all night and cavorting with Pauline in Alpine idylls, and cats in the rain, and the *riau riau* dancers in Pamplona.

The book should have had him telling his parents he was engaged to the movie star Mae Marsh even though he hardly knew her. Or shooting duck with Coop in Wyoming, or the boxing bout with John Huston that never happened.

What about the teething pains with Martha, and pretending they were not there because he wanted things to work so much with her he blocked them out. Or hanging Miro's 'The Farm' in his apartment for the first time and afterwards learning how to write from it along with the works of Klee and Cezanne and Picasso.

It should have him drinking at La Floridita and pontificating on how it was when his luck was good and the wind blowing from the right quarter and the sun coming up on the waves as he hooked another marlin with Pauline or Miss Mary. Maybe things were not quite as good now as they had been with Hadley in their time above the sawmill when he was starting out. He was able to forget that if the writing and the fishing were going well.

Why did the book not have him going to Italy with Mary in the '40s with the intention of defecating on the spot where he had been wounded? Or having the snow melting in the Abruzzi as the troops marched by, and the wind knifing through him as he climbed a mountain in search of a new nirvana or a new kill.

It should have had him writing the later novels in a standing position and laying off the sauce during the composition and not talking about what he was doing for fear he would talk it out of himself. And breaking John O'Hara's blackthorn stick over his head in one of his shows of temper.

What about him borrowing books from Sylvia Beach because he could not afford to buy them, but building up some mighty good ideas that way, and some kind of a goddamn library too.

Or when he interviewed Lloyd George in Canada the day Bumby was born, getting carpeted by Harry Hindmarsh afterwards for spending too much time at the hospital when he should have been writing articles for him.

A better book would have had sex and death and murder in an almost mystical union. It would have the taking of the Ritz via the Rambouillet route, and the lions that Santiago dreamed of, and the frozen leopard on Kilimanjaro and living in cold water flats that charged only sixty francs a month and skiing in the Vorarlberg and how he felt when Boni & Liveright said they were taking *In Our Time.*

It would have had him standing in his shorts and loafers in the Finca, his typewriter on a shelf opposite him, or rather his writetyper, struggling to find the right words and the right feelings, and wondering if his gift was disappearing, and if it was, how to get it back.

The book should have had him smuggling copies of *Ulysses* into the US and telling Ezra Pound that someday somebody would appreciate the gesture, before Ezra went mad like Zelda, and all the other beautifully mad people, and marriages that looked to be good ideas when he started them and things going to hell when he got greedy or selfish or successful, and not knowing who to blame when divorce loomed and not wanting to blame himself because he was getting the gold prize of a new wife but sad to be parting because each time a marriage died a part of him died too even if as the years went on it seemed easier to end them.

After each failed marriage, he told himself he could return to his books for company because he knew a book would not betray him like a woman could, or a critic, or friends he trusted before they got sucked into telling stories about him.

If this was enough of a book, it would have had him writing *The Fifth Column* in 1937 when the bullets were flying around him and staying cool under fire. It would have Aaron Hotchner meeting him for the first time in La Floridita to set up a lifetime friendship.

It would have had the excitement of seeing his name in print before he became famous, even if it was only in a cuckoo literary magazine that paid peanuts, or catching fish with his father and learning what to do with them afterwards, or being intoxicated with Pauline and not knowing whether to give in to it or not, or imagining he would be the greatest writer of all time and then cutting down on that ambition, or going a couple of rounds with Shakespeare and the great Russian writers before he found his own voice.

It would have had him giving boxing lessons in Kenilworth Avenue as his mother had her singing classes upstairs, or rushing away from Key West to sleep with Martha, and Pauline knowing something was up but not being able to say what. Or going to Spain with Martha and feeling bad about the relationship even before things had properly begun.

It would have had him running with the bulls in Pamplona, and meeting Dominguin and Ordonez and making them his heroes in a different way than writers were. Maybe it all gelled into one master plan, he thought, at least until the wars started and other things took over. Then there was all that stuff in the Mayo Clinic, the pills the doctors had that made him feel strange, but feeling stranger again if he did not take them.

The book should have had the first time he knew he could write novels and not just stories, and the rush he got when it was going well, and how he felt the first time one of them was on the bestseller list. Then another one was, and suddenly he knew what he was doing was important and would last, and he celebrated with one too many glasses of wine and afterwards his nerves were shot.

But what the hell. The books were out there, and many people were reading them and there were more where they came from, even though as time went on it got harder to write them. And then the critics started saying bad things about them, and making up things that were not there at all because they had nothing else to write about and he was an easy target.

The book should have had more about Hadley and Bumby in Paris, and Hadley playing the piano as he wrote, and him not being a good father when Bumby was young, but this was not because he did not love him, it was because he was too busy writing. He knew he could make it up to him when he grew up and they could go hunting together like he used to do in Michigan before things went bad with his father.

How could the book not have him falling into a bush fire two weeks after his plane crashed and not minding, or at least not seeming to, and not suffering any long-lasting symptoms either, though they said that was the case after the crashes too even though there was a lot of damage nobody knew about then.

The book should have had him being shelled in the Florida Hotel, the ceiling falling down on top of him, and this causing him only mild surprise as everyone around him frantically picked pieces of plaster from their hair.

He should have been sitting on the *Pilar* watching how the fish were running, the sun beating down on him as he tested the tension of his fishing line, boasting afterwards about the size of his catch like an adolescent but aware in a deeper part of himself that such things did not really matter. They did not matter any more than winning the Nobel Prize did, or marrying four times, or wanting to bed Mata Hari even though she was dead, or downing bottles of Valpolicella in the Gritti Hotel.

No, all that mattered when you came down to it was living your life from the ground up. All that mattered was taking your chances when they came, be it at the feria or in a secret part of your heart, the part where the magic resided, and the demons, and sometimes the magic and demons together in some mad communion that, like Yeats, was as cold and passionate as the dawn.

How could the book have missed him telling people not to write too much or too quickly, pacing himself like an athlete until there was always something left over for the next day, some departure point that would set the juices going rather than writing himself out in an empty flourish. Or brutally editing his own work, the early sketches that were too flimsy and the late ones that were too self-indulgent, all the while in search of that one true sentence.

He should have been fishing along the Irati in the book, or watching the sky change colour on the sierras, or looking at Ordonez going in over the bulls on muggy afternoons in San Fermin, or playing games of jai-alai in

Cuba, or bringing Hadley to Lake Walloon for the first time, or travelling to Lyons with Scott, or even that early weekend with Pauline in Paris when he wanted and yet did not want her.

What about the quick clear water in the irrigation ditches and the heavy green of the alfalfa? Should they not have been here too if the book was good enough? Should he not have been slaloming down the ski slopes at Schruns, or in the Abruzzi, or even in the Hurtgen Forest, beating his chest like Tarzan over yet another novel, or yet another wife. And then going into his tent to commune with *nada*.

A better book would have had him sauntering around the Finca like a benign tyrant, admiring the animal heads adorning the walls, or lost among his cats, those little tigers that reminded him of larger ones on mountain peaks, peaks he could not dream of scaling as he got older, just as he could not hunt or fish or do all the other things he took for granted when the world was simple.

The smell of smoked leather should have been here, and the smell of frozen roads, and the blue steel of the sky in the early morning shoots at Sun Valley, and the rush of excitement at the first kill, and the thrill of telling about it afterwards. But not too soon—and not too damned much either.

A better book would have had him waking up early in the morning in that country house in Paris to do his writing, the old military discipline standing to him as Hadley turned around for the second time. There would be few people about as he looked out the window during a break from his labours, only the goatherds and an occasional hobo, or maybe small pockets of people huddled round braziers, warming their hands off the embers as their breath fogged the air.

Such a book would have him waking Hadley to show her what he had written even if it was only a few lines. He would have been standing by her bed as proud as a child at some insight he showed into the forgotten people of the world, the ones he loved because he was one of them. He hoped he would not desert them if he became rich and famous.

A better book would have had him arguing with Dos Passos when he drifted to the left in the thirties, and telling Leicester that cats had 'absolute emotional honesty', and Leicester saying that his main ambition in life was to be 'Superman's older brother', and Gregory feeling guilty about the money he inherited after Pauline died, and Jinny telling Pauline to screw Papa for every cent after he divorced her, and the night he used a marlin he caught as a punchbag, and when he made a promise to break a critic's jaw every two years.

It would have had these things in it, and also the day Hadley placed a bet on a horse at 120/1 and nearly won. It would have Gertrude Stein using a bloodhound to keep him away from her when things went bad with her, and the night in Chicago with Katy Smith where he stated his view that women had their brains between their thighs.

There should have been something in the book about him conspiring with Winston Guest to help Bumby lose his virginity to a lady named Olga in San Francisco de Paula, not being aware that he had already done so the evening before. A better book would have had him talking about how drink proved both his nirvana and his nadir at different times of his life, giving him the courage to go on for a while and then stifling that very courage when its grip on him got too strong.

Such a book, finally, would have had the thoughts that were in his mind on that fateful morning of 2 July 1961 when everyone's world changed forever.

But it is not that kind of a book. There were just a few things to be said. There were just a few practical things to be said.

Endnotes

Introduction

1 Denis Brian, *The Faces of Hemingway* (London, Grafton Books, 1988), p. 61.
2 Arnold Samuelson, *With Hemingway: A Year in Key West and Cuba* (London: Severn House,1985), p. 11.
3 *Ibid.*, pp. 57-8.
4 First, one must last.
5 Lillian Ross, *Portrait of Hemingway* (London: Penguin, 1961), p. 45.
6 *New Yorker*, 4 January 1947.
7 Ross, *Portrait of Hemingway*, pp. 56-7.
8 *Paris Review 5,* Spring 1958.
9 *The Best of Bad Hemingway,* Florida: Harcourt Brace, 1989.

Chapter 1

1 Nagel, James, ed., *Ernest Hemingway: The Oak Park Legacy* (Tuscaloosa and London: University of Alabama Press, 1996), p. 25.
2 Marcelline Hemingway Sandford, *At the Hemingways* (London: Putnam, 1962), p. 78.
3 Nagel, ed., *The Oak Park Legacy*, pp. 12-13.
4 Kenneth S. Lynn, *Hemingway* (New York: Simon & Schuster, 1987), p. 19.
5 Peter Buckley, *Ernest* (New York: Dial Press, 1978), p. 98.
6 *Ibid.*, p. 99
7 Hemingway Sandford, *At the Hemingways*, p. 39.
8 James M. Mellow, *A Life Without Consequences* (London: Hodder & Stoughton, 1994), p. 8.
9 Lynn, *Hemingway*, p. 41.
10 Burwell, Rose Marie, *Hemingway: The Post-War Years and the Posthumous Novels* (New York: Cambridge University Press, 1996), p. 21.
11 Lynn, *Hemingway*, p. 41.
12 *Paris Review 5*, Spring 1958.

13 Carlos Baker, *Ernest Hemingway: A Life Story* (New York: Scribner's 1969), p. 5.
14 Anthony Burgess, *Ernest Hemingway and his World* (London: Thames and Hudson, 1978), p. 9.
15 Madelaine Hemingway Miller, *Ernie* (New York: Crown Publishers, 1975), p. 94.
16 *New York Magazine*, 28 December 1946.
17 James Fenton, ed., *Ernest Hemingway: The Collected Stories* (London: Everyman's Library, 1995), p. 387.
18 Mary Welsh Hemingway, *How It Was* (New York: Alfred A. Knopf, 1976), p. 102.
19 Letter from mother, 21 July 1918.
20 Henry Serrano Villard and James Nagel, *Hemingway in Love and War* (Boston: Northeastern University Press, 1989), p. 253.
21 Michael Katakis, ed., *Ernest Hemingway: Artifacts from a Life* (London: Simon & Schuster, 1918), p. xxiv.
22 Villard and Nagel, *Hemingway in Love and War*, p. 109.
23 *Ibid.*, p. 149.
24 *Ibid.*, p. 242.
25 *Ibid.*, p. 243.
26 Mellow, *A Life Without Consequences*, p. 90.
27 Michael Reynolds, *The Young Hemingway* (Oxford: Basil Blackwell, 1987), p. 40.
28 *Ibid.*, p. 57.
29 Letter to Jim Gamble, 3 March 1919.
30 Villard and Nagel, *Hemingway in Love and War*, p. 263.
31 Lynn, *Hemingway*, pp. 98-9.
32 Baker, *A Life Story,* Scribner's, p. 59.
33 Letter to Howell Jenkins, 16 June 1919.
34 Mellow, *A Life Without Consequences*, p. 23.
35 Gioia Diliberto, *Hadley* (London: Bloomsbury, 1992), p. 88.
36 Letter to Grace Quinlan, 8 August 1920.
37 Hemingway Sandford, *At the Hemingways*, p. 194.
38 *Ibid.*, p. 204.
39 Hemingway Miller, *Ernie*, p. 67.
40 Letter from mother, 24 July 1920.
41 Letter to Hadley, 12 January 1921.

Chapter 2

1 Alice Hunt Sokoloff, *Hadley: The First Mrs Hemingway* (New York: Dodd, Mead & Company, 1973), p. 10.
2 Lynn, *Hemingway*, p. 127.
3 Diliberto, *Hadley*, p. 89.
4 Sandford Hemingway, *At the Hemingways*, p. 210.
5 Diliberto, *Hadley*, p. 86
6 Ibid., p. 90.
7 Reynolds, *The Young Hemingway*, p. 196.
8 Nagel, ed, *The Oak Park Legacy*, p. 125.
9 Diliberto, *Hadley*, p. 88.
10 Sokoloff, *Hadley*, p. 40.

Chapter 3

1 Burgess, *Ernest Hemingway and his World*, p. 28.
2 *New York Herald-Tribune*, 29 December 1946.
3 Aaron Hotchner, *Papa Hemingway* (London, Mayflower, 1965), p. 56.
4 Sokoloff, *Hadley*, p. 51.
5 Leslie M. M. Blume, *Everybody Behaves Badly* (New York: Mariner Books, 2017), p. 47.
6 Aaron Hotchner, *Papa Hemingway* (London: Simon & Schuster, 1999), p. 57.
7 *Paris Review 5,* Spring 1958.
8 Ernest Hemingway, *By-Line* (London: Collins, 1968), p. 74.
9 Bernice Kert, *The Hemingway Women* (New York: W. W. Norton, 1986), p. 115.
10 Sandra Spanier, ed., *The Letters of Ernest Hemingway: Volume 2, 1923–1925* (New York: Cambridge University Press, 2013), p. 136.
11 Hotchner, *Hemingway and his World*, p. 105.
12 Ernest Hemingway, *A Moveable Feast* (London: Arrow, 1994), p. 182.
13 Letter to Sherwood Anderson, 9 March 1922.
14 Leicester Hemingway, *My Brother Ernest Hemingway* (London: Weidenfeld & Nicolson, 1962), p. 72.
15 Diliberto, *Hadley*, p. 133.
16 Samuelson, *With Hemingway*, p. 34.
17 Fenton, ed., *The Collected Stories*, pp. 739-40.
18 Paula McLain, *The Paris Wife* London: Virago, 2013), p. 167.

Chapter 4

1 Lynn, *Hemingway*, p. 191.
2 Mellow, *A Life Without Consequences*, p. 210.
3 Hotchner, *Papa Hemingway,* Mayflower, p. 137.
4 Diliberto, *Hadley*, p. 154.
5 Letter to Arnold Gingrich, 13 March 1953.
6 Hemingway Sandford, *At the Hemingways*, p. 216.
7 Letter to Maxwell Perkins, 31 August 1927.
8 Hemingway Miller, *Ernie*, p. 128.
9 Sandra Spanier, *The Letters of Ernest Hemingway: Volume 1 1907–1922* (New York: Cambridge University Press, 2011), p. 95.
10 Brian, *The Faces of Hemingway*, p. 44.
11 *Ibid*., p. 45.
12 Hotchner, *Papa Hemingway*, Mayflower, p. 80.
13 Katakis, *Artifacts from a Life*, p. 26.
14 Spanier, ed., *Volume 2: The Letters of Ernest Hemingway*, p. 135.
15 Spanier, ed., *Volume I: The Letters of Ernest Hemingway*, p. 68.
16 Baker, *A Life Story,* Scribner's, p. 224.
17 Lillian Ross, *Portrait of Hemingway* (London: Penguin, 1961), p. 44.
18 Mellow, *A Life Without Consequences*, p. 97.
19 *Paris Review 5,* Spring 1958.

Chapter 5

1 Diliberto, *Hadley*, p. 192.
2 Scott Donaldson, *By Force of Will: The Life and Art of Ernest Hemingway* (New York: Penguin, 1978.
3 Blume, *Everybody Behaves Badly*, p. 151.
4 Baker, *A Life Story*, Scribner's, p. 162.
5 Matthew J. Bruccoli, and Judith S. Baughan, eds, *Correspondence of F. Scott Fitzgerald* (Jackson and London: University Press of Mississippi, 2003), p. 183.
6 Anderson, Sherwood, *Letters of Sherwood Anderson* Boston: Little Brown & Co., 1953), p. 80.
7 Baker, *A Life Story,* Scribner's, p. 162.
8 Blume, *Everybody Behaves Badly*, p. 152.
9 Donald Ogden Stewart, *By a Stroke of Luck* (New York: Paddington Press, 1975), p. 132.
10 Hotchner, *Papa Hemingway,* Mayflower, p. 49.
11 Lucy Moore, *Anything Goes: A Biography of the Roaring Twenties* (London: Atlantic Books, 2008), pp. 250-1.
12 Spanier, ed., *The Letters of Ernest Hemingway, Volume I*, p. 177.
13 Lynn, *Hemingway*, p. 452.
14 Peter Viertel, *Dangerous Friends* (London: Viking, 1992), p. 255.
15 Letter from mother, 2 January 1927.
16 Mellow, *A Life Without Consequences*, p. 298.

Chapter 6

1 Sokoloff, *Hadley*, p. 80.
2 Sara Mayfield, *Exiles from Paradise: Zelda and Scott Fitzgerald* (New York: Delacorte Press, 1971), pp. 107-8.
3 Ruth A. Hawkins, *Unbelievable Happiness and Final Sorrow: The Hemingway-Pfeiffer Marriage* (Fayateville: University of Arkansas Press, 2012), p. 48.
4 Diliberto, *Hadley*, p. 247.
5 John Dos Passos, *The Best Times* (New York: New American Library, 1966), p. 204.
6 Diliberto, *Hadley*, p. 204.
7 *A Moveable Feast*, p. 14.
8 Diliberto, *Hadley*, p. 208.
9 *Ibid.*, p. 216.
10 Lynn, *Hemingway*, p. 341.
11 Diliberto, *Hadley*, p. 217.
12 Letter to Hadley, 18 November 1926.
13 Letter from father, 8 August 1927.
14 Richard Bradford, *The Man Who Wasn't There* (London: Tauris Parke, 2020), p. 141.
15 Paul Hendrickson, *Hemingway's Boat* (London: Vintage, 2013), p. 35.
16 Brian, *The Faces of Hemingway*, p. 135.
17 Letter from John Dos Passos, 10 November 1926.
18 Hawkins, *Unbelievable Happiness and Final Sorrow*, p. 155.
19 Scott Donaldson, *Archibald MacLeish: An American Life* (Boston: Houghton Mifflin, 1992), p. 60.

20 Letter from Gerald Murphy, 6 September 1926.
21 Matthew J. Bruccoli, *Fitzgerald and Hemingway: A Dangerous Friendship* (London: Andre Deutsch, 1994), p. 77.
22 Hotchner, *Papa Hemingway*, Mayflower, p. 52.

Chapter 7

1 Letter to Scott Fitzgerald, 15 September 1927.
2 Ernest Hemingway, *Men Without Women* (London: Penguin, 1967), p. 44.
3 *Ibid.*, p. 55.
4 Bradford, *The Man Who Wasn't There*, p. 86.
5 Lynn, *Hemingway*, p. 370.
6 Hemingway Sandford, *At the Hemingways*, p. 229.
7 Letter to Maxwell Perkins, 31 May 1928.
8 Hawkins, *Unbelievable Happiness and Final Sorrow*, p. 92.
9 Letter to Guy Hickok, 27 July 1928.
10 Mary V. Dearborn, *Ernest Hemingway: A Biography* (New York: Vintage, 2018, p. 259.
11 Lynn, *Hemingway*, p. 377.
12 Hemingway Miller, *Ernie*, p. 108.
13 *Ibid.*, p. 113.
14 Ernest Hemingway, *Selected Letters 1917–1961* (London: Panther, 1985), p. 283.
15 *Ibid.*
16 Hemingway Sandford, *At the Hemingways*, p. 231.
17 Leicester Hemingway, *The Sound of the Trumpet* (New York: Henry Holt, 1953), pp. 182-3.
18 Dearborn, *Ernest Hemingway: A Biography*, p. 270.
19 Ernest Hemingway, *The Snows of Kilimanjaro* (London: Arrow, 1994), p. 36.
20 Brian, *The Faces of Hemingway*, p. 80.
21 Mellow, *A Life without Consequences*, p. 368.
22 Dearborn, *Ernest Hemingway: A Biography*, p. 270.
23 Hemingway Miller, *Ernie*, p. 115.
24 Donaldson, *By Force of Will*, p. 137.
25 Hotchner, *Papa Hemingway*, Scribner's, p. 103.
26 Letter from Gus Pfeiffer, 5 February 1929.
27 Ernest Hemingway, *A Farewell to Arms* (London: Penguin, 1966), p. 7.
28 Ross, *Portrait of Hemingway*, p. 81.
29 Hotchner, *Papa Hemingway*, Mayflower, p. 48.
30 *Esquire*, December 1934.
31 Hotchner, *Papa Hemingway*, Mayflower, p. 169.
32 Hemingway, *A Farewell to Arms*, p. 193.
33 *Paris Review 5*, Spring 1958.
34 Hemingway Sandford, *At the Hemingways*, p. 228.
35 Hotchner, *Papa Hemingway*, Mayflower, p. 102.
36 Bruccoli, *A Dangerous Friendship*, p. 78.
37 Spanier, ed., *The Letters of Ernest Hemingway, Volume 1, 1907–1922*, p. 193.
38 Letter to Guy Hickok, 5 December 1931.
39 Brian, *The Faces of Hemingway*, p. 83.
40 Letter to Mary Pfeiffer, 8 January 1931.

Chapter 8

1 Tony Butitta, *After the Good Gay Times* (New York: Viking, 1974), p. 4.
2 Zeitz, Joshua, *Flapper* (New York: Three Rivers Press, 2006), p. 272.
3 Nancy Milford, *Zelda: A Biography* (New York: Harper & Row, 1970), p. 115.
4 Brian, *The Faces of Hemingway*, p. 53.
5 Scott Donaldson, *Fool for Love: A Biography of F. Scott Fitzgerald* (New York: Dell, 1983), p. 162.
6 Marty Beckerman, *The Heming Way* (New York: St. Martin's Griffin, 2012), p. 55.
7 Sylvia Beach, *Shakespeare and Company* (New York: Harcourt Brace, 1959), p. 116.
8 Donald W. Goodwin, *Alcohol and the Writer* (London: Penguin, 1988), p. 41.
9 Anita Loos, *Cast of Thousands* (New York: Grosset & Dunlap, 1977), p. 128.
10 Matthew J. Bruccoli. *Some Sort of Epic Grandeur: The Life of F. Scott Fitzgerald* (London: Hodder & Stoughton, 1981), pp. 276-7.
11 Arthur Mizener, *F. Scott Fitzgerald and his World* (London: Thames & Hudson, 1972), p. 72.
12 Mary Welsh Hemingway, *How It Was* (New York: Alfred A. Knopf, 1976), p. 219.
13 Bruccoli, *A Dangerous Friendship*, p. 26.
14 Mayfield, *Exiles from Paradise*, pp. 115-6.
15 *New Republic*, 7 June 1933.
16 Michael Reynolds, *The American Homecoming* (Oxford: Blackwell Publishers, 1992), p. 46.
17 Bruccoli, *A Dangerous Friendship*, p. 215.
18 Samuelson, *With Hemingway*, p. 40.
19 *Ibid.*, p. 42.
20 Carlos Baker, *Hemingway and his Critics* (New York: Hill and Wang, 1961), p. 42.
21 Samuelson, *With Hemingway*, p. 40.
22 Andrew Turnbull, ed., *Dreams of Youth: The Letters of F. Scott Fitzgerald* (London: Max Press, 2011), p. 329.

Chapter 9

1 Hawkins, *Unbelievable Happiness and Final Sorrow*, p. 141.
2 Michael Palin, Hemingway Adventure (New York: St. Martin's Press, 1999), p. 143.
3 John Hemingway, *Strange Tribe: A Family Memoir*, 2007, p. 19.
4 Jeffrey Meyers, *Hemingway: A Biography* (London: Macmillan, 1985), p. 321.
5 Earl Rovit and Gerry Brenner. *Ernest Hemingway* (Boston: G. K. Hall, 1986), p. 53.
6 Baker, *Hemingway and his Critics*, p. 143.
7 Frank M. Laurence, *Hemingway and the Movies* (New York, Da Capo Press, 1981), p. 62.
8 *Ibid.*, p. 60.
9 Hemingway Miller, *Ernie*, p. 127.
10 *Esquire*, February 1934.
11 Gregory Hemingway, *Papa* (Boston: Houghton-Mifflin, 1976), p. 25.
12 *Ibid.*, p. 19.
13 *Fame*, September 1989.
14 Hemingway, *Papa*, p. 18.

15 John Hemingway, *Strange Tribe: A Family Memoir,* 2007, p. 21.
16 Kert, *The Hemingway Women*, p. 269.
17 Hotchner, *Papa Hemingway*, Scribner's, p. 160.

Chapter 10

1 Hemingway, *Selected Letters*, p. 792.
2 Errol Selkirk, *Hemingway for Beginners* (New York: Writers and Readers Publishing, 1994), p. 112.
3 Buckley, *Ernest*, p. 153.
4 Hemingway, *The Snows of Kilimanjaro*, p. 1.
5 *Paris Review 5*, Spring 1958.
6 Mellow, *A Life Without Consequences*, p. 448.
7 Arnold Gingrich, *Nothing but People: The Early Days of Esquire, A Personal History 1928–1958* (New York: Crown Publishers, 1971), p. 279.
8 Bradford, *The Man Who Wasn't There*, p. 199.
9 James Plath and Frank Simons, *Remembering Ernest Hemingway* (Key West, FL: Ketch and Yawl Press, 1999), p. 116.
10 *Ibid.*, p. 101.
11 Hemingway, Leicester, *My Brother, Ernest Hemingway* (London: Weidenfeld & Nicolson, 1962), p. 106.
12 Kert, *The Hemingway Women*, p. 249.
13 *Paris Review 5*, Spring 1958.
14 Letter to Thomas Shevlin, 4 April 1939.
15 Turnbull, ed, *Dreams of Youth*, p. 331.
16 Bruccoli, *A Dangerous Friendship*, p. 7.
17 F. Scott Fitzgerald, *On Booze* (London: Picador, 2011), p. 20.
18 Bruccoli, *A Dangerous Friendship*, p. 208.
19 *Ibid.*, p. 165.
20 F. Scott Fitzgerald, *The Crack-Up* (New York: New Direction Books, 1956), p. 181.
21 Bruccoli, *A Dangerous Friendship*, p. 165.
22 Samuelson, *With Hemingway*, p. 20.
23 Hendrickson, *Hemingway's Boat*, p. 391.
24 Hawkins, *Unbelievable Happiness and Final Sorrow*, p. 186.
25 Plath and Simons, *Remembering Ernest Hemingway*, p. 62.
26 Hendrickson, *Hemingway's Boat*, p. 531.
27 Hawkins, *Unbelievable Happiness and Final Sorrow*, p. 186.
28 Brian, *The Faces of Hemingway*, p. 99.
29 Letter to Sara Murphy, 27 February 1936.
30 Letter to John Dos Passos, 12 April 1936.

Chapter 11

1 Brian, *The Faces of Hemingway*, p. 110.
2 Lynn, *Hemingway*, p. 464.
3 Janet Somerville, *Yours for Probably Always: Martha Gellhorn's Letters of Love and War* (Ontario: Firefly Books, 2019), p. 173.

4 James McLendon, *Papa: Hemingway in Key West* (Key West: Langley Press, 1993), p. 165.
5 Brian, *The Faces of Hemingway*, p. 101.
6 Somerville, *Yours for Probably Always*, p. 149.
7 Lynn, *Hemingway*, p. 468.
8 Hotchner, *Papa Hemingway*, Mayflower, p. 147.
9 Philip Greene, *To Have and Have Another: A Hemingway Cocktail Companion* (New York: Perigree, 2012), p. 131.
10 Baker, *A Life Story,* Scribner's, p. 268.
11 Laurence, *Hemingway and the Movies*, p. 84.
12 Carl Rollyson, *Beautiful Exile: The Life of Martha Gellhorn* (New York: Aurum Press, 2007), p. 73.
13 Baker, *A Life Story*, Scribner's, p. 309.
14 Kert, *The Hemingway Women*, p. 309.
15 *Newsweek*, 6 March 1937.
16 Morley Callaghan, *That Summer in Paris* (New York: Dell, 1964), p. 161.
17 *Esquire* 57, February 1962.
18 Somerville, *Yours for Probably Always*, p. 288.
19 Matthew J. Bruccoli, *The Only Thing That Counts: The Ernest Hemingway-Maxwell Perkins Correspondence* (New York: Scribner's, 1996), p. 277.
20 *New Yorker*, 26 December 1940.
21 Letter to Maxwell Perkins, 26 August 1940.
22 *New Republic* 103, 28 October 1940.
23 Turnbull, ed, *Dreams of Youth*, p. 332.
24 Hawkins, *Unbelievable Happiness and Final Sorrow*, p. 226.
25 Hemingway, *Papa*, p. 23.
26 Letter to Pauline, 26 January 1949.
27 Hawkins, *Unbelievable Happiness and Final Sorrow*, p. 241.
28 *New York Post*, Weekend magazine, 28 December 1946.
29 Carl Rollyson, *Nothing Ever Happens to the Brave: The Story of Martha Gellhorn* (New York: St. Martin's Press, 1990), p. 207.
30 Caroline Moorehead, *Martha Gellhorn: A Life* (London: Vintage, 2004), p. 206.
31 Burwell, *The Post-War Years and the Posthumous Novels*, p. 53.
32 Kert, *The Hemingway Women*, p. 422.
33 Letter to Mary Pfeiffer, 12 December 1939.
34 Hawkins *Unbelievable Happiness and Final Sorrow*, p. 223.
35 Letter to Patrick, 11 June 1952.
36 Letter to Gregory, 15 August 1950.
37 Letter to Hadley, 26 July 1939.
38 Meyers, *Hemingway: A Biography*, p. 347.
39 Hemingway, *Selected Letters*, p. 511.

Chapter 12

1 Andrew Shaffer, *Literary Rogues* (New York: HarperPerennial, 2013), p. 111.
2 *Los Angeles Magazine*, January 1964.
3 avid Thomson, *The Story of Orson Welles* (London: Abacus, 1997), p. 58.
4 *Cahiers du Cinema,* November 1966.

5 Aaron Latham, *Crazy Sundays: F. Scott Fitzgerald in Hollywood* (London: Secker & Warburg, 1972), p. 20.
6 Hemingway, *A Moveable Feast*, p. 129.
7 Letter to Arthur Mizener, 22 April 1950.
8 Milford, *Zelda: A Biography*, p. 222.
9 Latham, *Crazy Sundays*, p. 230.
10 *Ibid.*, p. 244.
11 Sheilah Graham with Gerold Frank, *Beloved Infidel* (New York: Bantam Books, 1968), p. 212.
12 Beckerman, *The Heming Way*, p. 167.
13 Connie Robertson, ed, *Wordsworth Dictionary of Quotations* (Herefordshire, UK: Wordworth Editions, 1998), p. 127.
14 Bruccoli, *A Dangerous Friendship*, p. 13.
15 Callaghan, *That Summer in Paris*, p. 22.
16 *Toronto Star*, Weekly magazine, April 1958.
17 *New Yorker*, 24 May 1999.
18 *Atlantic Monthly*, 16 August 1965.

Chapter 13

1 Dearborn, *Ernest Hemingway: A Biography*, p. 409.
2 Moorehead, *Martha Gellhorn: A Life*, p. 201.
3 *Ibid.*
4 Rollyson, *Beautiful Exile*, p. 239.
5 *New Yorker*, 24 May 1999.
6 Rollyson, *Nothing Ever Happens to the Brave*, p. 120.
7 *Ibid.*, p. 122.
8 Somerville, *Yours for Probably Always*, p. 285.
9 *Ibid.*, p. 286.
10 Moorehead, *Martha Gellhorn: A Life*, p. 204.
11 Hemingway, *Papa*, p. 41.
12 Rollyson, *Nothing Ever Happens to the Brave*, p. 236.
13 Moorehead, *Martha Gellhorn: A Life*, p. 235.
14 Rollyson, *Nothing Ever Happens to the Brave*, p. 185.
15 Ibid., p. 202.
16 Hotchner, *Hemingway and his World*, p. 154.
17 Hemingway, Papa, pp. 91-2.
18 Michael Reynolds, *Hemingway: The Final Years* (New York: W. W. Norton & Co., 1999), p. 90.
19 Bradford, *The Man Who Wasn't There*, p. 299.
20 Moorehead, *Martha Gellhorn: A Life*, p. 196.
21 Hendrickson, *Hemingway's Boat*, p. 433.
22 Moorehead, *Martha Gellhorn: A Life*, p. 221.
23 James Nagel, ed., *Ernest Hemingway: The Writer in Context* (Madison: University of Wisconsin Press, 1984), p. 15.
24 Greene, *To Have and Have Another*, p. 91.
25 Rollyson, *Nothing Ever Happens to the Brave*, p. 171.
26 Isabella Rossellini and Lothar Schirmer, eds, *Ingrid Bergman: A Life in Pictures* (San Francisco: Chronicle Books, 2013), p. 158.

27 Letter to Maxwell Perkins, 27 August 1942.
28 Ingrid Bergman, with Alan Burgess, *My Story* (London: Sphere, 1981), p. 105.
29 Charlotte Chandler, *Ingrid Bergman: A Personal Biography* (New York: Applause Theatre and Cinema Books, 2007), p. 93.
30 *New Statesman and Nation*, 13 November 1943.
31 Rollyson, *Nothing Ever Happens to the Brave*, p. 163.
32 Baker, *A Life Story*, Literary Guild, p. 535.
33 Lynn, *Hemingway*, p. 532n.
34 Moorehead, *Martha Gellhorn: A Life*, p. 273.
35 Letter to Buck Lanham, 23 July 1945.

Chapter 14

1 Rollyson, *Nothing Ever Happens to the Brave*, p. 215.
2 Hemingway, *How It Was*, pp. 133-4.
3 Hotchner, *Hemingway and his World*, p. 167.
4 Meyers, *Hemingway: A Biography*, p. 396.
5 Bradford, *The Man Who Wasn't There*, p. 347.
6 *Argosy*, September 1958.
7 *Newsweek*, 3 August 1964.
8 Letter to William Seward, 19 June 1947.
9 Dearborn, *Ernest Hemingway: A Biography*, p. 466.
10 Hemingway, *How It Was*, p. 281.
11 Royalty Statement, 30 August 1948, JFK Library.
12 *Kansas City Star*, 10 September 1950.
13 Viertel, *Dangerous Friends*, p. 270.
14 Letter to Charles Scribner, 22 July 1949.
15 Letter to Adriana Ivancich, 16 June 1950.
16 Viertel, *Dangerous Friends*, p. 81.
17 Hemingway, *How It Was*, p. 246.
18 Kert, *The Hemingway Women*, pp. 456-7.
19 Hendrickson, *Hemingway's Boat*, p. 454.
20 Hawkins, *Unbelievable Happiness and Final Sorrow*, p. 259.
21 Hemingway, *How It Was*, p. 246.
22 Letter to Adriana Ivancich, 3 June 1950.
23 *Kenyon Review13*, Winter 1951.
24 Letter to Harvey Breit, 8 July 1950.
25 Reynolds, *The Young Hemingway*, p. 209.
26 John Dos Passos, *The Fourteenth Chronicle: Letters and Diaries of John Dos Passos* (Boston: Gambit Publishing, 1973), p. 591.
27 Irwin Shaw, *The Young Lions* (New York: Jonathan Cape, 1948), p. 382.
28 Brian, *The Faces of Hemingway*, p. 203.
29 Andrea Di Robilant, *Autumn in Venice: Ernest Hemingway and his Last Muse* (London: Atlantic Books, 2019), p. 227.
30 *Esquire*, February 1962.
31 Hemingway, *Papa*, p. 103.
32 Meyers, *Hemingway: A Biography*, p. 570.
33 Letter to William Walton, 9 March 1950.
34 Moorehead, *Martha Gellhorn: A Life*, p. 305.

35 Letter to Bernard Berenson, 24 January 1953.
36 John Raeburn, *Fame Became of Him* (Bloomington: Indiana University Press, 1984), p. 136.
37 *Ibid.*
38 *New Yorker*, 24 May 1999.

Chapter 15

1 *Paris Review* 5, Spring 1958.
2 Charles A. Fenton, *The Apprenticeship of Ernest Hemingway: The Early Years* (New York: Farrar, Straus & Young, 1954), p. 1.
3 Letter to mother, 17 September 1949.
4 Lynn, *Hemingway*, p. 272.
5 *Little Review*, 12 May 1929.
6 Letter to Thomas Bledsoe, 9 December 1951.
7 Spanier, ed., *The Letters of Ernest Hemingway: Volume 2, 1923–1925*, p. 138.
8 *Paris Review* 5, Spring 1958.
9 *Atlantic Monthly*, August 1965.
10 Jack Hemingway, *Misadventures of a Fly Fisherman* (Dallas: Taylor Publishing Company), p. 321.
11 Letter to Harvey Breit, 23 July 1956.
12 Brian, *The Faces of Hemingway*, p. 210.
13 Raeburn, *Fame Became of Him*, p. 141.
14 Leonard Mosley, *Zanuck: The Rise and Fall of Hollywood's Last Tycoon* (London: Panther, 1985), p. 398.
15 Hotchner, *Papa Hemingway,* Mayflower, p. 90.
16 Mel Gussow, *Don't Say Yes Until I Finish Talking: A Biography of Darryl F. Zanuck* (New York: Pocket Books, 1972), p. 176.
17 Laurence, *Hemingway and the Movies*, p. 252.
18 *Ibid.*
19 Brian, *The Faces of Hemingway*, p. 127.
20 Kert, *The Hemingway Women*, p. 486.
21 Heminway Sandford, *At the Hemingways*, p. 241.
22 Hemingway Miller, *Ernie*, p. 130.
23 Kert, *The Hemingway Women*, p. 323.
24 Lynn, Hemingway, p. 476.
25 Burwell, *The Post-War Years and the Posthumous Novels*, p. 129.
26 Meyers, *Hemingway: A Biography*, p. 255.
27 Hemingway, *Strange Tribe*, pp. 18-19.
28 *Los Angeles Times*, 2 October 1951.
29 Hemingway, *How It Was*, p. 290.
30 Hemingway, *Strange Tribe*, p. 91.
31 Hemingway, *Papa*, p. 8.
32 Hemingway, *Strange Tribe*, p. 93.
33 Hendrickson, *Hemingway's Boat*, p. 568.
34 *Ibid.*, p. 603.
35 Valerie Hemingway, *Running with the Bulls* (New York: Ballantine Books, 2004), p. 120.
36 Hemingway, *Papa*, p. 10.
37 Hendrickson, *Hemingway's Boat*, p. 574.

38 Hemingway, *Papa*, p. 12.
39 *Holiday*, 27 February 1960.
40 Bruccoli, *The Only Thing That Counts*, p. 309.

Chapter 16

1 Baker, *A Life Story*, Scribner's, p. 272.
2 *Hemingway Review*, Spring 1992.
3 Brian, *The Faces of Hemingway*, p. 92.
4 Letter to Bernard Berenson, 13 September 1952.
5 *Paris Review 5*, Spring 1958.
6 Hendrickson, *Hemingway's Boat*, p. 569.
7 Beckerman, *The Heming Way*, p. 66.
8 Reynolds, *The Final Years*, p. 274.
9 *New York Times*, 26 January 1954.
10 *Washington Post*, 26 January 1954.
11 Selkirk, *Hemingway for Beginners*, p. 146.
12 Hotchner, *Papa Hemingway*, Scribner's, p. 93.
13 Raeburn, *Fame Became of Him*, p. 147.
14 Buckley, *Ernest*, p. 106.
15 Hemingway, By-Line, p. 426.
16 Adriana Ivancich, *La Torre Bianca* (Milan: Mondadori, 1980), p. 324.
17 Letter to Adriana Ivancich, 15 August 1954.
18 Letter to Archibald MacLeish, 22 November 1930.
19 Burgess, *Ernest Hemingway and his World*, p. 106.
20 Hemingway, *Papa*, p. 111.
21 Greene, *To Have and Have Another*, p. 127.
22 Letter to Harvey Breit, 27 June 1952.
23 *New Yorker*, 24 May 1999.
24 *London Sunday Times*, 19 December 1954.
25 Orson Welles and Peter Bogdanovich, *This is Orson Welles* (New York: HarperPerennial, 1992), p. 251.
26 Baker, *A Life Story*, Scribner's, p. 527.
27 Nobel Prize Acceptance speech taped by Hemingway and read out in Sweden on 10 December 1954.
28 Letter to Buck Lanham, 10 November 1954.
29 Baker, *A Life Story*, Literary Guild, p. 623.
30 Viertel, *Dangerous Friends*, p. 309.
31 *Ibid.*, p. 243.
32 Burgess, *Ernest Hemingway and his World*, p. 101.
33 Plath and Simons, *Remembering Ernest Hemingway*, p. 122.
34 Greene, *To Have and Have Another*, p. 204.
35 *Time*, 2 October 1958.

Chapter 17

1 *Holiday*, 27 February 1960.
2 Lynn, *Hemingway*, p. 593.

3 Baker, *A Life Story*, Scribner's, p. 277.
4 Bruccoli, *A Dangerous Friendship*, p. 9.
5 Beckerman, *The Heming Way*, p. 52.
6 Letter to Bernard Berenson, 20 March 1953.
7 Dwight Macdonald, *Against the American Grain* (New York: Random House, 1962.
8 Slim Keith, *Memories of a Rich and Imperfect Life* (New York: Simon & Schuster, 1990), p. 128.
9 *Toronto Daily Star*, 22 July 1922.
10 Hotchner, *Papa Hemingway*, Mayflower, p. 36.
11 *Saturday Review of Literature*, 7 September 1957.
12 Laurence, *Hemingway and the Movies*, p. 63.
13 Rudy Behlmer, ed., *Memo From David. O. Selznick* (New York: Viking, 1972), p. 448.
14 Laurence, *Hemingway and the Movies*, p. 79.
15 Dearborn, *Ernest Hemingway: A Biography*, p. 600.
16 Hemingway, *How It Was*, p. 471.
17 Letter to Alfred Rice, 15 December 1948.
18 *Paris Review 5,* Spring 1958.
19 Hemingway, *Running with the Bulls*, p. 91.
20 Hemingway Miller, *Ernie*, p. 65.
21 Hemingway, *Running with the Bulls*, p. 84.

Chapter 18

1 Hemingway, *My Brother, Ernest Hemingway*, p. 251.
2 *Ibid*., p. 252.
3 Kurt Singer, *Hemingway: The Life and Death of a Giant* (London: World Distributors, 1962), p. 26.
4 Hemingway, *Papa*, p. 116.
5 Hemingway, *How It Was*, p. 481.
6 Hemingway Miller, *Ernie*, p. 52.
7 Hemingway, *My Brother, Ernest Hemingway*, pp. 113-4.
8 Donaldson, *By Force of Will*, p. 304.
9 Hotchner, *Papa Hemingway*, Scribner's, p. 114.
10 Baker, *A Life Story*, Scribner's, p. 435.
11 Leslie Fiedler, *A Leslie Fiedler Reader* (New York: Stein & Day, 1977), pp. 153-64.
12 Lynn, *Hemingway*, p. 584.
13 Hotchner, *Papa Hemingway*, Mayflower, p. 234.
14 Brian, *The Faces of Hemingway*, p. 254.
15 *Ibid*., p. 255.
16 Lloyd Arnold, *High on the Wild with Hemingway.* (Caldwell, Idaho: Caxton, 1968), p. 333.
17 *Encounter18*, January 1952.
18 Hemingway, *How It Was*, p. 497.
19 Baker, *A Life Story*, Scribner's, p. 561.
20 Hemingway, *Papa*, p. 114.
21 Reynolds, *The Final Years*, pp. 358-9.

22 *Kansas City Star*, 10 September 1950.
23 Donaldson, *By Force of Will*, p. 282.
24 Mellow, *A Life Without Consequences*, p. 604.
25 Hemingway, *Misadventures of a Fly Fisherman*, p. 297.
26 Hemingway, *Papa*, p. 118.
27 Hemingway, *Misadventures of a Fly Fisherman*, p. 296.
28 Hotchner, *Papa Hemingway*, Mayflower, p. 125.

Chapter 19

1 Blume, *Everybody Behaves Badly*, p. 226.
2 Meyers, *Hemingway: A Biography*, p. 562.
3 Hemingway, *Strange Tribe*, p. 36.
4 Hendrickson, *Hemingway's Boat*, pp. 533-4.
5 *Ibid.*
6 Hemingway, *Strange Tribe*, p. 21.
7 *Ibid.*, p. 27.
8 Hemingway, *Running with the Bulls*, p. 265.
9 Hemingway, *Papa*, p. 116.
10 Letter to Carol, 15 August 1949.
11 Burwell, *The Post-War Years and the Posthumous Novels*, p. 230.
12 Robilant, *Autumn in Venice*, pp. 302-3.
13 Diliberto, *Hadley*, p. 281.
14 Plath and Simons, *Remembering Ernest Hemingway*, p. 160.
15 Letter to Frederick Saviers, 15 June 1961.
16 Hendrickson, *Hemingway's Boat*, p. 607.
17 Lynn, *Hemingway*, p. 57.
18 Hendrickson, *Hemingway's Boat*, p. 370.
19 Hemingway, *Misadventures of a Fly Fisherman*, p. 315.
20 John K. M. McCaffrey, *Ernest Hemingway: The Man and his Work* (Cleveland, New York: The World Publishing Company, 1950), p. 56.

Chapter 20

1 *McCalls 83*, May 1956.
2 Hemingway, *Papa*, p. xiii.
3 Brian, *The Faces of Hemingway*, p. 3.
4 Hemingway, *A Moveable Feast*, p. 91.
5 Selkirk, *Hemingway for Beginners*, p. 103.
6 Baker, *A Life Story*, Scribner's, p. 262.
7 Brian, *The Faces of Hemingway*, p. 181.
8 Burgess, *Ernest Hemingway and his World*, p. 94.
9 McCaffrey, *Ernest Hemingway: The Man and his Work*, p. 37.
10 Dearborn, *Ernest Hemingway: A Biography*, p. 321.
11 Brian, *The Faces of Hemingway*, p. 91.
12 *Ibid.*, p. 183.
13 Hemingway, *Misadventures of a Fly Fisherman*, p. 285.
14 Letter to Edmund Wilson, 8 November 1952.

15 Brian, *The Faces of Hemingway*, p. 66.
16 *Esquire*, February 1972.
17 Hemingway, *The Snows of Kilimanjaro*, p. 54.
18 Reynolds, *The Young Hemingway*, p. 102.
19 Baker, *A Life Story*, Literary Guild, p. 455.
20 Brian, *The Faces of Hemingway*, p. 73.
21 Burwell, *The Post-War Years and the Posthumous Novels*, p. 35.
22 Letter to Scott Fitzgerald, 1 July 1925.
23 Ross, *Portrait of Hemingway*, p. 85.
24 Bradford, *The Man Who Wasn't There*, p. 405.
25 Spoto, *Dietrich* (London: Corgi, 1993), p. 230.
26 *New Yorker*, 24 May 1999.
27 Singer, *The Life and Death of a Giant*, p. 209.

Bibliography

Anderson, S., *Letters of Sherwood Anderson* (Boston: Little Brown & Co., 1953)

Arbogast, C., ed. *Quotations of Ernest Hemingway* (Carlisle, Massachusetts: Applewood Books, 2018)

Arnold, L., *High on the Wild with Hemingway* (Caldwell, Idaho: Caxton, 1968)

Baker, C., ed. *Hemingway and His Critics* (New York: Hill and Wang, 1961); *Ernest Hemingway: A Life Story* (New York: Scribner's, 1969); *Ernest Hemingway: A Life Story* (London: Literary Guild, 1969); *Hemingway: Selected Letters, 1917–1961* (London: Panther, 1985)

Beach, S., *Shakespeare and Company* (New York: Harcourt Brace, 1959)

Beckerman, M., *The Heming Way* (New York: St. Martin's Griffin, 2012)

Behlmer, R., ed., *Memo from David O. Selznick* (New York: Viking, 1972)

Bellevance-Johnson, M., *Hemingway in Key West* (Ketchum, Idaho: Computer Lab, 1987)

Bergman, I., with Alan Burgess, *My Story* (London: Sphere, 1981)

Blume, L. M. M., *Everybody Behaves Badly* (New York: Mariner books, 2017)

Bradford, R., *The Man Who Wasn't There* (London: Tauris Parke, 2020)

Brian, D., *The Faces of Hemingway* (London: Grafton Books, 1988)

Bruccoli, M. J., *A Descriptive Bibliography of F. Scott Fitzgerald* (Pittsburgh: University of Pittsburgh Press, 1972); *The Notebooks of F. Scott Fitzgerald* (New York: Harcourt Brace, 1978); ed. *Conversations with Ernest Hemingway* (Jackson and London: University Press of Mississippi, 1978); *Some Sort of Epic Grandeur: The Life of F. Scott Fitzgerald* (London: Hodder & Stoughton, 1981); *Fitzgerald and Hemingway: A Dangerous Friendship* (London: Andre Deutsch, 1994); *The Only Thing That Counts: The Ernest Hemingway-Maxwell Perkins Correspondence* (New York: Scribner's, 1996)

Bruccoli, M. J., and Baughan, J. S., eds. *Correspondence of F. Scott Fitzgerald* (Jackson and London: University Press of Mississippi, 2003)

Buckley, P., *Ernest* (New York: Dial Press, 1978)

Burgess, A., *Ernest Hemingway and His World* (London: Thames and Hudson, 1978)

Burwell, R. M., *Hemingway: The Post-War Years and the Posthumous Novels* (New York: Cambridge University Press, 1996)

Butitta, T., *After the Good Gay Times* (New York: Viking, 1974)

Callaghan, M., *That Summer in Paris* (New York: Dell, 1964)
Carpenter, H., *Geniuses Together: American Writers in Paris in the 1920s* (Boston: Houghton-Mifflin, 1988)
Chandler, C., *Ingrid Bergman: A Personal Biography* (New York: Applause Theatre and Cinema Books, 2007)
Dardis, T., *Some Time in the Sun* (New York: Limelight Editions, 1988); *The Thirsty Muse: Alcohol and the American Writer* (London: Sphere, 1989)
Dearborn, M. V., *Ernest Hemingway: A Biography* (New York: Vintage, 2018)
Di Robilant, A., *Autumn in Venice* (London: Atlantic Books, 2018)
Diliberto, G., *Hadley* (London: Bloomsbury, 1992)
Donaldson, S., *By Force of Will: The Life and Art of Ernest Hemingway* (New York: Penguin, 1978); *Fool for Love: A Biography of F. Scott Fitzgerald* (New York: Dell, 1983); *Archibald MacLeish: An American Life* (Boston: Houghton-Mifflin, 1992)
Donnelly, H. M., *Sara and Gerald* (New York: Times Books, 1982)
Dos Passos, J., *The Best Times* (New York: New American Library, 1966); *Fourteenth Chronicle: Letters and Diaries of John Dos Passos* (Boston: Gambit Publishing, 1973)
Fenton, C. A., *The Apprenticeship of Ernest Hemingway: The Early Years* (New York: Farrar, Straus & Young, 1954)
Fenton, J., ed. *Ernest Hemingway: The Collected Stories* (London: Everyman's Library, 1995)
Fiedler, L., *A Leslie Fiedler Reader* (New York: Stein & Day, 1977)
Fitzgerald, F. S., *The Crack-Up* (New York: New Direction Books, 1956); *On Booze* (London: Picador, 2011)
Fuentes, N., *Hemingway in Cuba* (Secaucus, NJ: Lyle Stuart, 1984)
Gellhorn, M., *Travels with Myself and Another* (New York: Dodd Mead, 1979)
Gerogiannis, N., ed. *Ernest Hemingway: The Complete Poems* (London and Lincoln: University of Nebraska Press, 1992)
Gingrich, A., *Nothing But People: The Early Days of Esquire, A Personal History, 1928–1958* (New York: Crown Publishers, 1971)
Goodwin, D. W., *Alcohol and the Writer* (London: Penguin, 1988)
Graham, S., with Gerold Frank, *Beloved Infidel* (New York: Bantam Books, 1968); *My Hollywood: A Celebration and a Lament* (London: Michael Joseph, 1984)
Greene, P., *To Have and Have Another: A Hemingway Cocktail Companion* (New York: Perigree, 2012)
Griffin, P., *Along with Youth: Hemingway, The Early Years* (New York: Oxford University Press, 1985)
Gussow, M., *Don't Say Yes Until I Finish Talking: A Biography of Darryl F. Zanuck* (New York: Pocket Books, 1972)
Hawkins, R. A., *Unbelievable Happiness and Final Sorrow: The Hemingway-Pfeiffer Marriage* (Fayateville: University of Arkansas Press, 2012)
Hemingway, E., *For Whom the Bell Tolls* (Charles Scribner's Sons, 1940); *The Sun Also Rises* (London: Pan, 1965); *The Torrents of Spring* (London: Penguin, 1966); *A Farewell to Arms* (London: Penguin, 1966); *Green Hills of Africa* (London: Penguin, 1966); *Men without Women* (London: Penguin, 1967); *By-Line* (London: Collins, 1968); *The Essential Hemingway* (London: Penguin, 1969); *Islands in the Stream* (New York: Charles Scribner's Sons, 1970); *The Old Man and the Sea* (Herts, UK: Panther, 1976); *Selected Letters 1917–1961* (London: Panther, 1985); *The Dangerous Summer* (London: Grafton Books, 1986); *The Snows of Kilimanjaro* (London: Arrow, 1994); *To Have and Have*

Not (London: Arrow, 1994); *A Moveable Feast* (London: Arrow, 1994); *The Garden of Eden* (London: Flamingo, 1994); *True at First Light* (London: Arrow, 1999)
Hemingway, G., *Papa* (Boston: Houghton-Mifflin, 1976)
Hemingway, J., *Misadventures of a Fly Fisherman* (Dallas: Taylor Publishing Company, 1986)
Hemingway, J., *Strange Tribe: A Family Memoir* (2007)
Hemingway, L., *My Brother, Ernest Hemingway* (London: Weidenfeld & Nicolson, 1962); *The Sound of the Trumpet* (Henry Holt: New York, 1953)
Hemingway, L., *Walk on Water: A Memoir* (New York: Simon & Schuster, 1998)
Hemingway, M. W., *How It Was* (New York: Alfred A. Knopf, 1976)
Hemingway, J., *Strange Tribe: A Family Memoir* (Guilford, CT: Lyons Press, 2007)
Hemingway, V., *Running With the Bulls* (New York: Ballantine Books, 2004)
Hemingway Miller, M., *Ernie* (New York: Crown Publishers, 1975)
Hemingway Sandford, M., *At the Hemingways* (London: Putnam, 1962)
Hendrickson, P., *Hemingway's Boat* (London: Vintage, 2013)
Hotchner, A. E., *Papa Hemingway* (London: Mayflower, 1965); *Papa Hemingway* (London: Simon & Schuster, 1999); *Hemingway and His World* (London: Penguin, 1989)
Ivancich, A., *La Torre Bianca* (Milan: Mondadori, 1980)
James, C., *Fame in the Twentieth Century* (London: Penguin, 1994)
Joost, N., *Ernest Hemingway and the Little Magazines: The Paris Years* (Barre, MA: Barre Publishers, 1968)
Katakis, M., ed., *Ernest Hemingway: Artifacts from a Life* (London: Simon & Schuster, 2018)
Keith, S., *Memories of a Rich and Imperfect Life* (New York: Simon & Schuster, 1990)
Kert, B., *The Hemingway Women* (New York: W. W. Norton, 1986)
Kiley, J., *Hemingway: An Old Friend Remembers* (New York, 1965)
Latham, A., *Crazy Sundays: F. Scott Fitzgerald in Hollywood* (London: Secker & Warburg, 1972)
Laurence, F. M., *Hemingway and the Movies* (New York: Da Capo Press, 1981)
Loos, A., *Cast of Thousands* (New York: Grosset & Dunlap, 1977)
Loeb, H., *The Way It Was* (New York: Criterion Books, 1959)
Lynn, K. S., *Hemingway* (New York: Simon & Schuster, 1987)
Macdonald, D., *Against the American Grain* (New York: Random House, 19620
Mayfield, S., *Exiles from Paradise: Zelda and Scott Fitzgerald* (New York: Delacorte Press, 1971)
McCaffrey, J. K. M., *Ernest Hemingway: The Man and His Work* (Cleveland, New York: The World Publishing Company, 1950)
McIver, S. B., *Hemingway's Key West* (Sarasota: Pineapple Press, 1993)
McLain, P., *The Paris Wife* (London: Virago, 2013)
McLendon, J., *Papa: Hemingway in Key West* (Key West: Langley Press, 1993)
Mellow, J. M., *A Life Without Consequences* (London: Hodder & Stoughton, 1994)
Meyers, J., *Hemingway: A Biography* (London: Macmillan, 1985)
Milford, N., *Zelda: A Biography* (New York: Harper & Row, 1970)
Mizener, A., *F. Scott Fitzgerald and His World* (London: Thames & Hudson, 1972); *The Far Side of Paradise* (New York: Avon Books, 1974)
Montgomery, C., *Hemingway in Michigan* (New York: Fleet, 1966)
Moore, L., *Anything Goes: A Biography of the Roaring Twenties* (London: Atlantic Books, 2008)
Moorehead, C., *Martha Gellhorn: A Life* (London: Vintage, 2004)

Mosley, L., *Zanuck: The Rise and Fall of Hollywood's Last Tycoon* (London: Panther, 1985)

Nagel, J., ed. *Ernest Hemingway: The Oak Park Legacy* (Tuscaloosa and London: University of Alabama Press, 1996); ed., *Ernest Hemingway: The Writer in Context* (Madison: University of Wisconsin Press, 1984)

Noble, D. R., *Hemingway: A Revaluation* (Troy, NY: 1983)

Ondaaatje, C., *Hemingway in Africa: The Last Safari* (Ontario, CA: HarperCollins, 2003)

Palin, M., *Hemingway Adventure* (New York: St. Martin's Press, 1999)

Plath, J., and Simons, F., *Remembering Ernest Hemingway* (Key West, FL: Ketch and Yawl Press, 1999)

Plimpton, G., ed. *The Best of Bad Hemingway* (Orlando, Fl: Harcourt Brace, 1989)

Raeburn, J., *Fame Became of Him* (Bloomington: Indiana University Press, 1984)

Reynolds, M., *The Young Hemingway* (Oxford: Basil Blackwell, 1987); *The American Homecoming* (Oxford: Blackwell Publishers, 1992); *Hemingway: The Final Years* (New York: W. W. Norton & Co., 1999)

Robertson, C., ed., *Wordsworth Dictionary of Quotations* (Herefordshire, UK: Wordsworth Editions, 1998)

Robilant, A. di, *Autumn in Venice: Ernest Hemingway and His Last Muse* (London: Atlantic Books, 2019)

Rollyson, C., *Nothing Ever Happens to the Brave: The Story of Martha Gellhorn* (New York: St. Martin's Press, 1990); *Beautiful Exile: The Life of Martha Gellhorn* (New York: Aurum Press, 2007)

Ross, L., *Portrait of Hemingway* (London: Penguin, 1961)

Rossellini, and Lothar Schirmer, eds., *Ingrid Bergman: A Life in Pictures* (San Francisco: Chronicle Books, 2013)

Rovit, E., and Brenner, G., *Ernest Hemingway* (Boston, MA: G. K. Hall, 1986)

Samuelson, A., *With Hemingway: A Year in Key West and Cuba* (London: Severn House Publishers, 1985)

Sarason, B. D., *Hemingway and the Sun Set* (Washington DC: Microcard Editions, 1972)

Selkirk, E., *Hemingway for Beginners* (New York: Writers and Readers Publishing, 1994)

Shaffer, A., *Literary Rogues* (New York: HarperPerennial, 2013)

Shaw, I., *The Young Lions* (New York: Jonathan Cape, 1948)

Singer, K., *Hemingway: The Life and Death of a Giant* (London: World Distributors, 1962)

Sokoloff, A. H., *Hadley: The First Mrs Hemingway* (New York: Dodd, Mead & Company, 1973)

Somerville, J., *Yours For Probably Always: Martha Gellhorn's Letters of Love & War* (Ontario: Firefly Books, 2019)

Spanier, S., ed., *The Letters of Ernest Hemingway, Volume 1: 1907–1922* (New York: Cambridge University Press, 2011); *The Letters of Ernest Hemingway, Volume 2: 1923–1925* (New York: Cambridge University Press, 2013); *The Letters of Ernest Hemingway, Volume 3: 1926–1929* (New York: Cambridge University Press, 2015); *The Letters of Ernest Hemingway, Volume 4: 1929–1931* (New York: Cambridge University Press, 2017); *The Letters of Ernest Hemingway, Volume 5: 1932–1934* (New York: Cambridge University Press, 2020)

Spilka, M., *Hemingway's Quarrel with Androgyny* (Lincoln: University of Nebraska Press, 1990)

Spoto, D., *Dietrich* (London: Corgi, 1993)

Stein, G., *The Autobiography of Alice B. Toklas* (New York: Harcourt Brace, 1933)
Stewart, D. O., *By a Stroke of Luck* (New York: Paddington Press, 1975)
Thomson, D., *Rosebud: The Story of Orson Welles* (London: Abacus, 1997)
Tomkins, C., *Living Well is the Best Revenge* (New York: Museum of Modern Art, 2014)
Trogdon, R., *The Lousy Racket: Hemingway, Scribner's and the Business of Literature* (Kent, OH: Kent State University Press, 2007)
Turnbull, A., ed., *Dreams of Youth: The Letters of Scott Fitzgerald* (London: Max Press, 2011)
Viertel, P., *Dangerous Friends* (London: Viking, 1992)
Villard, H. S., and Nagel, J., *Hemingway In Love and War* (Boston: Northeastern University Press, 1989)
Wagner, L. A., *Ernest Hemingway: Six Decades of Criticism* (East Lansing, MI: Michigan State University Press, 1987)
Welles, O., and Bogdanovich, P., *This is Orson Welles* (New York, HarperPerennial, 1992)
Wood, N., *Mrs Hemingway* (London: Picador, 2014)
Zeitz, J., *Flapper* (New York: Three Rivers Press, 2006)